God made Jeremy a new creation, a man of many talents, and a humble man. There is so much value in this book. You will be blessed, as I was blessed.

–Mel Novak

… you will join Jeremy in his awakening; the relief and forgiveness he experienced by opening his heart to Jesus Christ, the ultimate giver of peace.

–Jeff DeVore

Do not be saddened by Jeremy's story; be heartened by it – what a glorious change a new heart makes! Only God can bring such beauty out of chaos.

–William D. Moore

The **Real** Comeback
A Life Transformed

Jeremy Rea Jackson
"The Scorpion"

Dedication

This book is dedicated to my mom, my hero.

No matter what trials she faces in life, she always finds a way to smile and to love others.

Mom, thank you for loving me the way you do.

Table of Contents

Acknowledgements

First and foremost, I thank God for rescuing me from destruction and sin, and for giving me the gift of eternal life through His Son Jesus Christ. Without Him I wouldn't have been able to write this book, because I'd still be blind. He kept me alive when I should have been dead.

I'd like to thank my mom and Robby for not giving up on me. They continued to pray for me and tell me about Jesus even when I didn't want to hear it. Now, they visit me in prison every weekend and build me up spiritually with Bible studies. They also helped with typing supplies, Internet research, and contacts.

I thank Tracy Buck for giving me the chance to share my story with the world. Tracy spent many hours typing, editing, and proofing this book; I am forever grateful. She is a child of the King, and I feel His presence when she is near. I would also like to thank her friend, Cathy Walsh, for doing the final proofing of this book. She gave her time and expertise willingly, and that means a lot to me.

I thank Adrian Torres, author of *The Walls Talk*, for introducing me to Ron and Tracy. He was patient with me as I bombarded him with questions about publishing a book. Thank you, Adrian.

I'd like to thank Mark Watkins for the graphic design and wonderful artwork that is the cover of this book, and also for taking his time to get it ready for publication. Thanks, Mark.

I'd like to thank my dad for all the stamps he sent me. These made it possible to mail pages of the book to Tracy and my mom. He also helped with typing supplies. Thank you, Papa, for teaching me to always work hard.

I thank my sister Sheila for the gift of a typewriter. She also helped with stamps and writing supplies. Thank you for your love throughout my incarceration.

I thank Diane in Nova Scotia for being such a good friend to me while I've been "inside." Her letters encouraged me when I was struggling through lockdowns and dark times. She also helped with typing supplies. Thank you, Diane.

I thank my Canadian friends Rick and Doug for their friendship and encouragement during these hard times.

I thank Hratch Baliozian for being a positive role model in my life. I attend his "Hispanic Life Skills Class: Parole Candidates," and he meets with me privately to help me gain insight into the bad choices I've made. I've grown tremendously since I've been working with him. Thank you, Hratch, for spending so many hours with me each week to help me become a better man.

I thank Dan who taught me how to write a book and who also helped me edit the first few chapters of this book. He gave me a love for English grammar.

I thank Rita, Nora, and George from V.O.E.G. Every Thursday they came and encouraged me to become who I am today.

I can't forget F.I.R.S.T. (Friends in Recovery Stand Together), which also played a role in my recovery. Thank you Todd, Stan, Jesse, Roger, Alberto, Ed, Robert, Frasier, Allen, James, Howard, Ezell, and Ramon for being my "accountability partners."

I thank Robert Ferguson for building me into a champion and for not giving up on me when I fell. Thank you, Mr. Ferguson.

I'd like to thank Grace Prison Fellowship and Pastor Dave for teaching me what love and unity look like.

I thank the faithful brothers at CIM C-Yard for exemplifying humility.

The following people I'd like to thank for helping with typing supplies and stamps: my sisters Corinna and Darla; my good friends Sami, Jacob, and Justin; Eric and my niece Jessika; Karen in Ventura.

I thank the following people for the part they played in my transformation: Arthur from Emmanuel Baptist Church; Elder Sand from Chinese Christian Church of Thousand Oaks; the brothers and sisters at Paul's Valley Church of Christ; Noel, Chris, Richard Garfield, Andrade, Jason, Aunt Pat, Uncle Dave, and Uncle Jack.

I'd like to thank Jeff DeVore, Richard Farrar, Bill Moore, and Mel Novak for taking the time to read this book and write short reviews.

Foreword

It would be fair to say that Jeremy Jackson's life has been one of transformation – from a young boy, who stuttered badly and was bullied by his peers, to the teenager who found the answer to the bullying in developing a strong body and working to become an MMA and UFC fighter, and IFC title holder.

The forward progression of Jeremy's career, spanning the six years between 2002 and 2008, shows his highs, particularly his defeat of Nick Diaz, and setbacks. These increasingly dragged him down – personal tragedy, turbulent personal relationships, professional disappointments, physical injuries and increasing addiction to pain killers and alcohol.

The emptiness he finds in living the life of a celebrity; his yearning for some greater meaning, reveal his inner spiritual struggles. Only when his life reached rock bottom, did his personal journey of transformation begin.

Jeremy's story offers a message of hope to anyone who has suffered from the ups and downs of life, or is trying to find meaning in existence. Jeremy found the answers in his commitment to Christ.

The transformation in Jeremy's life demonstrates that no human needs to be locked into a spiral of hopelessness, guilt and despair. Jeremy tells his story with depth, readability and humor, along with despair.

– Richard Farrar

**Mr. Farrar is a volunteer with the John Howard Society in Ontario, Canada, in a Restorative Youth Justice program, and is a retired college teacher.*

Preface

"The chief end of man is to glorify God and enjoy Him forever."
– Westminster Shorter Catechism

I am writing this book from a California State Prison. To date, I have been incarcerated for almost a decade and am looking at 25 years to life. Sometimes I forget there is a world out there. Every day I wake up to concrete walls and concrete floors. All around me I see razor wire and metal.

Today I write this from a level-two prison which is a lot safer than a level three or four. I don't see that much violence at this prison. Don't get me wrong. I still see violence, just not as much as I used to see. It was a nightmare at previous prisons because they were higher levels. Gun towers were inside and outside the buildings. I could hear other inmates kicking their doors and screaming at the tops of their lungs. Pepper spray would seep under my door because the guards had just broken up a fight. I could 'taste' the pepper spray, and it would be difficult to breathe.

It's hard to describe the feeling I get in my stomach when I hear the alarm go off. Did someone die in his cell today? Did someone get hurt at yard? Did someone get hurt in his cell? Since I have been incarcerated, dead inmates have been carried out in body bags, some have been murdered by other inmates, while others have committed suicide. Some of those carried out in those bags were my friends. Surprisingly, life continues on in here as if nothing has occurred. Inmates have become desensitized to death.

This is the world in which I live. It's not glamorous; it's not Hollywood; it's my life. Life in here is not like what you see on television or in the movies. It is a place I pray none of you ever end up.

Many of you know me as "The Scorpion." Maybe you saw me fight in person or on Pay-Per-View. You might remember me from "The Ultimate Fighter 4: The Comeback," a reality television show from 2006. Regardless of how you know me, you only saw glimpses of who I really was. You saw the image I had created for the world. The "Scorpion" became the image I hid behind.

I want people to know the truth about my life, not only my successes and accomplishments, but my failures as well. I want you to see my addictions and my motivations. I'd like for you to get a glimpse of my life through my eyes, so you can see what led me to where I am today.

It took me awhile to finally decide to write this book. For the past few years, people who have been close to me kept encouraging me, but inside I felt the time wasn't right until now. Why? There are many reasons, but I will only list three.

The first had to do with the fear of returning to the public eye. I have been out of the spotlight for a while, and I was afraid that if I wrote a book it would put me back in the mix and cause me to stumble.

The second reason was to make it clear to people that I was no "angel." I run into people all the time now who see the man I am today and have a hard time believing who I used to be. They say things like, "You are the most gentle and peaceful person I've ever met. I can't see you hurting a fly. What are you doing in prison?" It's difficult for them to see that I used to be a destructive man who was selfish and self-centered. They find it hard to believe that I drank vodka all day, every day, from 2004 to 2008. I stacked several kinds of steroids, stayed high with a variety of drugs, and I couldn't say one sentence without using cuss words. I was no angel.

And the third reason was that I heard what has been written about me on Internet sites such as Wikipedia, and I wanted to clear things up. Wikipedia only tells a few of my successes; then it makes it seem like my life ended in 2008 when I was arrested. But my life didn't end! That was the turning point in my life, and I became a NEW man.

People told me if I wrote a book explaining the truth of my life, the prison would never release me. They said people would lose respect for me. I'm not writing this book to try and gain respect! I am not writing this to glorify myself. My motivation to write this is to help you understand that there is more to life than chasing after sex, alcohol, drugs and entertainment. None of these things ever really satisfies. It always leaves you wanting more and more, wondering why none of it seems to fill that empty void in your heart. Only God can fill that spot.

I wrote this book thinking of you. It's to give you hope, that no matter what addictions you might have, you can be set free. No matter what your failures are, you can get back up and make a great comeback. I didn't start living until I surrendered my life to the One who created me. His name is Jesus Christ.

"For from Him, and through Him and to Him are all things. To Him be glory forever, Amen." –**Romans 11:36**

"The deepest desire of our heart is for union with God. God created us for union with himself. This is the original purpose of our lives."
Brennon Manning

Jeremy Rea Jackson
Chino, California

Introduction

Concrete is cold and hard. Sitting on the floor in a room about the size of a small closet, I wonder where I am and how I got here. To my left is an old concrete desk with a bed next to it. Bed? It's more like a slab with a yoga mat resting on it. To my right is a stainless-steel toilet with an attached sink. I hear a noise coming from outside, and it is indiscernible. It sounds kind of like doors opening. Standing up, I walk to a metal door and look out a window that is just four inches wide and twelve inches tall. A large black man in jailhouse blues walks up.

"How'ya doing?" he asks.

As I read the letters on his shirt, T-21248[1], it all begins to make sense and I remember. I'm in Ventura County Jail, California. The black man at my door taught me how to make Pruno, a homemade concoction of alcohol."Didja drink it? Whaddja think?" He has a pleasant smile.

"It's all gone. Why? You got any more?" I ask, noticing the cup in his hand.

"Here," he says, "slide a plastic bag under your door and you can have some of this."

"I don't think I have a bag. Just a sec' and I'll check."

Looking around I realize that I have a lingering buzz from the last cup I drank. There's no bag to be seen. "I don't have a bag," I say dejectedly.

"No problem. Grab that paper on the desk and slide it under," he says, pointing to the back of the cell where the desk is. "I'll make a funnel."

I slide the paper under the door; he grabs it, rolls it into a tube, and slides the pointed end into the narrow crack in the door.

"Put your cup under the tip while I pour," he instructs. A few seconds later, a quantity of Pruno is transferred to my small cup. I eagerly gulp it down.

"Jackson!" Startled, I jump and look around the cell.

"Crap!" I think to myself. "Caught!" Almost immediately, I realize it's just the speaker in my cell. I can relax.

---

1   Every inmate who enters the system is given a number. Mine is AG6940

"You ready for day room?" an authoritative voice asks. Each day I'm allowed out of my cell for one hour so I can shower or use the phone, preferably both. I inform the voice that I am ready. The man at my door retreats to his cell.

The section of housing I am in is known as Administrative Segregation, or Ad-Seg. Movies and television will portray this place as "The Hole." The Hole is for some people who need to be separated from the general population. Basically, The Hole is for the worst of the worst, the most dangerous. Conversely, The Hole is also to keep the general population away from some people.

Why am I in The Hole? For my own safety and the safety of others, I'm told; not for punishment. My cell door opens and I go straight to the phone. There's only one person a dangerous criminal held in a high-powered jail can call at a time like this.

"Mom? Bail me out! Please?" I beg. The conversation's always the same. I ask her to bail me out, and she tells me to give my life to God. "Jeremy, you need to pray, sincerely. Give your heart to God."

What is she talking about? I've been going to church throughout my entire life and dutifully prayed before every meal! I've been sitting in jail for three months and all she can do is talk about God?

"This isn't about God. I need to get bailed out. Quit bringing God into this," I said with mounting frustration.

"Son, you need to give your life to God," she said again.

"I gave my life to God a long time ago. What are you talking about? I am a Christian," I said. I've been a Christian since I was a child. I was baptized in 2006. Now two years later, she is telling me to give my life to God? Does she think I'm not a Christian?

Obviously she is not going to help me. We say our goodbyes, and I hang up, frustrated. Now for a shower. As I rinse the soap out of my hair, many questions run through my mind:

How did I end up in jail?

Where did my life go wrong?

How did I become an alcoholic in the first place?

Even more importantly, what does my mom mean by telling me to give my life to God when I already have?

Life had been great for me before my arrest. I had won my last MMA (Mixed Martial Arts)[2] fight, and I was preparing for bigger ones: both in venue and prize money.

Several years ago I had been part of a reality show on cable television called "The Ultimate Fighter: The Comeback." That show had generated a lot of calls for me. Powerful, important people were calling me. One asked me to star in another reality show that had already begun filming. Sixteen female fighters would live in a house competing against each other. It would be like The Ultimate Fighter but with girls. The show would be unique.

First, understand that it was not affiliated with the UFC. It was a completely separate organization that was trying out the same concept as The Ultimate Fighter. In fact, at that time, the UFC didn't even allow women into their organization to fight.

Second, I was asked to be the coach and live in the house with the fighters. I was chosen because the networks wanted drama, and the circumstances surrounding my eviction from The Ultimate Fighter: Season Four supplied that.

If that wasn't enough of a "lollipop" in my life, I was also part owner of an MMA gym in Ventura, California, and I was in the process of opening two more gyms: one in Venice and another in Ventura. I taught Martial Arts classes and was also a personal trainer. Life was fantastic, and I was on top of the world, enjoying mild celebrity status among those in the business. I often joked about getting my very own personal parking space.

Beautiful women sought my attention with sways and smiles. Men sometimes shook my hand and tried to show how strong their grip was. I always wondered if that was because of jealousy; I couldn't always tell by their eyes or their smiles when first meeting them. I was very happy with life, but was I really happy or was I just fooling myself? This is something you will find out as I take you back to the beginning of my life and tell you what went wrong, and how I ended up on this cold, hard cement floor in a Ventura jail cell.

---

2   *Total Combat 19*; March 31, 2007

1 The Beginning

I was born in Brawley, California, on Sept. 19, 1982, but I lived in Imperial which is a few miles south of Brawley. It's a small town near the border of Mexico in between Yuma, Arizona, and San Diego. The population was around 5,000 at the time and temperatures measured 126 degrees during summer months. I was born into a silent world. My ear canals were completely closed and no one knew, not even my parents.

As you can imagine, I didn't always obey my parents when they asked me to stop doing something. I simply didn't hear them and didn't know the difference. I was a frustrated little boy who couldn't understand what people were telling me and why they always seemed to get angry when I ignored them. Even the teachers became upset with me at times. Some thought I was retarded.

What is it like to be a deaf child? I didn't know I was deaf, so I assumed everyone was living my world. And, although I couldn't hear noise, I definitely could "feel" it. I felt vibrations all around me and even felt them within my body.[3] I knew when others were speaking because those vibrations were distinct from other noises. A man's voice is different from a woman's voice. I knew when doors opened and closed, or when a dog was barking. I felt every noise.

As we were on our way back from visiting Grandma in Oklahoma, my older brother Oscar and I played in the back of the camper on my dad's '69 Chevy step-side pickup. It seemed like forever to get home because of the speed my dad liked to drive, not because he got pulled over for speeding. It was the opposite. He drove very slowly and it made me batty. Sometimes he would even be pulled over by the police for creeping along on freeways.

While my brother and I played in the back of the truck, I decided to throw a Hot Wheels fire truck at his head! He grabbed his head and began to scream, though I couldn't hear him because of my hearing disability. I

---

3   Even today I am sensitive to sound vibrations. When people near me are speaking, especially those with deep voices, I feel it. When those in the next room are talking, I have a hard time sleeping because of these vibrations. Sometimes the beat of my own heart keeps me awake.

could sure tell by the look on his face, though, that I'd committed a huge error.

Tears were flowing and his mouth was agape. Let's just say he wasn't happy, at all. And neither were my mom and dad. My dad pulled over, and they took my brother out of the truck to examine the wound. I was three years old and Oscar was five. I saw my mom pressing a towel against Oscar's head, and it was at that point that I saw the blood.

As my mom tried to calm my brother, my dad turned around and made eye contact with me. I knew that look well. With one stroke, he removed his belt and held it as a whip as he made his way toward me. I watched from the passenger seat as my dad approached the truck, wondering if there was anything I could do to avoid the inevitable. A little knob on the door sparked a daring plan. I'd seen my parents press the knob, making the door inoperable. Maybe it would work now! I put my little hands on the lock knob and pressed down with all my might.

"CLICK!" went the locking mechanism. I couldn't hear what my dad was saying, but I had become very adept at reading lips. Most of what he said couldn't be repeated in a PG rated movie, but even at my young age I knew what was good for me, and opening that door right then probably wouldn't have been a very good idea.

"Boy, you'd better unlock this door right now!" my dad growled.

My terrified little head moved side to side repeatedly, "No way!"

My dad began looking through his pockets. The keys!

Oh crap.

After a few seconds of fruitless searching, he looked at the ignition. There hung his keys, taunting him with a gentle sway.

He walked around the front of the truck, heading toward the driver's side door. He didn't make it in time.

"CLICK!" My little hands had found the other lock knob. I had both doors locked now! My eyes followed the movement of his lips.

"I'm telling you right now, you better open this door! I'm going to blister your little butt!" Again my terrified little head shook. "No, sir!" I wouldn't be opening that door any time soon.

Then it dawned on me. I wasn't sure how long I could hold out in the cab of my dad's truck. How long could I postpone the inevitable spanking that was sure to follow? Eventually our family needed the truck to finish the drive home! Maybe I could negotiate with him? Probably not. But it didn't matter; I'd delay that spanking for as long as humanly possible.

Suddenly the "light bulb" look on my dad's face told me he'd thought of something else. Whatever it was, it was probably bad news for me. I watched as he walked toward the back of the truck. The camper shell! Oh no! There was a latch that could be released, gaining access to the cab of the truck!

Not good! The race was on. Could I get to the latch before the old man and his belt?

I crawled. He ran.

"CLICK! "

This time it was the sound of the latch opening. Definitely not good!

The largest hand I'd ever seen was reaching into the back of the truck and fishing for me, while I scrambled around like a rabbit in a barrel.

Sooner or later the unavoidable happened. The giant hand grabbed my ankle, and I couldn't wiggle free. With one firm yank, I was pulled from the safety of the truck, squirming like a pig in the jaws of a jungle cat.

I got a real good spanking that day. Well, it wasn't that good, but I never forgot it. That's one of my earliest memories of reading lips: three years old and self-taught! It was about two years later that my hearing impairment was discovered.

2 Twinkle, Twinkle, Little Star

It was my kindergarten teacher who discovered I couldn't hear. She called my mom and set up a parent/teacher conference. When a teacher calls a parent it's usually bad news, but this turned out to be my saving grace. Once there, she explained that every time she called my name, if I wasn't looking at her, I didn't respond. If I was looking at her, I'd respond. I was playing with the toys at the time, and she demonstrated by calling my name. I kept right on playing, completely oblivious to the world. My mom took me to a specialist later, and after some tests the doctor discovered my inability to hear.

He told my mom to imagine herself ten feet under water and someone is standing at the pool's edge trying to tell her something. How much would she understand? "That's what your son has been going through his whole life. He's not slow or incapable of learning. He just hasn't heard anything. It's a testament to his intelligence that he learned lip reading on his own."

I had the surgery that would open up my ear canals. Tubes were inserted to keep them open. I remember waking up in the hospital room surrounded by curtains. Everything was so loud I had to cover my ears! Even the footsteps of people walking hurt my eardrums. I felt like everyone was screaming. I was terrified and confused. Fortunately my mom came into the room and gave me a much-needed hug.

"M-M-Mom, I-I-I'm thirsty," I said. What was wrong with my voice? Why couldn't I talk without struggling? The opening of my ear drums had caused a new problem. The sound of my own voice distracted my mind, and whenever I tried to talk my speech center would jumble and cause me to stutter. The repaired auditory canals caused EVERYTHING to seem like blasts of brain-penetrating radio waves, which caused another issue. Sometimes it seemed as if I could see the incoming waves of sound, and it was horrifying. Imagine that for the next three years, everything in your life comes at you like an unexpected blast from a cannon, or like a rock band doing sound checks in your bedroom at all hours of the night.

For years I had nightmares. Any little sound was amplified to a point where it actually hurt a lot. Some weeks I survived on only ten total hours of sleep. Every household noise that most people grow accustomed to in their lives, I learned at a very tender age.

The teachers would call on me to read, and I would stutter my way through the sentence. "Th-th-the b-b-bird wa-wa-was...," and the entire class would fall out of their chairs laughing at me.

One time a teacher actually asked me, "What are you, retarded?" This was supposed to be a person who educated children. Yet this man had just "green-lighted" every student in the classroom, and ultimately the whole school, to tease and harass me to a point of suicidal depression. Childhood can be brutal enough without a homeroom teacher placing a stamp of approval on that brutality.

Recess is supposed to be a time of fun and play, learning to get along with others. For me it was torture. I spent most of my time trying to defend myself, or fighting because there was no other way around it. You see, my brother Oscar derived a great deal of pleasure provoking the other kids, and added to my woes it was almost impossible to tell us apart. So, I took a lot of flak for his evil doings.

I just didn't understand the world. Why me? Why was I tortured from all directions? Teachers, family, schoolmates, it seemed they all hated me. Why? What did I do wrong? Here I was, only a kid, and I simply didn't know what I'd done to make others enjoy tormenting me. If someone had just told me what to do, I would have tried my hardest to fix it.

Something that really confused me was that everyone else knew what was going on in the world. Although I was in the same class with the same kids, it felt like nothing was the same. Now that I could hear, it seemed like everyone knew so much and I knew so little. They were speaking of things I didn't know. It was like they were downloaded with all this information in one day, but they forgot to download me with the same information. They looked at me and expected me to know what they were talking about, but I didn't have a clue. I was frustrated! I wanted to know what they knew, but I didn't know how to get the information. If I opened my mouth to ask questions, everyone called me a "retard."

A few months after surgery, my family and I were traveling down a deserted back road in the Imperial Valley. I think we were probably frog hunting. We'd go hunting in canals at night and then have a feast the next day. They really do taste just like chicken! We weren't a bunch of rednecks out to save a dime; we just really liked frog legs. I guess at heart I'm a country boy.

Dad was driving his '69 Chevy step-side, while Mom sat in the passenger seat holding my younger brother who was about a year and a half old. Oscar and I sat on the floorboard in front of the heater. The floorboard was our usual spot during travel. My eyes gazed up through the front of the window, and I could see Orion's Belt and the Big Dipper. Of course I didn't know those names at the time. All I knew was that they were beautiful. My mouth hung in awe as I stared at those diamonds in the sky.

Who made all those stars?

What happened next was spontaneous. It was the first song I heard after my ear surgery. I began singing, "Twinkle twinkle little star, how I wonder what you are..."

No stuttering! My mom applauded as I held out the last note of the song. My eyes were still fixed on Orion's Belt as my older brother began to sing the "ABC" song. He was always competing with me, even at an early age. But I wasn't in "competition mode" at that moment because I was fixated on the stars. My mom began to cheer as Oscar kicked it up a notch and sang louder and faster. As he did, I just hummed my song and wondered who put those beautiful stars up there, just for me.

Throughout elementary school and junior high, I was picked on because of my speech impediment. I had two choices: put up with it or slug it out. As a one-time holder of full-contact fighting belts, I think it's obvious which option I chose as I grew older. I wasn't about to put up with ridicule and cruel teasing anymore. By the time I was nine, my mom was tired of seeing me bullied all the time, so she enrolled Oscar and me in boxing classes at a gym called "Sol De Oro." We trained five days a week. Eventually we competed all over southern California and Mexico.

When we weren't competing against each other in the ring, we would often be found swinging it out in the living room of our home. This usually led to another problem. There are many unsafe items in a living room that can be turned into weapons of mass destruction: end tables, chairs, and Dinky the family cat, complete with claws.

Dad didn't like seeing us boxing each other because he knew that it would eventually lead to a full-blown fist fight. The gloves would come off and anything close by became a weapon, including poor Dinky. Dad told our boxing coaches to make sure we sparred with others and not each other anymore.

But, before I learned how to defend myself, there were some very unpleasant events yet to happen in my life.

And, by the way, Dinky went the whole season undefeated, a perfect 38-0.

3 Raiders Jackets

When I was in first grade, Oscar and I each received Raiders jackets for Christmas. His was black and mine was purple -- yes, purple. Naturally I liked his black one best, but no amount of bribes could get him to trade with me.

"No way!" he exclaimed, "Yours is ugly and I wouldn't trade mine for a million bucks!"

"But if you had a million bucks you could buy thousands of jackets!" I cried.

"Look Jeremy, I don't want to trade my jacket for that sissy thing! Period." Then he strutted off as only an older brother who'd just won an argument can.

I was stuck with the sissy purple jacket.

Two weeks later I was playing during recess at school, wearing my new sissy purple Raiders jacket. Suddenly Oscar came running up to me, all out of breath.

"Still wanna trade?" he asked breathlessly.

"Trade what?" I asked.

"Your jacket for mine! C'mon, hurry up if you wanna do this!" He was already peeling off his jacket..

My eyes lit up like a Christmas tree, and I wanted to jump for joy. "For realzies?" "realzies" being the ultimate test-of-honor word.

"Realzies," he said solemnly.

We exchanged jackets. I almost couldn't contain myself!

"Thanks Oscar, you're the greatest!" My brother's not so bad after all. It was going to be nice having an older brother to protect and watch over me. I began to strut around the playground in my macho, black Raiders jacket.

Meanwhile, Oscar seemed to have vanished.

Wow! I still couldn't believe he actually did something nice for once.

Seconds later, several dark shadows suddenly eclipsed the sunlight. It was then I realized Oscar had been just a little too nice, which was totally out of character for my brother. The dark shadows were no eclipse. I was surrounded by sixth-graders. They were grinding their knuckles and looking very unhappily at me!

"We've got you now Oscar, you little punk!" one of them growled.

Instantly the pieces came together, and the outcome did not look too good for me.

Oh crap. Thanks, bro.

Throughout our young lives, especially elementary and junior high school, my brother and I were nearly identical. In fact we could have passed as twins except he was slightly taller. Even the teachers couldn't tell us apart most of the time. Worst of all, Oscar liked to annoy the sixth-graders every single day! But they couldn't catch him; fear makes a boy fast.

This explained why he wanted so badly to trade jackets with me. He knew that the sixth-graders would think that I was him and would lower a misguided "boom" on my head. Looking up at the biggest kid, I began to stammer that I wasn't Oscar, that I was his mild-mannered little brother – all harps, halos and wings. But, all that came out of my mouth was a staccato of indiscernible words.

"I- I- I- I'm- m-m- n-n-not--," and that's about as far as I got.

As I was being pummeled, the laughter from my brother across the field caused them to stop. The sixth-graders immediately realized they'd been had.

"If that's Oscar laughing, then who is this bloody little twerp?" one of them asked.

The tallest kid picked me up, dusted me off and said, "Sorry, thought you were somebody else." As they walked away, I checked the flow of blood coming out of my nose. Not too bad. I'd probably live.

Mom was waiting in the car after school to pick us up. As I was climbing into the car, my brother asked for his jacket back.

"Why did you do that to me?" I asked him, but he just laughed.

When we arrived home, he took his jacket back and there was nothing I could do. My anger was never a match for his wit.

"Man! You got blood all over my jacket! Thanks a lot!" he yelled.

"No, you're the reason there's blood all over your jacket."

You're welcome, bro.

Around this time my mom began working as an aide at the school. It didn't take long for her to notice that during recess I was often "on the fence," a form of punishment. Eventually Mom got tired of seeing me on the fence and decided to find out what I was doing to get in so much trouble. I explained to her that I wasn't getting into trouble. Oscar was the culprit and I was the fall guy.

"Then why don't you just tell them that you're not Oscar?" my mom inquired.

Sounds simple enough, but with my stuttering problem we would have been halfway through recess before I got my entire explanation out.

"Bu-bu-bu-but I-I-I'm n-n-n-not Ah-ah-ah-Oscar," I'd try to blurt out. By the time I got to the second "bu", the teacher would tell me to go stand against the fence until I learned my lesson.

"Bu-bu-bu--," I'd try again, only louder this time.

"I don't want to hear it, Oscar! Go stand by the fence right now or you can go see the principal!" she'd scold; then point the way to the fence. Pointing was the final gesture of a fruitless conversation.

Fortunately for me, Mom finally got to the bottom of the problem and set the record straight. But the die had been cast, and I was seen as a troublemaker by both students and faculty. For the next several years, all anyone had to say was, "Jeremy did it!" and my assumption of guilt was enough to warrant punishment. I had somehow become quite accomplished at being the scapegoat.

4 Imperial Backyard Baseball World Championships

A year and a half later, Oscar and I were playing baseball in the backyard of our home. I was standing by the back door, baseball bat in hand, ball cap pulled smartly to my eyebrows, eyeing my brother and waiting for the next pitch -- or the Yankees to call for me. I didn't really care which happened first.

He was standing about twenty feet away, glove on one hand and a tennis ball in the other. Ten feet behind Oscar was a gate that opened to an enclosure that kept some of our animals, including rabbits, chickens, ducks, doves, pigeons, and several other kinds of birds. Every day my dad would come home from work and go straight to the pens to feed them.

Oscar was about to pitch the ball when the back door of the house opened. Dad was home and would be making the trek across the yard for his everyday rendezvous with the hungry birds.

"Don't even think about pitching that ball, boys. Wait'll I get clear," he growled.

It would have taken all of two minutes to wait until Dad got out of the way, but Oscar was too impatient, so he pitched the ball.

I had only a split second to consider if I should swing. The pitch was soooo perfect, right down the tube! No pitched ball in the history of the Imperial Backyard Baseball World Championships had ever been more perfect! I just had to swing! Any kid on the planet would've swung at that pitch! Besides, I already had two strikes against me: it was deep in the ninth inning, bases loaded, and the Imperial Backyard Baseball Championship was on the line! I simply couldn't let my brother win again as usual! I was sick and tired of losing to him.

CRACK!!!!

No ball in the history of the Imperial Backyard Baseball Championships had been hit with such savagery! That tennis ball never stood a chance. Any other man-made object would have established a low-earth orbit at the velocity I'd just generated! I could almost imagine some soldier at the Strategic Air Command Base, deep in the heart of Colorado's Cheyenne Mountains, spotting the UFO on radar. I could even see him picking up the phone.

"Hello? Mr. President? This is Sergeant Smukatelli in Colorado. Yes sir, we've picked up something on radar. The aliens look like little green Penn tennis balls, sir. Yes, sir. Immediately, sir."

No tennis ball in the history of the Imperial Backyard Baseball World Championship had ever hit my dad squarely in the back of his head before. For a split second my Dad's hair looked like an explosion in a mattress factory, but in slow motion. Not good! Sorry, Dad. The ball was supposed to clear the East Coast. Honest! Like a bull that couldn't help but chase after a red cape, or a bass fish that could not resist hitting the lure, I couldn't help but swing.

My dad's head flung forward from the impact while the ball ricocheted toward Mexico, a place I'd love to have been right then! My dad calmly turned around, walked right past the true culprit, Oscar the pitcher, and headed straight for me! What about Oscar? He's the one who pitched that cherry! Why am I the only one getting punished? He is just as guilty for pitching the ball! My dad grabbed my wrist and escorted me into the house to give me my spanking.

"Daddy, please don't spank me hard," I said as we entered his room. He began rummaging through his fine collection of leather belts,[4] not saying a word.

When I finished crying he sat me down and said, "Son, do you know why I spanked you?"

I sat there thinking about the ball smacking him in the back of his head and tried not to laugh. Laughing right then would've been a death sentence for sure.

"Yes, I understand," I lied.

He went on to explain how it was my action that caused the ball to smack him in the head, not my brother's.

"But Oscar pitched the ball!" I pleaded.

"But you didn't have to swing, right?" he said.

It didn't make much sense to me at the time, but later on down the road it would. In the future I'd recall his words from that day.

---

4   My dad used to sell leather belts at the Swap Meet, so he had plenty to choose from.

5   Duct Tape Episode

By the time I was eight years old, Oscar had taken it upon himself to teach me how to be tough. I was standing in the backyard, and because of the 118-degree heat, I was only in my shorts. Here comes Oscar, stumbling out of the tool shed with five full rolls of gray duct tape. How is duct tape going to make me tough? I would soon find out.   Fifteen minutes later Oscar walked inside the house where our mom was on the phone with Gramma, fixing lunch for us. Oscar grabbed a soda out of the fridge and asked innocently,

"Hey Mama, where are the scissors?"

Mom, not paying attention, told him to check in the medicine cabinet in the bathroom. Oscar disappeared out the back door with the scissors, returning about ten minutes later with another question.

"Do you know where the tree trimmers are?" Oscar asked, sporting the face of an angel straight from the pearly gates of heaven.

Mom stopped talking to Gramma for a second and turned to Oscar.

"What exactly are you doing out there, young man?" she demanded, as only a mother who wants the truth can, but doesn't really expect it.

"I'm working on something," he said. Mom looked for deceit while studying his angelic face.

"On top of the shed," she finally answered and went back to talking to Gramma and fixing lunch. Oscar disappeared out the back door. Five minutes later Oscar was back.

"Mom, I'm gonna need the axe. Where is it?" he asked, as the choirs of heavenly angels sang ever-so-softly.

My mom's eyes widened at this latest inquiry, and she stood there, wondering what was up. "The axe?" she eyed him.

"Yeah, the axe. I gotta cut something out of the tree," and he smiled as big a smile as he could manage. She looked out the side window to see if she could see what he was working on, but didn't see anything out of sorts.

"What did you say you were working on?" she asked again.

"It's a project!" Oscar proudly proclaimed, looking her straight in the eye.

"A project?" she echoed. "Yeah, a project. Can I get the axe?" he repeated.

"No, now you know you're too young to be using the axe without your dad around."

"But Dad's not gonna be home for four more hours!" he complained.

"Well, you're just gonna have to wait!" Mom said. Then she told Gramma she'd talk to her later and hung up.

"Fine!" Oscar murmured and ran out the back door.

My mom stood there for a second, rewinding the conversation back through her mind. Curious, she walked out the back door to see Oscar standing in front of the huge tree with the axe she'd told him he was not allowed to use. She heard him say, "Well Jeremy, the only way I can get you loose is by cutting off some of your limbs. Lose the arms or the legs?"

And there I was, taped to the tree! It finally made sense to her. Oscar had used all five rolls of duct tape to secure me, leaving only a small slit for me to breathe through. It was 118 degrees. Each time he had left me, he returned with a bigger, sharper tool, finally informing me he had to remove body parts to get me free.

"Oscar!" Mom shouted at the top of her lungs. "Give me that axe! Now!"

She grabbed the axe from his hands, looking at him as if he'd suddenly sprouted horns belonging to the devil. She began trying to find the end of the tape so she could unwrap me. At 118 degrees Mom was trying to find the one piece of sweat-soaked tape that would begin unraveling the slimy tape.

It took a while to find the end of it, but she kept walking around the tree, going in circles. After about ten minutes, she was able to see my shoulders.

"Hang in there, son, just a few more minutes and I should have you out!" she said.

Twenty minutes later she removed the last strand of duct tape, only to discover I was naked.

"You taped him naked to the tree?" she asked, staring at Oscar angrily. He had no response. And I had no answer to the "why" either. It took two months for my eyebrows to grow back.

The next day I walked out the back door and into the backyard, to find Oscar digging holes in the sand with his best friend, James. The tunnels were about four feet deep, and it looked like they were just finishing up. Oscar stuck his shovel in the sand outside the entrance to the tunnel and climbed down into the dark cavern.

It was about 110 degrees, but much cooler down in the tunnel. I looked over at the coiled garden hose lying there next to the house, and a great idea popped into my head. I took that hose, quietly dragged it over to the opening of the tunnel, and stuck it down inside directly above their heads! Did I mention it was 110 degrees that day? The water coming from that hose was steaming hot!!

Savoring the moment, while whistling a happy tune, I calmly walked to the spigot, licked my lips, and let loose a steaming torrent of water on my brother's head. Then I ran back into the house, laughing hysterically and uncontrollably. Sorry, James, you were simply collateral damage.

I could hear Oscar and James screaming words that a sailor on a submarine in the deepest part of the ocean would use. "Jeremy!! You're dead meat!! #*%#!" they screamed as the blast of water scalded them both. I stayed close to Mom and Dad for the rest of the day, knowing it was only a matter of time before they'd beat the crap out of me. But, the satisfaction of the revenge far outweighed the fear of the coming beating.

6 The Tunnels

One time just before dark, Oscar invited me to go down the road to dig tunnels in the ground. Like rabbits, we would spend countless hours digging tunnels all over town. Unlike the tunnels in our backyard, these were much deeper. They were six to seven feet deep and had little rooms to hang out in. We even made a chimney for the fires we burned at night so we could roast marshmallows.

Oscar and I got to the tunnels after a long bike ride. I climbed down to the bottom of the tunnel and started digging with a small garden shovel. I would fill a bucket with sand, and Oscar would haul it up with a rope we had pilfered from our shed. After about the fifth bucket was being pulled up, I could hear Oscar shouting from the entrance. Curious, I climbed up out of the hole to see what was going on.

"Who are you talking to?" I asked.

"See those guys over there?" he asked, pointing down the road.

I looked in the direction he was pointing and noticed four big teenagers riding bikes on the other side of the road. They looked like they were over six feet tall and at least 200 pounds. Oscar and I were maybe 50 pounds soaking wet.

As I watched them riding closer, a dirt clod exploded on the biggest kid's head. As he fell off his bike, crashing to the ground, I wondered, "Who in the world is stupid enough to throw rock-hard dirt clods at these guys?"

I turned and watched Oscar as he picked up another dirt rocket and launched it toward the huge teenagers, tagging another one in the head.

This can't be good! Something tells me this will not end well.

The biggest one picked himself up off the ground and brushed the dirt from his eyes, looking around to see where the dirt clods were coming from. Then he made eye contact with me.

Oh crap!

"Yeah! It was us! What are ya gonna do about it?!" Oscar shouted from his scrawny body.

Before Oscar could finish what he wanted to say, their bikes were already in motion riding our way, like missiles flying toward their targets.

"Quick! Into the tunnel!!" Oscar said breathlessly.

I dove into the closest tunnel and waited for Oscar to follow. After a long minute or two, I realized he wasn't following me.

"Oscar?!" I whispered.

No answer came, but I could hear the sounds of bikes outside the tunnel as I tried to melt into the back wall of the cave. I was trapped!

"One of them is in a hole somewhere here! I saw him drop!" a voice from the surface said.

They didn't have a flashlight and couldn't see into the tunnels, so I decided to sit as still as a church mouse, quietly waiting, barely breathing.

"We know you're down there! You might as well come out!" one of them yelled in a booming voice.

"Are you sure he's still here?" another one whispered.

"Dude, I saw him dive into a hole right here! The other little punk took off on his bike!" a voice said with frustration.

Suddenly I could hear stomping above my head, and dirt was beginning to fall in my hair. They were trying to cave in the tunnels! I crawled to the other side of the tunnel, but one of them spotted movement and rocks started flying into the opening.

"There he is! Get him!" they shouted.

I curled into a ball and was hit a few times until I couldn't take it anymore. Crawling on all fours, I went into another chamber of the tunnel.

"There he goes! Come here, you little rabbit!" one shouted.

I made it to the chimney area where we lit our fires at night. I needed a distraction so I could climb out of one of our other openings.

We had matches, wood, and gasoline in this part of our cave. I had a great idea: I'd start a fire, they'd see smoke coming out of the tunnel, and then I'd be able to escape from another opening.

I poured gas on the wood and threw a match on it, hoping I didn't set myself on fire in the rush of things. I could hear them talking above ground. "Is that smoke?"

"Dude, there's a fire down there!!" one shouted.

While they were mesmerized by the smoke, I crawled to the farthest tunnel exit and poked my head out, like the little gopher from the movie *Caddyshack*. It worked! They had their backs to me as they stared at the smoke. This was my big chance -- the great escape! I looked around but couldn't see my bike. I was going to have to make a run for it!

I climbed out of that hole and sprinted toward my house. They immediately saw me and followed on their bikes. I couldn't outrun their bikes. I had to think of something quickly because they were gaining on me. Fifty yards down the road was a deep ditch that had no water in it, and I knew they wouldn't be able to ride their bikes into it; it was too steep. I slid down the side of this twenty-to-thirty foot ditch and realized pretty quickly it wasn't one of my best ideas.

There they were standing at the top of the bank. They had me surrounded. Each of them picked up a rock and asked me if I had any last words.

"Yes! I sh-sh-sure d-d-d-do! I di-di-didn't throw a, any r-r-rocks at y-y-you g-gu-guys. It wa-wa-was-s m-m-my b-br-br-brother." I begged them.

"Beautiful speech! But we saw you throwing rocks at us." the biggest one yelled angrily.

"B-b-bu-but I d-d-din-didn't thr-throw any r-rocks, honest!" I said.

"You calling us liars?" he asked.

"Y-y-yea, well-n-oo- n-no-not a l-li-liar. I'm j-ju-just say-saying y-yo-you're wrong" I said.

"You're calling us liars!" he shouted.

I think I realized there was nothing I could say to convince them I hadn't thrown the dirt clods, so instead I tried to talk them into throwing smaller ones; I even threw in a pitiful, "Please?"

But, before I got the words out the rocks were flying my way. The only thing I could do was curl into a ball and take it. Luckily none of them hit me on the head hard enough to cave it in -- most just landed all over my body.

Thirty minutes later I walked into the house, covered in blood and dirt. There sitting on the couch watching "Knight Rider" was Oscar, drinking Mom's sweet tea. He looked up, saw me, and broke out in a huge fit of laughter, saying I was the funniest thing he'd ever seen.

"Haha, v-ve-ver-very fun-funn-funny, Oscar," I said as I went to the bathroom to take a shower. I checked my wounds, and my ego.

I don't remember which one hurt worse.

7 Betrayed

A lot happened to me at the age of twelve; most of it is too brutal to write about, so I will only mention the "not so bad."

One day Oscar told me he wanted me to prove I was tough. First I made sure there was no duct tape in his hands. When I noticed his hands were empty, I relaxed a little.

"What do you want me to do?" I asked. "I want you to beat up Hector," he replied.

"Hector?" Hector was a school bully who didn't speak any English.

Oscar answered, "You've been boxing for a few years now. You need to put that training to use. Are you scared?"

"No way! I ain't afraid of nothin'," I bragged. But I was terrified, not only of Hector, but also of his brother Juan who was a year older than I was.

"You can beat him up after school today when he goes to get his bike," Oscar planned. The day went by so slowly. I sat in class counting the minutes and seconds. I was both nervous and excited. I was about to make my brother proud!

The final bell rang, and Oscar escorted me to the bike racks, along with his best friend Tommy.

"There he is. We'll stand here and make sure nobody jumps in," Oscar decided. Hector was walking toward his bike when he noticed I was following him. "I'm tired of you thinking you can just walk around bullying everyone," I challenged.

Hector looked over my shoulder, and I knew there was someone standing behind me; unfortunately, it was his brother Juan. I wasn't too worried, though, because Oscar was a year older than Juan, and I knew Juan couldn't match Oscar's boxing skills.

While Juan shoved me backward, Hector took his bike chain off and began to beat me with it.

"Oscar, help me!" I cried, as I fell to the ground. But Oscar and Tommy just stood there watching. As I covered my head with my hands, I caught a glimpse of them -- both had grins on their faces. I realized I had been set up by Oscar, and he was enjoying it. They kept grinning as they watched Hector continue hitting me with the chain. It probably lasted only two or three minutes, but it seemed much longer. Oscar never stepped in to help. Instead, he watched me roll on the asphalt, trying to escape the chain.

I felt confused, hurt, and betrayed.

A teacher saw what was happening and pulled Hector off of me.

My body hurt for a long time, but my heart hurts still. Why did Oscar enjoy seeing pain and brutality, especially inflicted on his younger brothers?

I never asked him, and now I can't.

8   The Walk of Shame

When I was eleven or twelve years old, my older brother wanted to teach me how to steal from the stores down the street. Though he made it look easy, I was still afraid.

"Don't be a chicken! I don't hang out with chickens!" he said. Despite all the bad things he did to me, I still looked up to him and wanted to be around him. So, I grabbed a pack of bubble gum and walked out of the store. "See how easy it is?" he said.

It wasn't long after this that he began stealing cigarettes and lighters so he could sell them. He kept them in the clubhouse in the backyard and put a chain on the door to keep Mom out.

"I want to go in the clubhouse too," I said to Oscar.

"You can't come in," he replied, as he put his hand on my shoulder.

"Why not?" I asked. He pointed toward another sign to the left of the door which read, "No Chickens Allowed."

"If I invite you in here, you have to be crazy like us," he said.

"OK, let me in," I said. He opened the door, and I followed him in. I noticed all the packs of gum, lighters, and cigarettes he had stolen.

"If you want to hang out in here, you have to steal lighters and cigarettes from now on," he told me.

"But I don't smoke," I answered.

"Then you can sell them," he said. I agreed and went to the store that same day. We shoplifted from three different stores down the street from our house. I wore baggy sweats, tucking the bottoms into my shoes. I tossed everything in my sweats and let them fall to my ankles. I could hear the boxes and plastic hitting against each other with every step, but I didn't care.

Before we could sell anything, Mom found out. She took some bolt cutters and cut the lock to our clubhouse. When we came home after riding bikes, we noticed two large buckets sitting in the middle of the living room floor, right in front of the couch. We sat on the couch as she screamed for an hour.

"Which store did you take them from?" she asked.

"Valley Market," Oscar admitted. "And AM-PM and El Sol Market," I contributed.

"Come on," she said. "You are taking them back."

"What?? Wait!" Oscar argued. "A lot of the stuff has been opened. They can't do anything with it now. It's no good!"

"It doesn't matter. You need to take it all back and confess your wrong. Whatever the consequences are, you will face them!" she demanded.

I chimed in, "It's going to be embarrassing!"

"I don't care how embarrassing it is. You are going to do what's right!" she said.

We sorted the stuff into three buckets, by store. I walked into Valley Market carrying one bucket, and my brother was beside me. All we could do was look down as we walked down the aisle of shame. Suddenly some big shoes appeared in front of us, and I knew it was the owner of the store.

"Go on, tell him!" my mom demanded.

"Um, sir, we s-t-t-ole th-th-is f-f-r-r-om y-y-our s-s-t-t-ore and we are returning it t-t-t-o y-y-you," I stuttered.

Mom prompted me, "What else do you want to tell him?"

I looked at Oscar, and he took over. "We are sorry, sir. What we did was wrong."

The owner of the store was a really big man in his fifties or sixties. He picked up the bucket and looked at all the things we had stolen. He took a deep breath, blowing it out with displeasure.

"Whatever the consequences, they are willing to face them," Mom assured him. I looked up at the owner, and his eyes locked with mine. I quickly looked away.

"Well, I'm not going to make you pay for all of this, nor am I going to call the police. But I do need to discipline you in some way or you won't learn a lesson. So, you are not allowed to come into my store for six months," he said.

"Six months??" Oscar blurted out.

"Should I make it longer?" the owner replied.

"No, sir," Oscar said meekly.

We walked out with our heads down, aware that we still had two stores to go. It was humiliating, but I learned an important lesson that day that would stick with me forever. When you do something wrong you must make it right by owning up to it and suffering the consequences, no matter what they may be.

9 Lifeguarding Days

When I was fifteen, I landed my first job as a lifeguard at the Imperial City Pool. My dad had been a lifeguard mostly at local lakes for over twenty years, which is where I received most of my training. I remembered being about seven or eight years old, sitting up in the lifeguard chair with my dad at Sun Beam Lake, in Seeley California. He would tell me what to look for and how to get to the victim quickly.

I sailed through my lifeguard training at Imperial Valley College. It was a great feeling to be able to save a life if I had to. I still vividly remember some of my rescues.

One time, while elevated eight feet in the air in the lifeguard chair, feeling very regal and official, I looked over at another lifeguard. I noticed he had a strange look on his face. He was sitting on the edge of the pool with his feet dangling in the water. This was his preferred spot because he hated sitting up in the lifeguard chair. He gestured absent-mindedly toward the pool. I followed the direction of his finger and noticed a little girl about three years old struggling to stay above the water. I knew it was just a matter of time before she would sink because I had seen this situation too many times. She was a lot closer to the lifeguard who had pointed her out; if she went under he could reach her in less than two seconds.

I looked back at him to see if he was going to jump in and save her, but he just pointed at her while staring at me. I looked back at the little girl and saw her take a last breath before sinking to the bottom of the pool. I looked back at the lifeguard again and noticed he hadn't moved a muscle! Leaping from my chair, I did the most perfect, Olympic-qualifying feat ever in the Imperial Valley Aquatic Event: a belly flop that caused an eight-foot tidal surge, and which slammed the air right out of my lungs. I was in such a hurry I'd forgotten how to jump feet first from the chair.

As soon as I got my breath back, I swam to where the little girl had been and went to the bottom of the pool. I brought her to the surface as quickly as I could, and I could tell she was okay because of the way she was moving. She began coughing and crying as I lifted her to the edge of the pool. I looked over at the guard who had pointed to her, and he was leaning back as if he were tanning himself! I still don't understand his inaction. Why do some people act that way? The good thing is a little life was saved, but it was no thanks to him.

Another time I was sitting in the lifeguard chair and heard the diving board groan with effort; then I saw it dip almost to the point of touching the water. An extremely large kid was perched on the end of the board, waving to his family! He was about twelve or thirteen years old and weighed close to two hundred and fifty pounds.

"Tio, Tio!" he called to his uncle as he looked down at the water. Hesitation! Oh crap! To a lifeguard that momentary delay is a giant red flag. A person who knows what they're doing will usually charge the pool or diving board. The way this kid was acting, he definitely was not related to Flipper and he wasn't exactly built like Michael Phelps either!

I remember thinking, "I sure hope this kid can swim because he's really, really big, and if I have to go in the water after him, we'll both be in trouble."

There had been numerous occasions where I'd had to risk my neck in order to save some large goofball who was trying to impress a pretty girl, only to find the water over his head. I've learned first-hand, adrenalin can give a drowning victim super-human strength. I'd already had many life-and-death battles in the deep end of a pool. While this kid's family counted to three, I counted with them, dreading the inevitable.

At "tres" he jumped; at "cinco" I jumped in. It only took three seconds for the bubbles to stop. He had all the aquatic grace of a concrete block. The poor kid must have been exhaling all the way to the bottom. When I saw the last medium-sized bubble break the surface, I knew he was out of air. This time, I did a proper feet-first jump from the chair and saved him. Life lesson: don't let foolishness trump common sense. Later in life that would be a lesson I wished I had remembered.

The following year, I went from the Imperial City Pool to the Imperial Valley College Pool, getting promoted to head lifeguard. Now I was really becoming the "Man"! All the pretty girls, even the fifty-year-olds, flirted with me. The other lifeguards weren't exactly happy having a sixteen year old as their boss, so no one listened to me.

With all this newfound attention from the opposite sex, I'd sneak out all night and be too exhausted to work the next day. As a result, I had to develop a clever disguise: dark sunglasses and a big straw hat. This prevented people from noticing that I was snoozing while sitting in the guard chair. One time I snuck back into my room at six o'clock in the morning, and I had to be at work by seven! I was so tired my mom had to drive me to work. As she drove she kept shaking her head at me and asking why I was having such a hard time keeping my eyes open. I was even contemplating propping my eyes open with toothpicks.

"You know, Jeremy, these people depend on you for their safety and, more importantly, for the safety of their children. You have an awesome responsibility; there is no greater honor in the world than being asked to care for someone's child."

As usual she was right. Who was I to jeopardize the lives of kids I was being paid to watch, just because I was having too much fun screwing around all night? Sure, I'd be the one who'd have to carry the memory of a dead child I should have saved, but for the family the pain would be unbearable, all because I thought I was a Casanova of the nightlife. That was a memory I didn't want.

Later that day I was sitting in the guard chair, and my eyes wanted to close. My mom's voice played in my head, "Jeremy, those people depend on you for their safety and, more importantly, for the safety of their most prized possessions: their children!"

My eyes snapped open, and I looked around to see if any of the other guards could relieve me so I could catch a few winks. No one was around. The other lifeguards were in the bathroom smoking pot.

Now what could I do? I climbed back up into the guard chair and thought about my mom's words. I had a huge responsibility, and I wasn't about to let my mom or any of the little kids down. I hunkered down, working solo the rest of the day because the other lifeguards were too stoned to be any help to a drowning victim. I learned a lesson that day. From then on I promised myself to be home and in bed at a reasonable time, assuring adequate sleep for the next day.

One day while sitting on a bench and enjoying my lunch break, one of the other lifeguards sat down next to me and began talking to me. He asked why he saw me drinking either chocolate milk or sodas at parties, instead of alcohol.

"Don't you like to have a good time?" he asked.

"Well, yes, of course I like to have a good time, but I don't need booze to do it." I replied.

"You know, you really should loosen up a little now and then," he said as he offered me a Styrofoam cup filled with beer. "Here, take a sip, see what ya think."

I gently pushed his hand away and remained firm, "I don't drink alcohol."

"Why not?" This guy was persistent.

"Because I have goals and dreams, and alcohol ruins lives!" I said.

"Well, what are your goals and dreams?" he asked.

"Someday, I'm going to fight in the UFC (Ultimate Fighting Championship) and become a champion!" I proudly proclaimed.

Laughing hysterically, he put his hand on my shoulder, "I hate to burst your bubble bro, but you're dreamin'! That ain't ever gonna happen!"

With mounting anger, I replied, "You don't think I have what it takes?"

"I know you can't!" he stated flatly.

"Why's that?" I asked.

"Jeremy," he began, "you simply don't have it. Fighting is more than big muscles and brute strength. You gotta have the mental game to go along with the strong body. In fact, this is how sure I am: if you become a champion then I'll give you ten million dollars. But, trust me, you won't even make it into the cage to fight! Those dudes are professional beasts who can twist you and break you in half! I hate to say it, buddy, but you're just Jeremy, a second-rate lifeguard at a third-rate pool."

Man, that stung worse than any bee sting I ever had.

"Listen," I said, with a measure of self-control, "Start savin' your money, cuz one day I will be a champion!"

"Yeah, I'll be holdin' my breath for that!" He walked off, still laughing.

Lesson: don't let someone steal your dreams. If you stay focused and want something bad enough, you can accomplish anything. You can reach your goals. All things are possible. I know this is true because one day I wouldn't hold just one champion belt, but multiple title belts: IFC (International Fighting Championship), CPW (Central Plains Wrestling Champion), and KOTM (King of the Mountain). "Focus" would become the key word I'd reflect back on much later. Life has a way of pitching a few curves at you.

10 Grooming to be a Fighter

As previously mentioned, I was nine when my parents decided to enroll Oscar and me in boxing. They were tired of seeing me bullied and beaten up because of my stuttering. Mom, Dad, and Dinky were tired of the out-of-control living room sparring sessions. We had no training and didn't know what we were doing, but Oscar and I sure had a lot of fun!

For the first year my formal training was really boring and disappointing. All we did was get our little fists taped up; then we'd jab our way across the gym, swinging at air and dancing the whole way. What are we trying out for, "Dancing with the Stars"? C'mon coach, I wanna punch someone! I wanna spar, punch a bag; punch something other than the wind!

Finally after what seemed an eternity, they promoted us to punching bags and sparring with real opponents! Eventually Oscar and I began competing locally. Then we began competing all over California, even into Mexico. I was stopping enemies dead in their tracks. I guess my coach knew what he was doing by having me jab at air for so long.

Lesson learned. Listen to the coach.

At thirteen years old I couldn't wait to get into wrestling. After enhancing my "ground game," Mom or Dad would drive Oscar and me to boxing class. I knew that if I wanted to be a complete fighter, I'd have to combine boxing and wrestling. It was during this same year that I got into a big fight with my older brother. It started like any other sparring session, but quickly escalated into a full-blown, two-man riot.

Oscar was a dirty fighter and right-hooked me in the groin. As soon as I caught my breath, I launched a kick that missed. He landed another right hook to my groin, and that's when I decided that this fight needed to go to the ground. By this time, one of the coaches had entered the ring and was desperately trying to break us up. Dad, sitting outside enjoying the fresh air, spied what was happening and made his way into the gym. He never liked it when Oscar and I went at it really hard; he knew it would become an all-out street fight.

"Let's go home!" Dad commanded, as he escorted us to his truck. We knew that we were both in trouble, but neither of us could guess what Dad had in mind.

Rather than face the consequences, I ran away.

I stayed gone most of the night until I realized that I wouldn't be able to make it on my own, and then I returned home.

Dad sat me down and explained that he didn't want me getting in the ring with Oscar anymore; we were both too competitive, and our fights always seemed to escalate.

The next day I found myself in my first real street fight. I was still pumped over the fight with Oscar and sort of looking for someone to take it out on. Naturally, my testosterone went looking for one of the biggest guys in my class.

While in the locker room at school, I approached Kevin, a kid who was famous for his unusual strength.

"You need to stay away from my girl!" I growled.

"Your girlfriend is all over me," he retorted.

Before Kevin could finish his sentence, I shoved him hard – real hard – Imperial Backyard Baseball World Championships hard!

Problem was that Kevin didn't move, not an inch, not even a nanometer! It was like pushing the Sears Tower while standing on a sheet of ice. He simply didn't budge.

Without a moment's hesitation, Kevin nailed me with a right hook.

IT'S ON!!! Yeah baby!! Now my skills were about to be tested. I was given a chance to prove myself in real combat! That year of throwing jabs at the air! All those hours of wrestling! The thousands of leg kicks! I was a beast! I was a killing machine! I was a Weapon of Mass Destruction! I was a coiled, steel-sprung animal waiting to strike! I was spinning through the air like a Raggedy Andy.

Kevin simply grabbed me with one hand and flung me across the locker room!

Perhaps some gymnastics training wouldn't 'ave hurt?! Eh, Coach?! Wasn't it against the rules to "Rag-Doll" your opponent?!

As it happened, I did a perfect flip in the air and landed on my feet, straddling one of the locker room benches. It was like a scene out of the Matrix movie.

I quickly jumped into my fighting stance, and my hands found their own marks.

Poor Kevin didn't stand a chance. My fists were like guided missiles, landing one punch after another, after another, after another, after another.

Eventually someone pulled me off. Looking at my hands, I saw that both were covered in blood; almost all of it was Kevin's.

My opponent's lip was split from mouth to nose. I could see a glint of bright white through all the blood; I realized the white was his front teeth.

It was then that I felt all-powerful. I'd finally benefited from all those hours of monotonous training. My whole body was a weapon, a finely-honed tool. This wasn't just a schoolyard kid winning his first real fight. I was a serious highly-trained fighting machine.

After that I went after every single bully I knew, past and present. The hunted had become the hunter, and I took them all down, one at a time. I never lost. All comers were easily dispatched. Word spread like a gutted feather pillow on a windy day, and it wasn't long before very large football players made very long detours to avoid crossing my path. Eventually there were no more bullies left to beat up. I'd vanquished all! Then it happened: I became that which I hated. I became a bully myself. I picked fights with anyone and everyone. Looking back, I despise myself for that.

But there was more of Martial Arts to learn, and eventually I'd become known almost the world over.

One day walking home from high school, I saw a karate studio named Seidokan/Shotokan. I watched from the window, observing the students in their karate Gi's, the white uniform of karate, executing Katas. A "Kata" is how and where you place your arms and legs for combat: a pose. Part of my new daily ritual was to stop and watch the fighters practice. Eventually the Sensei, the instructor, came out and invited me in.

I explained to him that I couldn't afford lessons. My only source of income was life-guarding, and besides all my money at that time went for something else. My older brother and I had shot out truck windows and street lights with our BB guns a few months prior. All my lifeguard money went toward the damages.

The Sensei worked out a deal whereby I could work for him, and he would train me in the art of Karate.

Just like in the movie The Karate Kid, I mowed my Sensei's lawn, washed his cars, painted his fences, cleaned his pool, planted trees, and helped teach some of his younger pupils.

By this time I had a full military-style workout regimen.

5:00 a.m.	100 squats 100 pushups 100 sit-ups Walk 100 yards on my hands
9:00 a.m. – 3:00 p.m.	School
3:30 p.m. – 4:00 p.m.	Run 2 ½ miles
4:00 p.m. – 5:30 p.m.	Wrestling
5:45 p.m. – 7:30 p.m.	Karate
8:00 p.m. – 9:30 p.m.	Boxing
10:00 pm - ???	Lift weights

I honestly don't know how I did it all, but I did. In fact, I was able to do all that and more. You see, girls suddenly began to gravitate toward me because I was the resident "Bad Boy." I started dating a lot then, and since I had no time during the day, nighttime became the "right" time!

When I was sixteen Oscar brought home some VHS tapes with fights on them. I watched Royce Grazie of the legendary Brazilian "Grazie" Clan, fight Ken Shamrock, a man built like a Greek god. These two warriors battled for thirty straight minutes! The only rules in the UFC at that time were no eye gouging, no biting, and no fish hooking of the mouth. Other than that, anything went!

But the most amazing thing that I saw had nothing to do with the actual fight; it was what happened afterward. The men, bloodied and bruised, HUGGED IT OUT!!

I fell in love with the sport right then. For me, there 'd be no turning back.

I'd been fighting guys on the street, then hating them, and being hated by them forever. What I really wanted, deep down in my heart, was to be able to fight someone of equal talent; then shake hands and be friends afterward.

I began searching online for Martial Arts training schools. Three caught my attention: Bart Vale, Ken Shamrock, and Robert Ferguson (the Prince of Leg Locks). All had studios, and all had some form of serious notoriety.

First I tried Bart Vale's studio in Florida, but all I got was an answering machine. I don't remember if I left a message or not.

Next I nosed around the Shamrock website, but it was too confusing and I couldn't find any contact information. Plus, I couldn't tell if his studio was in San Diego or in Lockford, California.

But the third name, Mr. Robert "Prince of Leg Locks" Ferguson[5], had a school about thirty minutes away from where an ex-girlfriend lived. His school was in Oxnard, California; my Maggie lived in Camarillo.

I called Maggie and explained the situation. She immediately said, "Sure, you can live with me!"

"Just until I find a place of my own…" I thought.

Her parents agreed that it would be OK.

I went home, packed my bags, and told Mom that I'd be moving north to live with Maggie. Of course, Mom was heartbroken and did everything, fair and unfair, to talk me out of it, but my heart was set and I wasn't about to change it.

"At least say goodbye to your dad. He is out at the lake," Mom was hoping that maybe Dad would be able to talk some sense into me.

As I drove to Sunbeam Lake where Dad worked as a park ranger, I cemented my resolve: I'd be one of the greatest UFC fighters in the world. Nothing would stop me.

Watching my dad's eyes tear up as I explained my plan left an impression that I carry to this day. Odds are I cried too. I'd never seen my dad so emotional.

---

5   At the time, Robert was a Submission Wrestling coach. Today he is mostly known as an author, certified nutritionist, and host of The Robert Ferguson Show.

When I arrived in Camarillo later that day, I grabbed the local phone book and thumbed through the Yellow Pages. Sure enough, there was only one MMA studio in the area: Robert Ferguson.

Maggie and I drove to his gym to see what it looked like. The lights were off, and I decided to leave a note. The words I wrote that day would change a lot of lives.

"My name is Jeremy Jackson. I want to be the next UFC champion of the world. Will you help me?"

I received a phone call from Robert Ferguson, and he agreed to take me under his wing and train me. He also got me a job busing tables at Spanish Hills Country Club in Camarillo. Thank you, Mr. Ferguson.

I explained to Robert that I'd been boxing since I was nine years old, that I'd studied Karate, wrestled in high school, and picked up a little Jiu-Jitsu.

"I think I'm close to being ready now, sir. When do you think I can get in a cage for a real tournament?"

Four and a half minutes later, one of his twelve-year-old students was tapping me out.

"You're not ready," was all Robert said. But evidently he saw something he liked because he didn't give up on me.

As the weeks went by, I had spaghetti-armed old men wrap me up like a pretzel and stomp me into the mat. Even the twelve-year-olds continued schooling me. I had a long way to go.

Even though I could out-power all of them, their techniques were absolutely textbook, and they defeated me over and over again. But my pride continued to preach at me, and I begged Robert for a cage match.

Finally he put boxing gloves on me. Now the tables were turned! No one could touch me! I was lightning in a bottle! Fast! Explosive!

"I wanna compete in a cage match!" I implored Robert. "I'll knock out my opponent!"

He figured out that I wasn't going to leave him alone about it, so he made some calls.

On September 9, 2001, I got my first real cage match.[6] It was to be held in northern California against a very strong wrestler from Caesar Gracie's camp. His name was Jake Shields, and he already had more than a few fights under his belt.

Robert gave me the layout: "Look, Jeremy, you gotta stick to the game plan if you wanna win. He is going to try and take you down. Don't let that happen! Keep the fight standing, no matter what. Beat him with your boxing skills, OK?"

"Got it, Coach! Keep my feet under me! Don't let the fight go to the mat! Outbox him!" I said, hopping back and forth. "This fight'll be over in less than ten seconds!" I yelled reassuringly.

"Do that, Jeremy! Make me proud!" Robert yelled back.

The announcer began making the introductions.

It sounded too easy! Use my hands! Don't throw kicks! Simply knock him out with my hands!

Two-point-two seconds into the first round, I threw a kick to my opponent's head.

Two-point-seven seconds, and I'm on my back.

Three-point-one seconds, everything my coach taught me goes out the window, and my wrestling instincts take over. Rather than use my Jiu-Jitsu skills, I used my wrestling skills instead. I turned my back to my opponent – a good thing to do in a rules-enforced wrestling match where you don't want to get pinned, but a very stupid thing to do in an all-contact fight.

Jake's arms closed around my throat, and I tapped out.

"Look Jeremy," Robert told me. "You have the potential to be a great fighter, but you've got to leave your ego behind and listen to me! I need you to trust me!"

Trusting people wasn't one of my strong suits, especially with all the stuff my older brother used to do to me. But in the years to come, I'd learn trust and become a world-class Mixed Martial Artist.

Robert would give me instructions before fights, and I'd stubbornly keep my own point of view. Deep down I knew that if I wanted to win, I'd have to listen. It took a while, but I finally learned he was right. He

6   Gladiator Challenge 6: Caged Beast

explained that I needed to focus on my Jiu-Jitsu and submission wrestling if I wanted to be an all-around fighter.

"Your boxing is strong. We just need to improve your ground skills," he'd say.

During training the next day, Robert yelled at me for the first time. I'd been trying to get people to tap out with wrist locks and pressure points, techniques learned in Karate. "Jeremy, that garbage doesn't work in the cage! You need to forget about Karate and focus on proven skills! Boxing, kickboxing, Jiu-Jitsu, and wrestling are proven tools! Focus on them!!" he roared. It was hard to let go of my Karate techniques, but in time I quit using them.[7] A few months after my fight with Jake Shields, I won my first cage match in an underground fight in Los Angeles: Kage Kombat. The guy I fought looked like a Skinhead who'd like nothing more than to rip my head off.

He made the mistake of trying for a standing guillotine, locking my head under his arm in an effort to clamp off my throat and make me quit. That proved to be a bad move.

I simply picked him up and slammed him to the mat. Then I worked my way around his body and wrapped myself around him. A few seconds later my arms were around his neck, and he tapped out.

I'd won.

It was my first MMA win. But, much to my disappointment, I found out that it didn't count on my overall record.

Not too long after that, I fought in the same event and won again. I knocked out Peter Delayo in overtime. This time it counted.

Throughout my career I would learn that this was normal. Some fights would count on my record, while others wouldn't. I still don't know or understand what the criteria are for when a win counts and for when one doesn't.

---

7   It's not that Karate is ineffective; it's just not the best choice in an MMA match. Wrist locks are effective in street fights, but in a professional fight they are nearly impossible to use because your opponent wears gloves. Similarly, pressure points work as distractions, but UFC fighters will never tap out because a pressure point is being applied.

I do wish they'd put all my fights on record.
But not the ones with Dinky. That cat was brutal!

11 First Title Shot

On June 21, 2002, I was working out at L.A. Workout in Camarillo with Justin, a good friend of mine from high school. Toward the end of our weight lifting, my phone rang. Much to my surprise the King of the Cage (KOTC) promoter was calling me!

"How would you like to fight Joe Stevenson for the Welter Weight Title Belt?"[8] the voice asked.

Wow! A title shot already?! I'd only had five or six fights by then, and most of those had been "underground." Nobody really knew who I was. Somehow this promoter had picked up my name, and now opportunity came knocking.

"Sounds good! What 'ave I got? A month? Two months?" I asked excitedly.

"Uh, how about tomorrow?" The promoter's voice kind of dropped a bit at that point.

"Tomorrow?? As in the day after today?" I asked incredulously. "Are you nuts?"

I was just finishing a heavy day of lifting. For the record, I never did any heavy lifting the week before a fight. I didn't want to be worn out. And the way it looked, I stood a real good chance of being too tired to put on a good show, not to mention that KOTC uses a smaller cage that favors a grappler. I was a boxer! Naturally, adding to my disadvantage was that Joe Stevenson was a master wrestler who would obviously try to take it to the mat. I would have difficulty keeping him at a distance for any length of time, even with my awesome jab!

It wouldn't be a good idea to fight tomorrow. Only a fool would do it.

My friend Justin put his hand on my shoulder and said, "Dude, take it! This will be my first time seeing you fight 'live'! I can get you there before noon tomorrow."

I put my hand over the phone. "No way! I need to rest. We can't get there before noon tomorrow anyway," I explained.

"I'll get us there before noon, and I'll drive safely while you rest! You'll see!" he begged.

The promoter had offered a bonus if I could make it to the event before noon the next day because he wanted me to do interviews and a photo shoot.

"Listen, sir," I began saying into the phone. "I'd really like to do this. I would, but it would be absolutely insane for me to jeopardize my health and career over one..."

"I'll pay extra," said the promoter.

"DONE!"

"OK, tell you what. You get us there by noon tomorrow, in one piece, and I'll give you some of the bonus," I said to Justin.

I saw my life flash before my eyes nine times on that trip. We almost wrecked eleven times, but during two of 'em this ruthless killing machine had his eyes closed and was squealin' like a little girl. I not only left claw marks on the dashboard, it's even possible I tinkled a little. But Justin actually got us there in one piece before noon.

After the interviews Justin and I were sitting in the Star Wagon fight trailers watching old Rocky movies. I still hadn't seen Joe Stevenson. Was he even going to show up? I remembered seeing his fights on video. He was a chubby but effective fighter who took his opponents to the mat and won with "ground and pound."

About an hour before the match, I was warming up behind the stands when people began asking me for autographs.

My autograph! A first sign that I was someone! I was on my way to the top! I hadn't even been in ten fights, and already my adoring fans were asking for the autograph of Jeremy Jackson! This is so cool!! Yes! Come to me, my fans!

"Sign here, Dwayne! Take a picture with me, Dwayne!" all the fans were screaming.

Dwayne??

I looked around for anyone who might resemble a Dwayne. There was just me, Justin, Brian, and Herb Dean – no one even close to resembling a Dwayne.

Crap.

Stupid Dwayne, whoever you are.

More people approached. "Mr. Ludwig? Can we get a picture with you?"

Oh! Dwayne Ludwig! Why didn't you say so? Dwayne was a popular fighter who trained with legendary fighter Bas Rutten. I had trained with both of them throughout my career.

Finally I'd had enough. "I'm not Dwayne Ludwig!" I yelled, more than a little miffed. "I'm Jeremy Jackson!" I proudly proclaimed.

"Uh, who's Jeremy Jackson?" someone asked.

Guess I'm still a nobody.

Herb Dean, one of my training partners,[9] went to get something out of his car. When he returned he had a very curious look on his face.

"I just saw Joe Stevenson," Herb said solemnly. "He's changed, and not for the better. Look Jeremy, I'm not trying to scare you or anything, but you should consider breaking a leg or something."

"C'mon, I'm a killing machine!" I objected.

"Let's just say that he isn't the Joe Stevenson I remember. The dude is out in the parking lot, and they are trying to calm him down." Herb said.

"Calm him down?" I asked with a confused look on my face. "What do you mean, 'calm him down'?"

All Herb did was point toward the parking lot.

Standing in the center of a small crowd was a guy shouting, growling, stomping, and punching himself in the face, with great force! Herb shrugged his shoulders.

I was the first one to enter the cage, and I could hear the crowd shouting, "Come on, Dwayne! You can take him! You're the man, Dwayne Bang!"

---

9   Herb Dean is a popular referee for the UFC. He and I were friends and trained together from 2001-2006.

Aw, shut up. For the last time, I'm not Dwayne "Bang" Ludwig!

The lights dimmed, and I could see the silhouette of a monster standing in the smoke at the top of the ramp. That couldn't be Joe Stevenson!! Please, let it not be. The beast that was racing down the ramp was definitely not the Joe Stevenson I'd seen in videos.

I looked at Herb and saw his lips moving. He was trying to say something.

"What??" I yelled over the crowd.

"Don't touch gloves with him at the start of the match. He'll draw you in and try to take you down. Do not touch gloves with him! Do you understand me?? Do not touch gloves with him!" Herb even mimed the act of touching his fists together and vigorously shaking his head. "Don't do it!"

It is customary to touch gloves at the beginning of a match to show respect. At the sound of the bell, we met in the center of the ring. Joe extended his glove, and I reciprocated.

Woops. Joe closed the distance quickly and took me down: Ground-and-pound.

The referee stopped the fight in the first round when my corner threw in the towel.

As the fog in my head lifted I remembered, "Oh yeah, don't touch gloves. Now I get it." Some lessons sink in better than others.

Herb just shook his head and looked down.

I stood there and watched as they put the KOTC belt around Joe's waist. I couldn't believe how close I'd come to getting a title belt. I'm not saying I almost won the fight because it was pretty one-sided, but if I'd listened to my teammates it might have gone the other way.

I was happy that I was offered a title shot so early in my career because it meant that somewhere, in someone's office, my name had come up, a good sign. I knew that more offers would come my way, and next time I'd do it right: no fights on short notice and listen to your corner.

After the fight, I was standing with Justin when another good friend of mine from high school walked up. "Jacob!" I said with a surprised look on my face. "I didn't know you were here."

"I wouldn't have missed it for the world, bro. You think I could get an autograph?" he said with a smile. I could see it in my friend's eyes that he looked up to me. He and Justin were my closest friends throughout high school. People called us, "The Three Musketeers."

I took off my MMA gloves and signed them for my friend. Even today he has those gloves in a glass container.

12 CPW Open-Weight Champion

A month later I knocked out Eddy Ellis in the IFC (International Fighting Championship) and was offered another title shot. It, uh, wouldn't be in KOTC, IFC, or even in California. It would be in Kansas, surrounded by fake wrestlers.

The biggest highlight for me was that it was my first time on an airplane. My entourage included good friends Robert Ferguson and Herb Dean. No one seemed to know much of the event. In fact, the only thing we did know was that it was to be some kind of submission fight.

We eventually pulled into a large dirt lot, and I looked for a stadium, or at least something resembling a small gym. It looked more like rodeo grounds than a championship fight venue. Then we saw it: a wrestling ring right in the middle of the rodeo grounds. We all looked at each other and laughed. Are you serious? At least the bleachers completely encircled the ring. There wouldn't be a bad seat in the house.

To add to our dismay, we saw men in the ring wearing frilly outfits that resembled Lucha Libre wrestlers. They were bouncing off the ropes body slamming each other.

"I'm going to find out just what is going on here," Robert said as he trotted off. "Be right back!"

Fifteen minutes later Robert returned and filled us in.

"They are going to do some wrestling matches and some submission matches."

"Wrestling matches?" I exclaimed. I hadn't come all this way to do any of that fake garbage. "You mean like Freestyle or Greco wrestling?" I asked hopefully.

"No. Well, not exactly." Robert couldn't help but smile. "Other guys will demonstrate some old-school WWE-like wrestling. You, my friend, will not be doing any of that stuff."

Whew!

"You," Robert went on, "will be part of a tag-team tournament." Now I was thoroughly confused. Tag-team wrestling? Sounded fake to me, but we'd already come this far. "All right, what are the rules? What do I do?" I asked.

As it turned out, it was OK. It would be an open-weight competition, and the winners would be the Central Plans Wrestling Champions. Best of all, the winners would get belts! Most people in the tournament were a bit bigger than I was; I only weighed 170 pounds.

My partner wore a Gi, and I chose to wear my tights. I was sure my partner and I would dominate this event. No one would stand a chance. I was a killing machine, and my partner was a local hero, so we had the hometown crowd on our side.

"Here's the game plan, partner: I will double-leg my first opponent and then pick him up and carry him to our corner. After I tap your hand, we will have about ten seconds to submit him. It'll be a two-on-one for 10 seconds. We'll clean up!" I promised.

My plan worked brilliantly. We won the whole thing. In fact, at one point I was sinking in a leg lock while my partner simultaneously worked an arm bar. Nobody stood a chance!

I was so proud of my new belt that I wore it all around Kansas, until we had to board the plane. Before leaving, the promoter said that he needed the belt back to "do some work on it." I should 'ave known better.

I never saw that belt again. But no one can take away the stats and the win that went along with it. The belt is only a symbol. Everyone knows who the Central Plains Wrestling Champion was.

Eventually I'd discover that the promoter was going through a divorce, and his wife was entitled to half of his property, including half of my belt.

The experience was much more valuable than any leather and metal belt. Besides, after watching the fake wrestling matches, I became a fan of the sport. Not everything they do is fake. I made a goal to see a WWE event live.

13 Home is Where the Heart Is

By 2002 Maggie and I were having problems with our relationship. I never invited her to any of my events; I was always training, working, or competing. I didn't give her the love she deserved. I cared only about myself. I told myself that I was focused on being the UFC champion, and I didn't have time to show love to anyone. But it wasn't really that I didn't have time; it was that I didn't know how to show love to anyone. I was too busy admiring myself. This led to loneliness on her part, and she looked for attention from other men.

One day I was sitting on our bed playing the guitar, hoping to finish a song that I was writing for her. This was the best way that I knew to express what was in my heart. All those years of stuttering and being teased had led me to express myself in ways that were not traditional. When I sang I didn't stutter. As my eyes wandered the room, while mentally searching for just the right words, I caught sight of my big wall calendar on which a message was written with a big blue marker.

"Jeremy, home is where the heart is. It is what it is. Pack your bags and leave. I don't want to see you when I come home. I'm sorry. Maggie." The writing included a big blue frown-face.

My heart sank. What now? I couldn't go back to my hometown and live with my parents. I couldn't fulfill my dreams of being a UFC champion from there. There were no MMA gyms in Imperial Valley at that time. I needed to stay close to Robert Ferguson if I wanted to accomplish my dreams.

I began packing my bags and stuffed everything into my '86 Toyota Celica. The poor car was so packed I could barely drive. A friend of mine had a small place he shared with his girlfriend in Silverstrand, California. He said the best they could offer was a 6'x6' shed in their backyard. It would have to do.

I crawled into the shed later that day and squeezed myself in between some trash bags full of leaves and grass. Also in the shed were bikes, surfboards, tools, and other things. It was the "other things" I was worried about.

Yes, this title-belt-holding killing machine was afraid of spiders! Quit laughing! It's not funny! I hate spiders!

As I was lying on my back that night, I could see three bright stars through the opening of the shed: Orion's Belt! My old friend! I was immediately transported across time and space. I unconsciously started humming "Twinkle, Twinkle, Little Star."

"Whoever You are up there beyond those stars, if You can hear me, please help me get the UFC Title and a decent night's sleep. Please?" I prayed.

I usually sleep on my back when it's hot, and that night was no exception. Sometime into the wee hours, I felt something large crawling across my forehead.

SPIDER!

I quickly swatted it away and heard it land on a plastic bag somewhere in the distant night. Usually at that point I'd be running off, crying like a little girl while wiping imaginary critters off of me. But this time I didn't even move. I was too broken. My heart ached so much from the loss of Maggie, I just didn't care.

A few minutes later I felt the spider crawl back onto my forehead. Great!

It was probably pissed at me for the last unscheduled flight, and it's here to exact revenge.

What to do? I can't kill it. I've tried to kill spiders before, but I've always been too scared to get that close. This was really the closest I'd ever been to a spider. If I flung it off again, he or she would likely be even angrier. Maybe if I leave it alone it won't bite me.

I closed my eyes and fell back to sleep, fully expecting to find a web spun across my head that said, "Eight legs are better! Stupid hairless two-legger! It is what it is!" It actually kept my forehead warm that night.

When I awoke the next morning, it was gone and not a single bite mark could be found anywhere on my body, nor any unpleasant "web writings."

14 King of the Mountain

In August 2002, Robert Ferguson called me to the side during training to let me know about a big event coming up.[10] It was an eight-man tournament, stacked with some tough fighters. The fighters were from well-known schools: Caesar Gracie, Team Punishment, and Shark Tank, to name a few. Frank Trigg had one of his undefeated kickboxers in this welterweight tournament.

"Jeremy, the Ultimate Athlete Organization is putting on an event called 'King of the Mountain.' The IFC title will be given to the winner." Robert said.

He shared with me a little information about some of the fighters, and I was familiar with most of them. Nick Diaz was from the Gracie camp and was undefeated at the time. I had seen him compete in a submission tournament in Las Vegas not too long before and knew his ground game was really good. I had also watched him beat Chris Lytle, a UFC veteran, in the IFC a couple of months before, so I knew he had good stand-up skills as well. He was a well-rounded fighter.

Zack Light, a UFC veteran from Tito Ortiz's camp, was a strong wrestler. In fact, we studied his fights the most since we could find the most footage on him.

Adam Lynn and Mike Penalber were also well-rounded fighters. This tournament seemed impossible to win, but Robert Ferguson is a great motivator.

"Jeremy, none of these guys belongs in the same ring with you. They don't stand a chance against you. Go in there and knock all of them out, putting your name on the map. You want to make it to the UFC and become a UFC champion? Show the world what you're capable of. This is your chance! Two years ago you slipped a note under my door saying you wanted to be the next UFC champion, and you asked me to help you. Well, I've invested my time and energy into you. I believe in you. I'm canceling all my appointments so I can travel with you to this event. I'll be losing a lot of money, but it's worth it. You can do this, Jeremy!" Robert exclaimed.

---

10   Ultimate Athlete 4: King of the Mountain

That was all I needed to hear. Robert Ferguson believed in me, and I agreed to join the eight-man tournament.

We began training for the event, and we tried something new. Along with my regular MMA training, he had me work out in all his cardio kickboxing classes. He had me eating the right stuff, and I had incredible energy. By fight time I was in great shape.

The event was outdoors, and instead of a cage it was an octagon-shaped ring. The weather was really cold, 48 degrees, and I couldn't get warmed up for my fights. There were no warm-up rooms; everything was outdoors.

My first match was with UFC veteran Zack Light. Immediately, I felt his strength when he took me down. After the first round Robert spoke to me in the corner.

"Don't let him hold you down. He will win on points. If he takes you down get back up. Also, you are throwing single punches. Instead, throw your combos: one, two, hook! Let your hands fly, Jeremy!" Robert exclaimed.

As soon as the round started we exchanged a few blows and, sure enough, I landed a jab cross-hook, sending Zack to the canvas.

By the time I left the ring I knew my left hand had to be broken. My fingers were turning blue, and my hand was swelling quickly. I chose to continue on with the tournament.

My next opponent was Mike Penalber, who had also won his first match that evening.

"Let your hands fly, Jeremy!" Robert shouted from the corner.

Within the first minute Penalber went down after I landed a stiff jab. I landed a few more shots while he was down, and the referee stepped in to stop it.

Nick Diaz defeated two tough fighters that night, and it would be him and me in the finals. The goal was to keep the fight standing, no matter what. We knew how good Nick was on the ground, and I wasn't going to play to his strengths. Although I knew how dangerous Diaz was, I felt unstoppable that night.

"Jeremy, this is it! Knock him out, and you are the IFC champion!" Robert said to me as we made our way toward the ring.

I could hear the crowd shouting my name over the loud music: "Scorpion!"

I was a little surprised because I knew Diaz was the favorite. I knew at that point I was stealing the show.

Standing in the ring, I looked across at Nick and noticed he had no fear in his eyes. He was ready for a battle. As soon as the fight began, I was expecting him to try and clinch to get the take-down. But to my surprise, he came out striking with me which was a big mistake. I sent him to the canvas with a left hook. As I stood over him hitting him, he was attempting a leg-lock, and I remembered the game plan: don't play with him on the ground.

"Let him up, Jeremy!' Robert shouted.

After letting him back up I landed another left hook, but this time I finished him off. And of course, what most people remember is Nick trying to get back up and stumbling. I moved as quickly as I could to catch him, and he pushed me away. That's just the way Nick is. It's the "Bad Boy" mentality. But after fighting two more times in the future, Nick and I would be cool with each other.

Nick doesn't like to let people get too close to him. It takes time before he gets comfortable around someone. He didn't show me any respect until our third fight. Even today I am a fan, not of his attitude, but of his skills and the warrior within.

I couldn't do much after winning King of the Mountain because I had two broken hands. I couldn't open doors or drive my car, but I was eager to show off my new title belt and accepted every invitation to be a special guest. Wow! A special guest!

The first call came from a good friend who lived in the area. He was hosting a seminar at his gym for some local Tae Kwon Do master. I was excited because it was my first time being a special guest.

I walked in thinking I would be surrounded by fans, but nobody even knew who I was, nor did they care. They only knew I was some cage fighter. They were there to see the Tae Kwon Do master.

During the middle of the seminar, the instructor called me to stand in front of him as he introduced who I was.

"This is a cage fighter. You all know what cage fighting is, right?" the instructor said.

"Yes, sir!" the students shouted in unison.

"OK, Mr. Jackson. I want you to pretend like you are trying to take me down, just like you do in the cage," he said.

I was about to do a double-leg take down, when he stopped me to say something. "Put your head down and go slow."

Now I want to make something clear. When you are going for a double-leg take down, you never put your head down and stare at the floor, and you definitely don't go slow. But I wanted to be a good guest, so I put my head down and went real slow so he could show his technique. Before I explain what happened next, I want to inform you that this guy was easily 300 pounds and owned black belts in a few arts.

As I slowly stepped forward with my head down, he quickly swung into Necko Datchi, the Cat Stance, and landed a hammer-fist to the back of my head.

I don't know if I was knocked out for one second or ten seconds. All I remember is being on my knees, looking at the blue floor. When I realized what had happened, I wanted to jump up and roundhouse kick him to the head, but I was too dizzy. As I was on all fours staring at the floor, I saw his bare feet walking next to me as he calmly spoke to the class.

"You see, this is a cage fighter and the hammer-fist stopped him. It works every time," he said.

I quickly hopped to my feet so that people wouldn't think I was hurt. "Now, Mr. Jackson, I want you to do the same thing. Pretend like you are going to take me down. Remember to go slow and put your head down," he murmured with a soft voice.

No way! Is this guy crazy, or does he think I'm stupid?? I hesitated, because I didn't want another hammer-fist to the back of my head.

"Don't worry. I promise I won't hammer-fist you again," he assured me.

So, I took his word for it and slowly stepped forward with my head down, not knowing what was coming next. He placed both of his hands on the back of my head and locked his arms as he took a giant step forward, pressing my head toward my stomach. I landed on my butt with my legs spread, and he pressed my head into my crotch with all his might.

"KIIIAAAAAA!" he shouted.

I heard a loud "Pop! Pop! Pop!" in my neck and felt a sharp pain shoot down my spine.

I climbed back to my feet in humiliation. At this point I was beginning to realize that I was no special guest. I was the "guinea pig" and joke of the seminar. Traditional arts like Karate, Tae Kwon Do, Kung Fu, and others didn't get along with MMA during this time. MMA fighters made fun of traditional arts. I had a lot of respect for them, but I didn't think they were the best arts for the cage.

As I walked out of the martial arts studio that day, I couldn't turn my neck, and I was bent over. I knew I was hurt badly, and for the rest of my career my neck bothered me.

I told my teammates what had happened, and they were fired up. One of my buddies on the team, who happened to be a bodyguard for a famous rapper, was bothered most.

"Where is this guy?? Show me where his gym is, and I'll teach him a lesson!!" he said.

"Don't worry about it. I'll be fine," I assured him.

"The guy hurt your neck! Let me hurt his!" he said.

"Look, let him have his moment. It isn't worth pushing this any further. I'll be all right. Just drop it," I said.

This didn't stop me from accepting invitations to be a special guest. I made appearances at MMA events all over California. Soon I would learn that to do this with two broken hands and an injured neck was a bad idea. Every person that came up to me saw my IFC title belt around my waist and wanted to shake my hand. I was so excited to be taking pictures that I shook every hand offered to me. I can't describe the pain I felt every time someone would squeeze my hand. As a result my hands never did heal up the way they should. I didn't even have them in casts because I still wanted to be able to train.

Just like my neck, my hands bothered me throughout my career. They were significant injuries since I needed my hands to punch and grab. My neck would lock up to the point of not being able to turn it. These injuries affected my fight career as well as my personal life. Daily activities like brushing my teeth, shaving, writing, typing, texting, bathing, or picking up a cup of coffee became challenges for me. It was painful!

One time while shopping at the 99¢ Store with my girlfriend Tarah, she called to me from a different section of the store. "Jeremy, did you get any milk?" she asked.

When I turned to look at her my neck locked up, and I almost fell to the floor in pain. This happened several times at the 99¢ Store; as a result, Tarah began calling the injury "The 99¢ Store Injury."

In February of 2003 I worked at a gym in Camarillo as a personal trainer. When I trained my clients on the bottom floor, I noticed a woman in her early twenties staring at me as she exercised on one of the elliptical machines on the second floor. She had dark hair, light skin, and an amazing figure. She was beautiful!

Each day as I looked up, she was staring. I told one of my friends about her, and he told me he used to date her mother. He took the mother and daughter through weight workouts a couple of times a week.

"Why don't you go up and talk with her?" he suggested.

"Are you crazy? I can't do that!" I replied.

"Why not?"

He had a good point. What's there to lose? Sure, she could call me a creep and tell me to get lost. But then I could say, "Then quit staring at me, stalker!!" And what if she was staring at me because I was staring at her? What if she was staring at the guy behind me? I was obviously a little intimidated and tried to talk myself out of it.

I finally decided to go up and talk with her. As I was about to walk up the stairs and approach her on the elliptical, my friend stopped me.

"Where ya going?" he asked.

"To talk with my future girlfriend," I said confidently.

"Well, you better hurry up because she just left," he said.

"What?!?"

"Hurry up! She is outside getting in her car to leave!" he shouted, while pushing me toward the front door of the gym. I ran out the front door, and there she was getting into her car.

"Ex-c-c-use m-me," I said, while walking toward her.

My stuttering was obvious, and I was worried she'd think I was weird. I tried to focus and slow down so I wouldn't stutter, but it didn't help. She didn't say anything as I walked toward her. She just stared at me with her car door opened.

"S-s-s-so you l-l-live ar-round h-h-here?" I asked.

This is not going well at all! Quit stuttering!! My heart was racing, and I couldn't help but stammer each word that came out of my mouth. She was definitely going to think I was a weirdo.

"Yes, I live in Camarillo," she replied. I stuttered worse when I invited her out for dinner. She stared at me with a blank look as I struggled to spit each word out. Then she reached in her car for something. Great! Probably some pepper spray.

"Here is my number," she said as she grabbed a pen and paper to write it down.

I called her later that day against my friend's advice. He told me I should wait two days and then call, so that I wouldn't seem desperate.

"Hello?" a voice answered.

"Tarah?" I asked.

"Yeah?"

It's the creepy guy from the gym who stutters.

"It's Jeremy," I said. "We spoke earlier at the gym."

"I remember."

"Look, I know there is some kind of rule where I should wait two days before calling, but I think that rule is stupid. Why would I wait two days? Unless you think I should have waited two days? Should I call back in two days?" I said with a laugh

"No, I don't think you should have waited two days. You made the right choice," she said.

We talked for a while, and I tried my best to impress her. I told her about my limo, Lamborghini, and private jet, all of which were lies; I owned a 2002 Toyota Echo, and that was it.

The next day I pulled up to her house in my Echo to take her out for our first date together. When she sat in the passenger seat, she had to ask the question: "Where's the Lamborghini?"

"Oh, it's in the shop getting fixed," I replied.

"And the limo?"

"It's in the shop too," I said.

"The jet?" she said with a smile.

"Shop."

Tarah and I hit it off and began dating. Two and a half years later, we would have a son.

At this time I was preparing for a big fight in WEC[11], World Extreme Cage-fighting, which took place in March 2003. It was a big event because Frank Shamrock was making his return, which is why the event was called "Return of a Legend." I would be facing Shonie "Mr. International" Carter from Chicago. He had been on a winning streak and hadn't lost since he fought Pat Militich in the UFC. Shonie had beaten some of the best, even knocking out Matt Serra with a spinning back fist in one of the earlier UFCs. I had seen his fights on VHS tapes as a teenager when I still lived in Imperial Valley. This was a big opportunity for me. I was told I'd be fighting for the WEC super-fight title.

I was a big fan of Shonie Carter and couldn't believe I'd be stepping into the cage with him. I had defeated some tough fighters, but it was never enough to make it to the UFC. This was back when you really had to earn your way to the UFC. The talk on the Internet was that Shonie would eat me up and spit me out. They said I didn't stand a chance.

March 27, 2003, I was in the back trailer getting warmed up for my fight. I recognized some of the other fighters getting warmed up: Nick Diaz, Gill Castillo, Poppies, and of course Frank Shamrock.

By this time in my career, I had my first fight manager. Don was from Reno, but lived in Camarillo. He found sponsors for me and set up my fights. This took the pressure off of Robert, and Robert could focus on the coaching part of it.

"Ten minutes until show time, Jackson!" a man with a headset on said as he peeked in the room of the trailer.

I made my way out of the trailer and toward the arena. The event was outdoors; held in a large white tent next to the casino in Fresno, California. I stopped before I entered the tent and looked up, seeing all the stars in the sky.

"Help me win this fight, so I can make it to the UFC," I prayed. Tito Ortiz walked by as I finished my prayer

---

11   WEC 6: Return of a Legend. Frank Shamrock was the main event.

"Hey, what's up Jeremy?" Tito said as he passed by. " 'Sup, Tito!" I said with my cool voice.

Did Tito Ortiz just say my name? Tito is a legend in MMA. I looked at Robert and Herb Dean, and they both had smiles on their faces. Looks like my name was finally on the map. He didn't call me "Dwayne!" He called me "Jeremy!"

Less than thirty minutes later my hand was raised in victory. I won by unanimous decision, proving the world wrong. My body ached all over, and I could barely move my arms. Shonie made sure that I would remember this battle.

I looked around to see if someone was going to bring in the WEC belt to put it around my waist, but no belt ever came. Something better came running into the cage. My mom ran in and wrapped her arms around me.

When I went to pick up my paycheck from the promoter, I left my IFC belt (the one I won at King of the Mountain) with my older brother Oscar. He had wanted to wear it. My coach Robert asked the promoter why I didn't receive the WEC belt, and the promoter wouldn't give a straight answer. So, we left it alone and walked away after getting the check.

The next day we were ready to leave the hotel when we ran into Shonie Carter. He and I became good friends after that day. In fact, he began calling my mom, "Momita."

I couldn't find my IFC belt, and I began to panic. I looked down at the parking lot and noticed my older brother was wearing it around his waist. I walked over and put my arm around him.

"I'll help you win your own, old bro!" I said.

He took it off, put it on my shoulder, and then gave me a big hug.

"I love you, Jeremy. I'm so proud of you!!" he exclaimed.

17 Bonding

Around this same time I visited my hometown to see my family. While there, my older brother Oscar wanted me to go with him to shoot some pool. It was a very special moment. My older brother wanted me around?

While we were playing our first game of pool, he walked over and put his hand on my shoulder. "Let's put some music on," he said.

We both walked over to the jukebox and scanned the selections. Without hesitation, we selected "Stand By Me" by Ben E. King.

When the song began, a group of Hispanic men started complaining about the music. These guys looked like gang members and were up to no good.

"What a gay song!" one of them said. Oscar looked at me to see my reaction.

I ignored what the men were saying and continued to shoot pool.

"Man, we gotta listen to this gay music?" one of them repeated.

"D-d-d-d-dude, it's j-j-just a s-s-song," I stuttered. Most of the time I was able to hide my stuttering, but when I was angry or nervous my stuttering would show.

"W-w-w-what, you c-c-can't t-t-talk right?" one of them mocked.

Oscar slammed his stick down on the table and raised his voice. "Hey, that's my brother you're making fun of! You mess with him, you mess with me!"

What? Oscar was defending me? Was this real? "It's OK Oscar. It don't bother me," I said.

It did bother me, but I didn't want to fight outside the cage or ring. I was a pro fighter. Sure, there were about five of them, but they didn't stand a chance against us unless they had weapons.

"No, they need to be taught a lesson," Oscar said.

"Look, how about I buy everyone a soda and call it even," I said as I walked over to the counter to purchase some drinks.

As the employee was setting the drinks on the counter, I turned and saw Oscar walking outside with all the men. I quickly paid for the soft drinks and followed them outside.

"Don't you ever disrespect my brother like that!" I heard Oscar shouting as I walked out the door. He was surrounded by five men cracking their knuckles.

Before I could say anything, Oscar socked one of them in the face. They quickly assumed their fighting stances and were about to jump him until they saw me walking up.

"Guys, come on! This ain't worth it. Look, I gotta be honest. I'm a pro MMA fighter, and he is a pro boxer!" I said.

Their eyes widened as they all took in what they just heard. They stared at one another, wondering what they should do. "We don't want no trouble," one of them said with fear in his voice.

"Neither do we," I assured them.

They slowly backed away and disappeared into the parking lot.

At that moment I felt an arm around my shoulder. "Nobody messes with my little brother," Oscar said.

I wanted that moment to last forever. For once in my life my older brother was willing to stand up for me; not only that, he treated me like I was his best friend. It was like he enjoyed having me around. I could see it in his eyes; he was proud of me.

18 The Rematch

In April 2003, my fight manager Don wanted to meet up with me at a local coffee shop. Whatever it was, it sounded like it was important.

"Nick Diaz wants a rematch, and I told him he would get it," Don said.

"What? Rematch? Why would I want to fight him again? Let's move on," I replied.

Don took a sip of his coffee and then leaned forward in his chair.

"The same night you beat Shonie Carter, Nick broke Joe Hurley's arm. Nick came up to me after his fight and said he wanted his rematch and that he would snap your arm too!" Don said with a frustrated voice.

"Don, I'm not giving him a rematch." I answered.

A few days later my phone rang while I was at the gym. It was the UFC!! My dream was coming true. Chills ran throughout my body and my heart was racing. "We have been following your career, Jeremy. We want you to fight Dennis Hallman in UFC 44-Undisputed," Joe Sylva, the UFC matchmaker, said.

I didn't hesitate to say yes. This was what I had been looking for. I was one step closer to getting that UFC title. But I had to ask him how he got my number. His response was, "We have our ways, Jeremy. We are the UFC!" That was good enough for me.

The fight wouldn't be until September 26, 2003, in Las Vegas, which gave me plenty of time to get ready. However, a couple of weeks into my training my manager dropped some big news on me.

"I set up a rematch with Nick Diaz. It will be in the IFC." Don said.

"What?? I'm fighting against Hallman in the UFC in September!" I replied.

"Jeremy, I set the rematch with Nick in July. It will be a tune-up fight for you. Go in there, knock him out, and you'll be ready for your UFC fight in September." he said.

"I think it's a dumb move. I don't need to fight Nick Diaz again. I am signed to fight Hallman in the UFC," I replied.

"Jackson, this guy has been running his mouth since you knocked him out! Shut him up for good!" he answered.

"Diaz is no joke. He is not a tune-up fight. You saw what he did to Hurley's arm. Hurley is a tough fighter! I saw Diaz beat Chris Lytle, a UFC veteran. This is a bad idea. It will be a hard fight for me. What if I get hurt?" I said in frustration.

We went back and forth for hours, but eventually I gave in when he told me another title belt was being put up.

Robert Ferguson wasn't happy with my decision. He thought it was a bad move, also. My phone rang, and it was someone else who wasn't happy with the news: it was the UFC.

"Jeremy, if you lose this fight with Diaz, we will pull you from your fight with Hallman. It's best to cancel your fight with Diaz," Joe Sylva said.

He was absolutely right. I needed to cancel my fight with Diaz and focus on Hallman. But, I was still a young man and was easily influenced by my manager. I continued with the plan to fight Diaz.

I began training for the fight, but quickly ran into a huge problem. I had nobody to train with. Robert Ferguson was caught off guard and was going to help me prepare for the September match in the UFC. He didn't have time to help me prepare for the July rematch against Diaz. So, I did the only thing I could do. I punched the bag at the gym while Tarah timed me.

One day a man walked into the room where I was punching the bag and offered to hold the mitts so I could punch them. He looked familiar, but I didn't know where I knew him from. Come to find out, he was in the movie "Snake Eyes" with Nicholas Cage, and he also boxed for the Mexican Olympic team.

After training he would take me to Carl's Jr., which was totally off my diet. Robert Ferguson had me on a strict diet and would have had a heart attack if he saw what I was eating. Robert was a nutrition expert and had me eating like a machine since 2001. But, it was all about to change as I sat at Carl's Jr. with my new boxing coach Adam Flores.

"I can't eat this," I said to Adam.

"Why not? Champions eat this stuff," he replied.

It was hard to argue with him while a burger, fries, and a soda were being placed in front of me. This became my new diet.

The day before my fight we were supposed to fly in a private plane that one of my sponsors owned. But he said it was in the shop. Why did that sound so familiar? Oh, yes! I used that same line on Tarah. So, we rented an SUV and drove to the event in northern California. But first we had to pick up my new boxing coach who happened to be at a T-shirt shop in Ventura. We pulled up, and he invited Don and me inside because he wanted to show me something.

"Look!" Adam said as he lifted up a white T-shirt with red letters that read, "Scorpian."

My manager grabbed the shirt in anger.

"Scorpian?? You can't even spell scorpion right!!" he yelled.

Adam turned the shirt around to look at it.

"Whoops! Hey, poh-tay-toh, poh-tah-toh. It will be unique! You can be the Scor-pee-aaan," Adam said.

"No! He is not the Scor-pee-aan! He is the Scorpion! Now leave the shirts here and let's get going!" my manager grunted.

I've never seen him so ticked before. But he was even more ticked when Adam told him he was bringing a friend, and that his friend was running a little late.

"We don't have time to be inviting everyone! We need to leave!" Don shouted.

But Adam insisted that since the fight would be on an Indian reservation, it would benefit us to have his friend who was a Native American. I didn't mind since it's always good to have a little juice. But my manager was tired of waiting and in a bad mood. I went and sat in the SUV while they argued it out.

Eventually Adam's friend showed up, and we were on the road. Adam volunteered to drive. I thought I was going to die, or vomit, during the car ride. I have serious vertigo, so I sat in the back gripping the seats.

"Can you tell him to slow down? I don't feel good," I said to my manager.

Don told Adam to slow down, but he wouldn't listen. In fact, it seemed like he drove faster. By the time we arrived I was sick to my stomach. We stopped at a restaurant, but I couldn't eat anything without wanting to vomit.

While we sat at the table at the restaurant, my manager answered his cell phone and began to argue with my coach Robert Ferguson, who would be showing up later that day. My head was spinning.

Also during this time, I was being followed by a film crew that was doing a documentary on me. I was stressed out because I didn't have any privacy. I tried my best to smile for the camera and act like nothing was wrong. To spice things up I decided to send a gift to Nick Diaz's hotel room. We packed a basket full of candy bars, and I autographed a picture to go with it. Nick wasn't too happy when he got it.

The next night I lost to Nick Diaz in the first round[12]. The entire event was one big mess. Nick entered the cage first while they played my entrance music. I waited and waited until it was my turn to walk toward the cage, but I never got the go-ahead. The event staff kept telling me to wait a little longer. Meanwhile, the crowd was wondering if maybe I had chickened out: maybe I got scared and ran back to the dressing room.

Fans of Nick Diaz were less than twenty feet away shouting at me.

"You're scared! Nick is going to break your arm! You're finished!" his fans shouted over and over.

"What's going on?" I asked Robert.

"I don't know. Stay focused, Jeremy." Robert replied.

"I'm just going to walk out there and enter the cage," I said.

"Focus, Jeremy. Don't let it get to you." Robert answered.

But it was getting to me. I was far from focused.

I was standing in the area where the fighters wait to walk out to their music. My team stood to the side and watched as I shadow boxed to stay warm. After a minute of shadow boxing, I walked around the area and tried to clear my head. I had a lot on my mind. First, I knew I didn't properly prepare for the fight. Nobody was available to train with me because the fight wasn't supposed to happen. Second, I knew Nick had trained like a

---

12   IFC 18: Big Valley Brawl; July 19, 2003

madman for this fight, as I read in his interviews. Third, I felt sick to my stomach from my boxing coach's reckless driving. Fourth, if I lost the fight I would lose my contract with the UFC. Fifth, my team wouldn't stop arguing with each other. Sixth, I needed some "alone time." And seventh… well, it was about to start.

At this time in my life I was very superstitious. As I was walking around the area, I almost kicked an empty beer can on the ground. A voice in my head said, "If you kick that can, you will lose."

"That was a close one," I thought. I made sure to stay far away from that beer can. But because I was trying so hard to get focused, I forgot all about the can. I heard the sound of aluminum rolling across the ground in front of me, and I knew instantly what had happened.

"Oh no, what have I done? Now I'm going to lose. It's a done deal. Stick a fork in me. I am going to lose this fight, and there is nothing I can do about it. It doesn't matter how good my boxing skills are, I'm finished. Stupid beer can!" I didn't realize it at the time, but I was already defeating myself, so by the time I stepped in the cage I felt like my mind was paralyzed. It was like having an entire arsenal of nuclear weapons, but the system was malfunctioning and they wouldn't fire.

Warning: be aware of your internal dialogue. Is it helping you or hurting you?

After what seemed like forever, the event staff gave me the green light to make my way to the cage. Once the fight started I noticed something different about Nick. He had his right hand practically glued to the right side of his head to block any left hooks I'd throw at him. Also, he wasn't as cocky.

He would eventually take me down and get the mounted position. He stayed busy by throwing light punches until the ref stopped it.

Later that night I was sitting in front of my hotel room with my teammates, manager, and coaches. A familiar face walked up and joined us. It was Nick Diaz. It was the first time I had seen him alone without his teammates around. He was just a normal dude who loved the art of fighting. He autographed a backstage pass for me, and I still have it.

The next day my phone rang, and it was the UFC. They let me know that I would no longer be fighting against Hallman in UFC-44. Instead, Nick Diaz was invited to take my place.

I stood on my balcony in Port Hueneme, California, looking up at the stars. I could smell the ocean and feel the breeze on my face. The ocean was about a hundred yards away. I stared at the stars and felt like the biggest fool in the world for taking the rematch against Diaz.

"Give me another chance," I asked, as I stared at the stars.

The next morning the UFC called and told me Dennis Hallman wouldn't be fighting against Diaz. Nick and I would square off for the third time, and it became the trilogy.

19 UFC 44: Undisputed

What is the meaning of life?

This question was heavy on my heart as I stared out of my window at the Mandalay Bay Hotel in Las Vegas. It was September 23, 2003. The next day I would be stepping into the cage to fight Nick Diaz.[13]

Looking through my window, I was blown away by how big Las Vegas was. People below looked like ants going in and out of casinos. Here I was, twenty-one years old, living my dream. I was making a name for myself.

My palms were sweaty, and I had a lot on my mind. My manager had just left the room to go buy some alcohol. It bothered me that his focus was on getting drunk. I felt alone. My coach, Robert, stepped out of the room to make some phone calls. My mind drifted as I was near the top of the Mandalay Bay Casino, my hands on the window looking out at this city full of flashing lights. The question came to my mind again.

What is the meaning of life? Where did I hear this before? And why didn't I know the answer? Then it hit me.

In 2000 Robert Ferguson sat with me at a restaurant in Oxnard, California. We were talking about the sport of MMA when he surprised me with a question.

"Jeremy, what is the meaning of life?" he asked, after taking a sip of his coffee.

I was only eighteen years old, and nobody had ever asked me that before; if they did, I wasn't paying attention. My mind searched for the answer, but I was puzzled.

What was the meaning of life? It was a question that would surface again and again throughout my career, usually when I least expected it.

I have stared out of many hotel windows in different cities, asking the same question. I've stood on the beach looking out at the Pacific Ocean in awe, wondering who made something so amazing. Where did it all come from? What is the meaning of it all?

---

13   UFC 44: Undisputed

As I looked at the dancing Las Vegas lights from my hotel room window, my childhood memories would come and go. I was trying to put the puzzle together, hoping to find the answer to the question. "What is the meaning of life?" I said to myself.

Was I still that little kid who was known as "Stutter-boy" or "Retard"? No way! I was now the Scorpion, Jeremy Jackson! This was the image I worked so hard to build. The Scorpion wasn't a stutter-boy or retard! He didn't stutter anymore! He was now the Scorpion who "stung his way to victory!" That's what it said on the front of an MMA magazine.

But even though I was now the Scorpion, I knew who I really was on the inside. I was still a terrified little kid longing to be accepted. I may have hidden my stuttering with a few cuss words, but I still saw myself as that little boy who couldn't talk. I tried so hard to convince myself that I was the Scorpion and that my younger years were just a dream, but as the years passed I became confused and didn't even know who I was anymore. So I held on as tightly as I could to what I did know; people liked the Scorpion. So I held on to the Scorpion image.

September 26, 2003, I was in my dressing room waiting to be called out so I could step into the cage with Nick Diaz for the third time. Andre Arvloski and I were assigned to the same dressing room, and I was amazed by how calm he was. He was playing cards and speaking in Russian, while I sat there trying to clear my mind.

"Jackson!" a man with a clipboard said. "You're up!"

Security escorted me down a long hallway while Robert Ferguson and some of my other teammates walked beside me. I looked up at the posters on the walls of all the rock stars and famous people who had walked down this same hallway before they performed on stage. We seemed to walk down this hallway forever, until I was able to hear the crowd screaming.

This was it! Now I was in the big show!

The game plan was simple: we knew Nick would try to take me to the ground. The goal was to keep the fight standing and knock him out. If he took me down, I was trained to get an under-hook and get back to my feet. I was to keep him in my world.

The first and second round went as planned. Any time he took me down, I created space for the under-hook and got back to my feet. I had one more round, and according to my corner, I was ahead on points.

Before the round started, Robert reminded me to stay off the ground with Nick. All I had to do was keep the fight standing, and I'd walk away with a win.

The third round was almost over when Nick went for another submission hold, but I escaped it, ending up in his guard. I could hear my corner telling me to stand back up.

"Stand back up, Jeremy! Don't stay down with him!" Robert screamed.

But I felt confident; I was stronger than Nick and felt that I could escape all of his submission attempts. I was going to stay on top of him and punch him until the end of the round.

This was a big mistake! I should have listened to Robert and stuck with the plan. Nick was an expert on the ground. This was his world. He swung his leg around and sank in a textbook arm bar. He promised that he would break my arm if he got the chance, and this was his chance. There was no escaping the arm bar because it was executed perfectly. I tapped out.

The trilogy was finally over.

Nick and I had a lot of respect for each other. When you fight a guy three times you learn a lot about him. I had studied all his videos and knew his strong points and his weak points. Nick's coach, Caesar Gracie, traded phone numbers with me, and we kept in touch after that.

"The person who becomes committed to a particular outward image can be entrapped by it to the extent that his inward feelings are inconsistent with that image."
– Les Carter

"We all have an image which we attempt to maintain – a way in which we want others to view us."
– Steve Gallagher

20 Help Me

After my fight with Nick Diaz, I went back to my hometown for a family visit. It was then that I learned of my brother's crystal meth addiction. It was shocking! He was a professional boxer in great shape.

As soon as I arrived, Oscar pulled me aside. "Jeremy, can we talk?" he asked.

We walked into our old bedroom, the one we'd shared as kids. I gazed out of the bedroom window while he sat on the bed looking down at the floor.

"I saw you fight on Pay-Per-View last week," he began. "You looked good out there. You almost had him. Look, Jeremy, I need your help. I'm caught up in some bad stuff. I want to change, but I can't do it while living here in the valley. I need you, brother. Let me come and live with you in Camarillo. I can't do this alone." Tears rolled down his face.

The only other time I'd seen him cry was the time I threw the toy fire truck at his head when I was three years old.

"Oscar, I can't help you right now. I'm sorry. I have a big fight in Hawaii next month. I'm busy. I don't know what to tell you," I said.

"Jeremy, please. Let me come and live with you. Please help me, brother," he said with a shaky voice.

My career was just beginning to take off, and I was scheduled as the headline fight in Hawaii. I didn't have time to babysit.

"I can't, Oscar. I'm sorry," I replied.

It was tough telling my brother no because I had always looked up to him. But I didn't know how to help someone with an addiction.

A few weeks later he moved to Louisiana and lived with our older sister, his two kids, and his girlfriend. Even though he was able to quit using crystal meth, he was still an alcoholic.

On November 22, 2003, I faced off against Mark Moreno as the main event in Hawaii.[14] I won by submission in the first round. Before I got on

---

14 Ring of Honor 1

the plane to head back to California, I agreed to fight Thomas "The Wildman" Denny as the main event in Mississippi. Since the event was several weeks away, it would give me plenty of time to prepare, but that fight would never happen. Thomas Denny pulled out at the last minute because he was sick. Instead, I was invited to be a special guest and say a few words in the ring.

I called Oscar and my sister in Louisiana and asked if they would come to the event.

I arrived in Mississippi and sat alone in the stadium seats. I was deep in thought as I stared toward the ring in the center of the room. To this day, I don't know why I didn't sit closer to the ring.

Why was I sitting in the back? Maybe because I'd forgotten what it looked like from back here? Lately I had been watching fights from the front row.

I thought I was alone, when I noticed a young black kid, about 18 years old, sitting a few rows behind me.

"You're Jeremy Jackson, aren't you?" he said with a grin.

"I am," I answered, reaching for a handshake.

He asked me several questions, including what it was like to fight in the UFC.

"Do you train?" I asked him.

"Every day! In fact, I'll be fighting right here tomorrow," he said with confidence.

I should have known he was a fighter by the way he was talking. He shared that his goal was to fight in the UFC.

"What's your name? I'll be cheering for you tomorrow," I said.

"Melvin Gillard," he answered, while shaking my hand again.

This kid went on to build a name for himself in the UFC. We spoke for about twenty minutes, and then I told him I had to get going.

During the event the following day, my older brother sat in the front row staring intently at one of the title belts on display next to the ring. I was up in the ring speaking on the microphone and had to cut my speech short so I could go talk with my brother.

"Hey, bro! So what do you think of the event so far?" I asked him.

"Jeremy, see that title belt? I could walk out with that and nobody would know," he said as he put his arm around me.

"Look Oscar, please don't embarrass me. Leave it alone. I'll get you a title belt, but leave that one alone." I said.

"Yeah, but it's right there! I could just grab it and walk out," he replied.

"Please don't, Oscar. I promise I'll get you one of your own, all right?" I said.

At the after-party I was taking pictures with fans, when someone came up and tapped me on the shoulder. I turned and noticed a cute blonde woman in her late twenties.

"Well, hello there. Would you like a picture with me?" I asked.

"Um, actually, I came to ask you if that is your brother over there?" she asked, while pointing toward some security guards who were escorting some shirtless white guy out of the club.

It was my brother! I followed them outside and asked what was going on. Apparently he was taking his shirt off in the club, which the ladies liked, but it was against the rules. He had been warned several times, but he just wouldn't listen.

Oscar put his arm around me and begged me to get him back in. "Jeremy, get me back in. Tell them who you are," he said, while rubbing my shoulder. Turning to the security guards he said, "This is the Scorpion! He's a special guest here at the casino!"

"We don't care who he is! Rules are rules!" one of the security guards barked.

"Oscar, why don't we just call it a night?" I said.

"At least have a drink with me?" he asked. He always tried to get me to drink, but I hated alcohol and avoided it.

"You know I don't drink. I'll have an iced tea or Pepsi with you," I promised him.

"OK, but get us back in!" he begged.

I convinced the guards to let him back in, which turned out to be a big mistake. He was kicked out of the club a few more times. Finally, I couldn't take it anymore; I led him back to my hotel room.

21 Professional Boxing Career

At the beginning of 2004, I decided to take a break from MMA to compete as a professional boxer. Because of my MMA reputation, I was picked up quickly by a local boxing gym in Ventura, California. Since I wouldn't need my MMA manager anymore, I let him go and signed with a boxing manager. Now that I no longer trained with Team Freedom, my MMA team, I also hired a new boxing coach.

I began sparring more than I ever had when I used to prepare for an MMA fight, and this put a lot more pressure on my already-broken hands. The only thing that kept me going was the therapy I went through each day.

Every night before bed, I'd soak my hands in ice water for seven minutes. Then I'd take them out and wrap a heating pad around them for five minutes. Then it was back into the ice water. I repeated this cycle several times. The pain was horrific, but I had to do it if I wanted to continue fighting. I also had electroshock therapy and ultrasound therapy for my hands every day.[15]

On July 3, 2004, I had my professional boxing debut in Monterrey, California.[16] The guy I fought had a lot of experience as a professional boxer; that gave him a huge advantage. He'd also done his homework and studied my MMA fights. His game plan was to keep away from my left hook and not allow me to get in close. His plan worked until the third round. What he didn't know was that I also had a vicious straight right as well.

I threw a left hook which caused him to move to my right. Then I turned over a right hand and knocked him out cold!

After the fight I told my boxing manager and boxing coach that I needed to let my hands heal because the broken bones in my hands were causing too much pain. Not even therapy was helping anymore. They told me that it was normal for boxers to have pain in their hands.

15 Therapeutic ultrasound and neuro-stimulation help speed up the healing process.

16 Riot at the Hyatt

"It's called 'Boxer's Hand'," they said. I was familiar with the term because I'd had it several times when I boxed as a kid. I tried to explain to my coach and manager that my hands were actually broken, but they continued to say the same thing: it's just "Boxer's Hand."

I went to a sport doctor who'd helped famous fighters in the past. He took some x-rays and put the films on the wall. Then he gave me the confirming news. "Mr. Jackson, you have breaks here, here, here, and here. Basically, your hands are a mess," he said as he pointed to the x-rays.

"Can I still fight with them?" I asked.

He looked at me like I'd just asked if I could still get pregnant. "If I were you," he said, "I'd take some time off and let your hands heal. They're badly broken and should be in casts. If you fight with those hands you'll probably ruin them forever."

That was a scary thought. My hands were my moneymakers! I needed them! If I didn't allow them to heal I would ruin my career.

I set up a meeting with my coach and manager the next day, and shared what the doctor said. Amazingly, they continued trying to convince me that it was only "Boxer's Hand," and that the doctor was either wrong or lying.

"Why would the doctor lie?" I implored. "I saw the x-rays. I saw the breaks!"

"I don't trust that doctor!" my manager replied.

During the meeting, my manager let me know that he had two more fights booked in July. This would be a total of three fights in one month.

"My hands are broken!" I blurted out.

"Jeremy, don't believe that doctor. Trust us," my coach said.

I went to a different doctor and got the same opinion. Both of my hands were broken. "Doc, what would happen if I fought this month?" I asked.

He almost fell out of his chair; then looked me straight in the eyes. "What? I don't think you hear what I'm saying, young man. Your hands are broken. I highly recommend that you take time off to let them heal. You'd be crazy to fight with hands like that!" the doctor said.

The next day I was in another meeting with my boxing coach and manager. "This doctor doesn't know what he is talking about either.

Jeremy, it is normal to have hands like that in boxing." They were very reassuring.

I was shocked! These guys didn't care about my well-being. What was I going to do? I was a fighter and didn't want to let my coach and manager down. So, I went against the doctors' advice and continued to prepare for the upcoming fights.

As my coach was taping up my hands before training, he filled me in on my next match. "Scorpion, your next match won't even count on your overall record. This will be more like a sparring match, you know, to help you get ready for the big match in Vegas," he said.

A sparring match? It's just another day of training. I spar four to five days a week already! "Is this guy coming here?" I asked.

"No, we gotta go up north. It'll probably be at his gym. The guy is a top-notch south paw," my coach said.

We drove up north. Tarah came with us so she could watch. We pulled up to a park and noticed a boxing ring out in the open surrounded by a crowd. Surrounding the crowd were booths and food stands. "This isn't a gym! This looks like a regular event, crowd and all!" I said.

The guy I was fighting had his "fight shorts" on: the ones he'd use for actual fights. He looked like he was competing in a professional television bout. As for me, I was sporting the "tight whites" that I used for sparring. Normally, nobody was around when I sparred except my training partners, so I usually didn't care how I looked in my "Daisy Dukes." You wouldn't catch me wearing 'em in public! No sir!!

"All I have are my white shorts!" I said to my coach.

"Nobody cares how your shorts look," he said.

Yeah, easy for him to say. He wasn't walking around in "booty shorts."

"I care how I look in front of all these people! I thought this was only sparring!" I exclaimed.

"It is! It won't count on your record, and it will be good experience," he said.

I stood in the ring looking at my opponent. His nice shorts had his name written across the front. Know what mine had written across the front? "Embarrassed." I kept trying to stretch my white shorts and pull them down as far as I could, so they wouldn't look so much like "Daisy Dukes." I felt like I was wearing a thong.

My opponent walked up to me and held out his glove.

"It is an honor to be in the ring with you. I saw your fight with Nick Diaz," he said.

I touched gloves with him and told him I wished I would have dressed for the occasion. He looked down at my shorts and grinned.

As soon as the bell rang, he was all over me with punches! All I could do was cover up and defend myself. This was no sparring match. This guy was trying to take my head off. He wasn't giving me an opportunity to punch back. The crowd was cheering him on, which made things worse. I had to do something. I timed the rhythm of his punches and found an opening that would give me just enough time to dip to my left and throw an uppercut, then follow it with a straight right. It worked to perfection and sent him to the canvas. I helped him up, and we finished the rest of the round with him throwing punches non-stop.

The second round started the same way as the first, and I had to find his timing again. When I did, I knocked him down again. I was so glad that I didn't have to throw too many punches with my broken hands. But I made the few punches I did throw count by knocking him to the canvas every time. The many punches he threw were mostly blocked by my gloves and didn't land on my face or body.

My next fight would be at the end of the month in Las Vegas. My boxing manager filled me in with the information I needed to know.

"The guy you are fighting is a little bigger than you are, but don't worry. He is just coming back from an injury," my coach said. I looked online at the guy's record and was blown away by how many people he had knocked out.

"This is only my second fight as a pro boxer! You think I'm ready to fight a guy of this caliber: one who's bigger than I am? I gotta do this with broken hands?" I wondered.

"Jeremy, you are ready to fight the top dogs in boxing. You're a champion!" he said.

"A champion in MMA, not in boxing!" I reminded him.

During the weigh-ins, my opponent's coach said something that really bothered me when I got on the scale.

"Oh, he is just a little-bitty guy!" he said out loud.

I wasn't little, but compared to my opponent I was. He was so much bigger that the athletic commission almost didn't allow us to fight. The contract was rewritten, and we agreed to fight at a heavier class even though I was underweight.

When the fight started I landed a jab on his elbow, causing a shooting pain to go up through my arm, and my left hand began to throb. Finally, it went numb.

At the end of the first round, I told my corner crew that my left hand was done.

"I gotta switch to south paw. My left hand is finished!" I said.

"You're winning the fight, Jeremy. Just beat him with your right hand. You're way too fast for him," my coach said.

I remember landing a lot of shots to his body until the third round. He eventually noticed that there was something wrong with my left hand and became more confident. He landed a right hand and knocked me under the ropes. I stood back on my feet and let the referee know I was fine.

He was about to restart the fight when he noticed I was still out of it. That's when the ref stopped the fight. It was a good call because I really was out of it.

22 There is Something Out There

In the summer of 2004, Tarah and I were leaving our apartment on the Channel Islands University campus in Camarillo. I was driving down a long winding road that led out of the university, while Tarah sat next to me in the passenger seat writing down what we needed from the store. Soft music was playing on the radio, and I was deep in thought.

I had been searching for something my entire life, but I didn't know what it was. Was it the UFC title belt? Maybe it was Tarah I was searching for? No, it was something else, but I couldn't figure it out. "Tarah, do you ever feel like maybe there is something more to life?" I asked.

She stopped her writing and looked at me, her face a blank. "What do you mean?" she answered.

"I can't explain it really, but I feel like there is something else out there: another world or something, a world better than this one, a perfect world," I said.

"OK, you're weird," she said with a laugh and continued making her store list.

"No, I'm serious! I was sitting here listening to this music, and I began to imagine something like..." I looked off into the distance, searching for the right words.

"Like what?" Tarah asked as she stopped writing.

"Like a paradise: everything is alive and green; animals are tame; everything is perfect. The world we live in now is crazy. I feel like this isn't the way it was supposed to be," I said.

In the distance were some deer eating grass on the side of the road. "Look! Deer!" she said with excitement.

"I know. I saw them before you did," I answered.

"I'll give you a cookie when we get home."

"Whatever," I responded. I didn't want to change the subject. I needed to share what was on my heart.

"So what do you think?" I asked.

"About what?" she responded as she started writing again.

Frustrated, I said, "About what I was talking about."

"I don't know, Jeremy. You're not making any sense," she said as she wrote the last few lines.

"You don't feel like there is something out there that is better than this world?" I asked.

"You mean like aliens? Because I think you're an alien," she said and laughed.

"Tarah! Can't we have a serious conversation for once?" I said in a solemn voice.

"What do you want me to say, Jeremy? You're talking crazy!"

"I just feel like there is something. Something we are not seeing. I'm telling you, I can feel it. There is something better than this world, Tarah. You can call it paradise or call it another world. I don't care," I said.

"OK, but it all sounds pretty weird to me," she said while handing me the list.

I realized she wasn't feeling the same way I was. In fact, she was beginning to think I was crazy. What was I feeling? I didn't understand it myself. It felt like someone was drawing me. But who, or what, was it? I felt a strong pull on my heart. Someone was trying to get my attention.

But then again, it does sound a bit crazy. Maybe Tarah was right. I was probably just stressed out, or it could have been all the punches to my head from MMA and boxing.

I turned up the music and continued to think my crazy thoughts, but kept them to myself.

Later that night I decided to go for a run. I had several locations where I ran depending on what kind of routine I planned on doing. If I wanted to do sprints, I'd go to a mountain in Newbury Park, sprinting up and jogging down at least eighteen times. If I wanted to go for distance, I'd go down the street to a mountain near my home or go to Ventura and run up a mountain near Main Street. On this day I chose Ventura.

The mountain has a road that leads to the top where people like to park and enjoy the view. I ran up this winding road as fast as I could and reached the top in less than ten minutes. I decided to turn around and go back down so I could run up again. I repeated this about five times.

After my last time up the mountain, I stood near a statue at the very top and looked out at the amazing view. I could see miles and miles of ocean, and some islands in the distance. I looked out toward Main Street and noticed all the cars traveling to and from work.

I felt like I was missing something. What was it that I needed so badly? I scanned the city, but the more I looked, the further I felt from what I was searching for. Whatever it was, I knew it was foreign to me. It was something good and pure. It was the opposite of what I was. Does something like that even exist?

I looked back toward the ocean and noticed that the sun was setting. It was beautiful. As I moved a little closer to the statue I leaned my hand on it to rest. "Eventually I'll find what I'm looking for," I said as I turned around to head back down the mountain.

It wouldn't be until 2016, sitting in my prison cell, that I would realize it wasn't a statue I was leaning on. It was a giant cross! Now I understood why some call the mountain "The Cross."

23 The Phone Call

In September of 2004, I received the phone call that would turn my world upside down. I could hear someone crying on the other end of the line.

"Mama, you all right?" I asked. Why was she crying?

"Jeremy, something happened to Oscar! He's, he's, he's….he is d, d, d," she mumbled as the phone hit the floor.

What was going on? Dad picked up the phone, and he was also crying.

My dad crying??! He never cries!

"Son, Oscar is…" My dad tried speaking, but he got choked up.

"Yeah, I'm here. What's going on?" I asked.

"Son, Oscar is gone. He was in a car accident. He's dead, son," he said with a choppy voice.

Those last words echoed in my head. "He's dead. He's dead. He's dead."

Oscar was gone. Just like that.

I was flooded with all our childhood memories. It was overwhelming. But most of all I remembered him asking me for help, and I didn't even lift a finger to help him. Suddenly a huge weight was on my shoulders, and I didn't know what to do about it. As my dad was describing how my brother died, the world began falling from under my feet. I wasn't sure how I was supposed to feel. I felt alone. Was this how I was supposed to feel?

Apparently a big rig had clipped my brother's car, causing him to flip and land against a rail on a bridge. When he climbed out, he fell over the railing to the highway below.

Tarah was at work when she received my phone call. I told her the news and that I was heading back to the valley to be with family. She offered to go with me, but I told her I needed to go alone.

"Jeremy, let me go with you," she begged.

"I need to be alone with my family," I insisted.

"Are you going to be OK?"

"I'll be fine," I mumbled.

"Babe, let me drive you!"

No matter how hard she tried to be there for me, I wouldn't accept her help. I wouldn't accept anyone's help. I was too prideful and thought I could do it all on my own.

I drove home to attend the funeral and bury my brother. The hardest part was seeing how Mom was taking it. I didn't know how to help her. I can't even count how many times she fell to the kitchen floor, crying. No parent should ever have to bury a child.

I sat in the living room in a daze, absorbed with my own heartache. Rather than talk about it, we just stared off into space, preoccupied with our own pain. How does a person prepare for something like this?

During the viewing I placed my IFC title belt around Oscar's waist and kissed his forehead. "I promised I'd get you a title belt. You can have mine. I always looked up to you, whether you knew it or not. I love you, Oscar." I whispered.

It was so painful helping to carry his casket. Knowing he was inside this box, and was about to be buried underground, made me sick to my stomach. That day as they buried him I felt like a piece of me was buried, too.

A month later I was invited as a special guest at Lake Havasu, and I brought my younger brother Bodi with me. As we sat in the hotel room, I told him what was on my heart.

"I'm a mess, Bodi. I don't know what to do," I said.

He walked over to the liquor cabinet and pulled out a bottle of vodka. He poured two shots, and I just sat there staring at the shot glasses. I was deciding if I should try it. I had always avoided alcohol and hated the smell of it.

We each grabbed a shot glass, lifted it into the air, and said, "Cheers."

"Here's to Oscar!" he said. My first drink of hard liquor was to my dead brother.

It tasted like I was swallowing gasoline or rubbing alcohol. Who in his right mind would want to drink something so disgusting? I wasn't in my right mind, so I drank shot after shot.

Then it happened.

I felt a buzzing sensation in my brain, and suddenly my body was numb. It took away the pain; not just the physical pain of broken bones and a bruised body. It also removed my broken heart after losing my brother. I was able to forget the pain and escape reality. But there was a huge flaw with this coping mechanism. I no longer cared about other people's feelings, nor did I care if I hurt them. Most of all, I became even more self-centered. All I cared about was staying numb so that I could cope.

I drank until I could barely walk. I had to be at the nightclub that night to judge a bikini contest and say a few words into the microphone, but I couldn't make it on my own. Eventually my little brother helped me walk to the club. When the owner of the club saw how drunk I was, he was hesitant to let me go up and speak. My little brother agreed, "I don't think he can do anything tonight. I need to get him back to the room."

"I got this!!" I said, as I jumped and did a perfect spinning kick in the air; then I wondered what I was doing on my butt.

"I'm taking him back to the room," my brother said as he led me away.

After a long weekend of heavy drinking, Bodi and I traveled back to Imperial Valley where he lived with Mom and Dad. I dropped him off and drove back to Camarillo. Before I got back to the apartment, I stopped and bought a few bottles of rum.

Tarah was shocked to see me at the kitchen counter pouring shots. "Why are you doing this? What happened to you, Jeremy?"

"All you do is complain! Blah, blah, blah! I'm a grown man, Tarah! If I want to drink, I can drink!" I shouted.

By December I had packed my things. "I need to do some thinking," I said as I walked out the front door.

I wanted to be free to do whatever I wished. I wasn't going to be told how to live. I wasn't going to sit around and let my heart ache with each beat. I was going for instant gratification, and no one was going to stop me.

I slept in the back seat of my 2002 Toyota Echo parked in random places around town. I found a night job working as the head of security at a night club in Ventura. After work I'd drive to Thousand Oaks and park within a few miles of a gym where I trained clients. I'd crawl in the back seat at around 3:30 in the morning and fall asleep.

One time I climbed out of the car to stretch and a van was parked next to me. A man stepped out and did a double take. "Didn't you fight in the UFC?" he asked.

I turned bright red. He could obviously tell that I'd been sleeping in my car. After that I quit sleeping in the back seat and began to sleep in the trunk. Inside the trunk was a glow-in-the-dark handle that I could open from the inside. I parked behind businesses or on side streets in Moorpark or Thousand Oaks. Most of my clients were at gyms in those two cities. During the day I coached people in weight training and cardio kickboxing. At night I bounced at the night club. By 3:30 a.m. I was in the trunk of my car spooning a bottle of vodka.

One morning when I woke up, I wasn't exactly sure where I had parked. Then it dawned on me. The night before I had decided to park in front of the gym so I could be closer to work. I figured it was a brilliant idea. This particular morning I woke up and climbed out of the trunk in my boxers. It was early; nobody showed up at the gym until about 6:00 a.m. I did my normal routine and began to urinate on the ground outside my car.

SLAM!! A car door shut about 20 feet away. Oh, crap! I opened one of my eyes and quickly stopped peeing so I could cover myself. My eye was blurry, so I pried open my other eye.

"Oh, no!" I said to myself.

The parking lot was full of cars! I had slept in. A man was sitting in a car parked directly behind me, and with him was one of my clients closing her trunk. She looked at me and blushed.

I had to find a better place to park. I started parking in the fields by some train tracks. All night, trains would come screeching by, honking their loud horns; causing me to jump and hit my head on the trunk of the car.

This wasn't going to work.

I found another place even farther from the city. It was a small campground and well away from all the noise. I sat on the hood of the car playing my guitar and drinking a bottle of vodka. My eyes were getting heavy, so I put the instrument in the back seat; then climbed into the trunk with my friendly bottle. As I was falling asleep I heard something outside of the car.

"What's that sound? A raccoon or something?" I whispered to myself. Then I took a gulp of the vodka.

Whatever it was, it came closer. I could hear heavy breathing, and its feet walking on the gravel. Maybe it's a person trying to steal my car?! I was about to pop the latch and jump out, ready to teach this clown a lesson, when I heard the steps come toward the trunk. I decided to wait and see what he did next. If he opened the trunk he'd get a kick right to his mouth.

The breathing got heavier and heavier until I heard someone or something sniffing the trunk. A dog? Maybe a really big dog?

The back of the car started bouncing. An enormous weight was rocking my car! "That is no dog. It's either a T-Rex or a bear!" I whispered to myself.

It was still sniffing the trunk, growling. It continued bouncing my car up and down, as if trying to make me fall out, or it was doing pushups on the trunk. My guess is it wanted to eat me. After a few minutes it gave up and left. I took a few more gulps of vodka and fell asleep. In the morning I opened the trunk slowly, looked around, but saw nothing but mountains, dirt, and bushes. I obviously had to find another place to park, This wasn't going to work either.

I bounced around from spot to spot for months, never staying in the same place for very long. Something always happened, and I'd have to move.[17]

---

17 I never really considered myself homeless because I knew that I had plenty of homes to go back to. I could've gone back home with Tarah, or moved back in with my parents. But I wouldn't be able to spend my nights on wild escapades if I was home. All my life I had lived a disciplined lifestyle, and now I wanted to live with no restraints.

24 Training with Nick Diaz

In February, after finding out she was pregnant, I moved back in with Tarah. I wanted to be a good father to my child due in September. I wanted to turn my life around, but no matter how hard I tried to stop drinking I failed. It seemed like the more I tried to change, the worse I became. I'd sleep in the trunk of my car for a few days and then come home to Tarah for a day or two.

Four months later, I met someone at the nightclub where I was working. I was checking IDs at the door when a handful of Hispanic women approached me. One of them was staring at me until her cousins embarrassed her. "She likes white boys!" her female cousins blurted out.

She turned bright red but didn't take her eyes off of me. I asked her for her ID to make sure she was twenty-one. "Elizabeth," I said, as I read the name off of the ID.

"No, don't say my name! I hate my name!" she replied.

"Why don't you like your name?" I asked.

"Just call me Liz," she insisted. One of her cousins asked if she could see my cell phone, so I handed it to her. She started pressing numbers which worried me. What if she was responding to a text from Tarah?

"Here!" she said, handing me back my phone. "Now you got Liz's number! Call her when you get off work." I didn't call her after work. Instead, I went home and continued to try to make things work with Tarah.

A week later, I traveled up north to train with Nick Diaz. I was able to stay sober for a whole day so Nick and I could train together. But there was a big problem: I was out of shape! It had been almost two years since I had competed in MMA and a year since I stepped in the ring. But Nick was training for a big fight, and I wanted to do what I could to help.

I stayed at Caesar Gracie's house, and we talked about a lot of things. I was considering moving up north to join his team. He had some of the best fighters in the world at his school, but I'd have to give up my drinking, which I wasn't ready to do.

The next day, without warming up, Nick and I jumped in the ring to spar. It was straight to business. At the end of the first round my neck locked up on me. It was the worst my neck had ever felt. But I didn't drive seven hours to give up after one round.

"You all right?" Nick asked after round one.

"Yeah, I'm all right," I replied.

"Let me know if you need a break, and I'll have my brother step in," he mumbled through his mouthpiece.

Rounds two and three made my neck even worse. I was beginning to get dizzy from the pain. I called it a day, and his brother stepped in to take my spot. They must have slugged it out for ten more rounds because they were still going at it after I got out of the shower.

I hung out with Nick and Mr. Grazie for the rest of the day. Then after dinner, I headed back to Camarillo. Before I jumped in my car, I opened the trunk, pulled out all the vodka bottles, and put them on the floorboard on the passenger side. I opened the first bottle and drank as much as I could, then started back to Camarillo. While I was driving I was looking through my phone and noticed a name.

Liz.

It was the woman from the club. Her cousins had programmed her number in my phone. I called her, and she remembered me. We talked on the phone during my entire drive back to Camarillo, and we met later that night. I remember sitting in the passenger seat of her car, parked in front of a sporting goods store in Oxnard. I was holding a large bottle of vodka as if it was my life support, probably not what she expected on her first date. What exactly did she see in me? I'm not quite sure. A drunk? A loser? A player? Or could she see past all the alcohol and see my potential? One thing was obvious: I was full of ambition, but the poison in my hand was extinguishing what was in my heart.

As I spoke about my dreams, she listened intently, staring with curiosity. It was as if she was getting a glimpse of the pain I felt, but she wasn't sure; maybe she was thinking, "How do I get this guy out of my car?" though the look on her face said otherwise. She was interested in me.

What was I doing? I had Tarah who was pregnant waiting for me at home. But I wasn't ready to be a father. I wasn't even capable of being a faithful boyfriend. I wanted to have my freedom and didn't want to commit to anything.

So, I broke up with Tarah which was painful. I had been seeing Liz for about three weeks and needed to break things off with her, too. I didn't want any commitments.

I went to Liz's apartment and told her I needed a break, and she did something I will never forget. She wrapped herself around my leg and wouldn't let me walk out of the door.

"I know you are living in your car. I saw all the stuff in the back seat. I'm not dumb! You can stay here with me! Please don't leave!" she cried.

She knew I was living in my car. How humiliating.

"I can't stay here. Let me go!" I said, while trying to take a step with her latched onto my leg.

"Nooo!! Stay with me! I can't let you live in your car!" she cried.

She wasn't going to let me go. I felt something in my heart that day. No matter how hard I tried to walk out of the door, she was glued to my leg. Now, maybe she really cared about my well-being, or she was just crazy about me; I don't know. But the fact that she wasn't going to let me get away without a struggle made me feel wanted. I was still hurting, missing my older brother and needing to be comforted. She helped me get my mind off of Oscar's death and showed me the affection that I was craving.

I agreed to move in with Liz and immediately realized it was a big mistake. She and I both had a lot of pride. We also had some unresolved issues in our lives. She had a lot of pain from her past, and she took it out on me. At the same time, I was an alcoholic who continued to let her down again and again. I'd promised her that I would change, but in reality I was getting worse.

25 Hooked on Pain Killers

In 2005, I was doing a light-weight workout at a gym in Westlake, California. "Light" means fifteen-pound dumbbell curls in each hand. Normally I'd curl forty to sixty pounds, but not with my neck hurting so badly. It had been locking up on me and getting worse over the years.

A man about my age started working out next to me. He kept staring at me, so I assumed he was either gay or he saw me fight Nick Diaz in UFC 44.

"You got any fights coming up?" he asked.

He's a fan!

"Actually, I plan on fighting in October," I answered.

"My name is Mike. I'm a fan. You're the only one ever to knock out Nick Diaz," he said as he shook my hand.

"Nice to meet you, Mike. Nick Diaz is a tough dude. I just got back from training with him. I injured my neck while sparring with him and had to cut training short," I said.

"Is this fight in October in the UFC?"

"I wish it was, but it's going to be in Total Combat. I'll be the headline fight," I said while doing a few more curls. "But I hear the UFC wants me back, so I gotta win this fight."

"You used to fight all the time from 2002 to 2003; then you just disappeared," he said.

"Well, in 2004 I took a break from MMA to compete in professional boxing. Then my older brother died. Add to all of that, I have a lot of injuries getting in the way," I explained.

"Sorry about your brother. I didn't know you lost a brother. I can't help ease that pain, but I can help take away the pain of your physical injuries," he replied.

"You can?"

"You ever heard of Norcos?" he asked with a grin.

"No. What are they?"

The only pain killer I knew about was Vicodin. I never was really big on pain killers. I took a few here and there after some big injuries, but that was about it.

"Norcos are better than Vicodin. They take away ALL the pain," he said.

I liked those words, "Take away all the pain." I had a pinched nerve in my neck that hurt so bad it was making me dizzy. My two broken hands were always hurting, and on top of that I was still healing from a broken rib. I would love to stop feeling pain! At that point I was willing to try anything.

"They'll take away all the pain, and I'll be able to train?" I asked.

"Bro, you will feel like Superman! Call me after you leave the gym," he said, handing me his number.

I got hooked on Norcos – instantly. They took away the pain, and I was able to train as hard as I wanted. I didn't feel a thing!

I started off with one pill every six hours and was up to fourteen a day by the end of the month. Then it got worse because they also made me sleepy. To offset the drowsiness, I started drinking Rockstar energy drinks to stay awake so I could accommodate my training and my night job.

This was where my addiction to pain killers began. I started buying every Norco pill the guy had. He also gave me a few phone numbers so I could buy pills from other people. I had Norcos in my system as long as I was awake.

Although the pills took away the physical pain, they didn't help with the emptiness that I had within, so I filled that with vodka.

Around this time, my younger brother was trying to find something to take away the anguish of losing our brother. He had been smoking marijuana for a while, but it wasn't enough. He began sniffing morphine and got hooked.

I didn't know he was snorting drugs. I wouldn't find that out until 2009, when he wrote me a letter explaining how his addiction began. He said he couldn't deal with the loss of our brother and didn't know what to do. I was his only brother left, but I lived hours away from him; even if I had lived with him, I wouldn't have been able to help. I couldn't even help myself.

26 Jeremy Jackson versus Christian Vargas

On October 14, 2005, I visited my brother's grave in Imperial Valley. The next night I was scheduled to fight Christian Vargas as the main event at a casino not far from my hometown.[18] I hadn't fought in MMA in 23 months, so I'd probably be a bit rusty.

Liz stood next to me as I gazed at my brother's tombstone. Liz never got to meet him because Oscar died nine months before she and I met. By now she was beginning to realize that this event was what changed my life. This was why I turned to alcohol.

She held my hand as we stared at his name etched in stone. "Will you give me a minute alone?" I asked her.

She kissed me on the hand and walked back to the car. I continued staring at the grave. It was hard to imagine that he was six feet under the grass I was standing on.

"Oscar, I don't know if you can hear me right now. I have a big fight tomorrow. I'm the main event at a casino up in the mountains. I haven't fought in MMA since I fought in Hawaii. A few months ago, I went up to train with Nick Diaz, and I injured my neck again. It still hurts, but I think I'll be all right tomorrow. Look, I want to tell you something," I said, as I glanced at my grandpa's grave marker a stone's throw away. My eyes looked toward the sky as I tried to hold back the tears. "You know, I've been a real mess since you left." Now the tears really began to flow. "I want to reach my dream and get the UFC title, but I feel like everything is against me. My heart aches every day. It's my fault you are gone. If I had let you come live with me, you'd still be here today. I spend my days drinking my life away now. It seems to be the only thing that can cover the pain and guilt. I'm so sorry, Bro. I let you down. Where do I go from here? I guess I'll just keep pressing forward no matter what. I'll get that UFC title; then I know I'll be happy. I love you," I said, as I wiped my eyes and walked back to the car. I left a pack of Juicy Fruit gum on his grave. Every Christmas we used to get a pack of Juicy Fruit from our grandparents, so we always had Juicy Fruit on us everywhere we went.

18 Total Combat 10

Liz and I sat in the car in front of my parents' house. I needed to tell her something. She knew I had a son who'd been born a month prior. She didn't know I wanted to get back with Tarah and try to be a better father.

"Liz, I think I made a mistake," I said.

"Mistake? What are you talking about?" she asked, confusion on her face.

"You know I have a son who was born a few weeks ago. I walked out on Tarah while she was pregnant. And to be honest, I still have feelings for her. I should go home and be with them," I said, staring out the window into the distance.

She began to cry and hold me with all her strength. "No, please don't leave me! Don't do this to me!" she cried.

My heart was aching, and I was torn between the two worlds: Tarah and my son, or Liz. All this was bad timing. I had a big fight the next day, and I didn't need this on my mind. "Liz, I'm a mess. I feel so broken down," I said as I put my arm around her. "I'll stay with you. I'm sorry about all this crazy talk."

The next day I fought Christian Vargas and won by submission. The plan was actually to knock him out, but nothing ever goes as planned, right? At the start of the first round, I was hit by something heavy which knocked me to the canvas.

BAM! My knees buckled and my vision was blurred.

What smacked me on the right side of my head to do this kind of damage? I thought someone might have thrown a full beer can into the ring and hit me in the head. Or it could have been a big right hand from Vargas. I had studied all his fights and knew he had a heavy right hand.

But I was watching his right hand and knew it didn't hit me. Come to find out, he had landed a left roadhouse kick to my head, which surprised me. I was dazed and on my back, with an undefeated opponent standing over me raining down punches. He knew I was rocked and this was his chance to finish me off.

What do you do when life roadhouse-kicks you to your jaw, knocking you to the ground? You can just stay down and go to sleep, or you can find a way to get back in the fight. It's difficult to get back in when you're dazed, with punches flying toward your face. But sometimes you have no other choice but to continue to press forward, even when you can barely see. It's what a warrior does when all is against him. You find a way to get back on your feet, even if you have to absorb a few more blows.

My first reaction was to try and submit him from my back, with a triangle choke. As he escaped my submission attempt, I saw an opportunity to try to get back on my feet. Back up, I took him down and ended up on top. It didn't take me long to get his back and sink in a rear choke at 3:56 of the first round.

After this the UFC began calling again.

27 I Want to be Famous

I was standing in the living room of Liz's and my apartment when the phone rang. I recognized the number right away: it was the UFC! They wanted me to fight Josh Koscheck in January of 2006 at the UFC Fight Night. Without hesitation, I said "YES!"

Karo Parisyan, one of my training partners, helped me prepare for the fight. We were training like animals each day, and I pushed my body to the limit. Although I was drinking vodka and popping pain killers, I was in amazing shape. I was ready for Koscheck.

One day after training, I received a phone call from the UFC. Josh Koscheck was injured and would be pulling out of the fight. Jonathan Goulet from Canada would be stepping in to take Koscheck's spot.

I didn't need a change in plan. We believed that Goulet would try and take me down, just like Koscheck would have. The game plan was to keep the fight standing and knock him out: you know, my usual game plan!

I was rinsing off in the showers at the gym after a hard night's training with Karo, when suddenly I felt like I was having a heart attack. I grabbed my chest and leaned against the shower wall.

I'm too young to have a heart attack!!

I tried to take a deep breath, but couldn't because of the pain. I walked over toward the sinks and looked at myself in the mirror. My chest was bruising. I needed medical attention.

The diagnosis was a torn pectoral muscle. I found out I hadn't injured myself in the shower. It actually happened during training with Karo. I just didn't feel the pain when it happened. How could I not feel my pectoral muscle tearing during training? I had plenty of strong pain killers in my system and didn't feel a thing. By shower time the pills were beginning to wear off. That was when the pain hit me full force.

I had to make a decision whether I could still fight with a torn pectoral muscle. Fighters are always fighting with some kind of injury. The question is, how much will it affect you during training and, more importantly, during the actual fight?

I chose to pull out which was probably a wise choice. Dwayne Ludwig, who was a former training partner of mine, stepped in to fight Jonathan Goulet.

Where would I watch the fight? I didn't like watching from home because Liz would always be shouting from the back room about something she saw on someone's MySpace page.

"Jeremy! Come see what this b**** said about me!" Liz would shout.

Now, don't get me wrong. I definitely wanted to know what the "chisme" (gossip) was. Just not during the fights!

I found an old dive bar in Ventura that would be showing the fights on its TV. I never even knew this bar existed until that day. I sat at the bar that night watching the fights on a TV directly in front of me. Sitting around me were several drunk guys, most of whom were completely out of control. During the Ludwig and Goulet fight, which lasted only eleven seconds, the men around me were saying disrespectful things about the fighters.

"Hey! How about showing a little respect? These guys are pro athletes!!" I blurted out.

They laughed and said, "What do you know about pro athletes?"

"I was supposed to fight against Goulet tonight, but I was injured. Ludwig took my spot," I said with a serious expression. It was dead quiet for about five seconds, and then practically everyone fell to the floor laughing.

"No, I'm serious! I'm Jeremy Jackson, the Scorpion," I proclaimed.

One of them interrupted me and said, "Right! And I'm Tito Ortiz! I was supposed to fight tonight against the Iceman." At this point, the entire bar thought it was the funniest joke on the planet. Everyone was pretending to be a UFC fighter and cracking jokes. They thought I was a crazy drunk.

I looked at the bartender and said, "Two shots please, your cheapest vodka." As he was pouring the shots, I asked, "How much for the whole bottle?"

As I sat there watching the rest of the fights, and drinking my life away, I knew I had to build a bigger name for myself. People recognized me at MMA events, but seldom outside. I wanted to be able to walk into a bar and have everyone turn their heads to say, "There's Jeremy Jackson, the Scorpion!"

Celebrities get recognized everywhere they go. No matter where they are, they are surrounded by a crowd wanting a photo. That's the type of attention I wanted. I considered that to be true power, and with true power come money and women.

Anyone who is competing in sports, or acting in movies, wants to be famous. I know some may disagree with me, and that's OK, but I think Kevin Bacon said it best during an interview with the Daily Telegraph: "Show me an actor who doesn't want to be famous, and I'll show you a liar."

28 The Ultimate Fighter 4: The Comeback

While I was recovering from my torn pectoral muscle, I received another call from the UFC. Joe Sylva filled me in on the good news. He wanted me to be on "The Ultimate Fighter," a reality TV show. To be honest, I was a little insulted.

Those of us who had made it to the UFC the "old-fashioned way" did not like The Ultimate Fighter show at first. We saw the TV series as an easy-in to the UFC, without having to put in the work. We had to fight our way to the UFC, while those on the reality shows just needed personality, not fighting skills. The Ultimate Fighter show was for guys hoping to make it to the UFC.

So why ask me to be on the show? I'm a UFC veteran!

Joe explained that Season Four would be different. It would be for veterans who'd somehow fallen off the map and were no longer fighting in the UFC. The winner of the show would get a shot at the UFC title; hence the title, "The Comeback."

So this was it! My lifelong dream was within my grasp: a shot at the UFC title! This was why I had left home straight out of high school: to be a UFC champion.

The UFC flew me to Vegas so that I could meet with the producers. They gave me a quick rundown. There would be other UFC fighters that I would recognize, but most importantly, I was not to talk about this with anyone.

As I sat quietly in a room next to some buffed-out older guy, UFC fighters began pouring into the room, taking seats around us.

Wow! There's Matt Serra! I saw him fight in the earlier UFC. And there are Dean Thomas, George Rivera, Mikey Barnette, Chris Lytle, Pete Spratt, Shonie Carter, and many other big names. I was amazed at the talent in the room.

I turned to get a better look at the older dude. It was Keith Hackney! This guy fought Royce Gracie when the UFC first began. I was a fan of all these guys. But I had to keep my cool and act like it was no big deal.

The show's representatives told us that we would be taken to different medical facilities and get checked out. When we weren't doing interviews or getting medical work done, we were supposed to stay in our hotel rooms. They didn't want the secret getting out about who would be on Season Four.

Now, most UFC fighters don't take orders very well, and these guys were no exception. A lot of us went to malls and clubs, while those who were married or had girlfriends went to a store down the street, then directly back to their rooms.

When we left Vegas we were told to wait for a phone call that would tell us whether or not we'd made the cut for the show. Out of all the UFC veterans, only sixteen would make it. I went home and waited.

Almost immediately Liz and I started fighting, so I began sleeping in the trunk of my car again. I didn't want to train for the Ultimate Fighter while sleeping in the trunk of my car. I also needed to stop drinking and popping pills, so I accepted an offer from Mom to come back and live with her. I felt that this was the only way I could give up drinking and prepare for the show. The next day I packed my things to go back home.

When I arrived in Imperial Valley, I still had vodka in my system since I had been drinking during the entire drive. I went straight to my old bedroom, which now belonged to my younger brother Bodi, and walked around looking at all my old trophies from boxing, karate, and baseball. My little brother was my biggest fan. He had "Jeremy 'The Scorpion' Jackson" posters all over his walls.

Would I be able to stop drinking and win this show? Would I get a shot at the UFC title?

I stood up, walked to the window, and looked out. There was the backyard I'd grown up in. I had put in countless hours of martial arts training there. I briefly saw my dad's hair explode from the impact of the green tennis ball that I had batted. The memory brought a playful smile.

Turning around, I felt my mind drifting back to that that day in 2003, seeing my older brother Oscar sitting on the edge of the bed, looking down in shame. He'd begged me to help him with his addiction to drugs, and I hadn't lifted a finger. Eleven months later he died.

As I stood there staring at the bed, the guilt was unbearable. I could have helped him, but my career was more important than my own brother. My selfishness won.

I walked out of the room and headed for the front door.

"Where you headed?" Mom asked.

"Oh, I was just going to go for a drive," I answered.

"I'll go with you," she said.

"No, I'll be all right. I'm fine, really," I said as I continued on my way.

"All right. If you need me, I'm here for you," she exclaimed.

She knew. We both knew.

I drove down the street to a liquor store and parked in front. "Fight it, Jeremy!" I said to myself.

My mind kept flashing back to my brother crying. Before I could stop, my car door opened and my feet were marching toward the entrance. I walked in, grabbed a basket, and began to fill it with large bottles of vodka. I set the basket on the counter, then heard my name.

"Jeremy Jackson?" a voice inquired. Usually when someone says my full name, it is either a fan or a jealous husband. Sometimes it was because I was in trouble with Mom. But this was a man's voice coming from behind the counter. I couldn't see the person because all the bottles were blocking my view of the clerk.

"You're Jeremy Jackson, the Scorpion!" he pronounced. "I've followed your career ever since you won the IFC title in 2002 when you knocked out Nick Diaz!"

I slid the bottles to one side. Hey! I know that face! It was an old friend I used to hang with when I was a kid. "Daniel?" I asked in shock.

"Yep! You remember me! You know, I heard you visited your hometown every now and then, but I never seemed to catch you," he said. I noticed that he was staring at the bottles, and I realized how it looked.

"Oh, uh, these are for a wedding party, not my wedding, someone else's. They like vodka," I said, clearing my throat.

"Yeah, I can see that," he said as he was ringing them up. He asked if we could take a picture together, and I agreed. Though he wanted to talk, I told him I needed to go.

"Daniel, I'd love to catch up some time, but I really gotta get going," I said. I walked out the door carrying way too many vodka bottles for one person. I drove to a place where I used to ride bikes with my brothers. I was sitting on the hood of my car drinking vodka, when I noticed a vehicle coming down the road. It was my little brother.

He pulled up and parked next to me. "I thought I'd find you out here," he said, while closing his car door.

"I needed some fresh air," I explained. He walked over and sat next to me. It was nice having my little brother beside me. We sat together watching the sun set over the mountains.

"It's crazy," I said.

"What is?" he asked.

"How fast a life can change. One second I'm focused and driven, and then BAM! Everything changes. Sometimes I pretend that he's still in Louisiana, but deep down I know that I'll never be able to talk with him again," I said with tears in my eyes.

"I know what you mean, Jeremy," Bodi said, as he stood up and stared into the distance. I could tell he was deep in thought. "But you still got me." After making eye contact with me, he turned around and walked back to his car, but before he opened the door he had one more thing to say.

"Mama told me to tell you that dinner is ready," he said.

"I'll be home in a bit. I'm just gonna kick back here a little longer. Hey, don't mention anything about me drinking, all right?" I said with a smile.

As soon as he drove away I gulped down the rest of the vodka in the bottle. I was about to open the second; then remembered I had to be home for dinner, so I put the bottles in the trunk and drove home.

29 Show Time!

For the next couple of weeks, I punched the bag in the backyard of my parents' house or went for a run down the dirt roads. After my workouts I gulped down a bottle of vodka and passed out. Obviously my rehab was not going so well, but I didn't think the producers would call me to be on the show anyway.

I walked into the living room to tell my family I'd be driving up north to see Tarah and our son. They were all gathered around the TV watching season three of The Ultimate Fighter.

"Hey Jeremy, want to watch season three with us?" Mom asked. I told them I needed to see my son and Tarah. The room fell silent.

"For how long?" she asked. "I don't know," I answered.

We hugged and said our goodbyes. Before I walked out the door, I watched about thirty seconds of the show. I watched as the fighters sat around the fireplace and tried picturing what it would feel like to see myself on the show. Then I turned and walked out.

I met Tarah and our son at a hotel in Camarillo. Because I was so excited to see him, I tried my best to stay sober, but I failed. As soon as he fell asleep, I chugged the first bottle I could find.

Early the next morning, Tarah shook me awake to tell me something important. I opened my eyes and realized I was lying on the hotel bed.

"Jeremy, call your mom. It's important," she blurted out. My phone was turned off because I didn't want Liz calling. I turned my phone on and called Mom.

"Jeremy, The Ultimate Fighter show has been trying to get hold of you. Here is their number. Call them ASAP. They said it's urgent!" Mom shouted into the phone.

I hung up and called the number. As soon as someone answered, I cut them off. "This is Jeremy Jackson," I said.

"Jeremy Jackson? You're one tough guy to reach. We need you on a plane to Vegas. The show starts this morning. You're on The Ultimate

Fighter, Season 4.[19] We need to get you here now. What airport are you near?" the voice answered.

"LAX or Burbank," I offered.

"We'll fly you out of Burbank. Can you be there in two hours?"

I looked at Tarah. "Yeah, I believe I can," I replied.

This was my life: I was constantly being rushed from one place to another, with no time to absorb what had just happened. It was like watching a movie in fast-forward. Life was becoming one big blur.

"Jeremy, we need you here ASAP! Make sure you don't miss your flight," he said.

After hanging up, I asked Tarah to drive me to the airport. I took the bottle of vodka and downed it. On the way to the airport, I kept wondering if maybe it was all just a dream. It was happening so fast.

During the flight I asked the stewardess for a glass of vodka, and she made me a cup of orange juice with vodka. I chugged it and asked her for another. She looked at me and said it would be a while until she made me another one.

"Look Ma'am, I'm terrified of flying. Alcohol calms me. Now, unless you want me freaking out on this plane, I suggest you give me more vodka to help me out," I said. She stared at me for a few seconds, and I could tell she was about to either tell me no or slap me. So, I interrupted her and showed her my patented "Jeremy Jackson Hurt Puppy Dog" look: guaranteed results or your money back.

"Please?" I said with a pouty lip.

She smiled and poured me a cup of straight vodka. No orange juice.

"Thank you," I said as I lifted the cup. Pouty-lip works every time!

When the plane landed, I stumbled off and went to get my luggage. Standing out front was a man holding a sign that read, "Jeremy Jackson."

---

19   The Ultimate Fighter show had already picked their sixteen fighters, but one of the fighters, Nick Diaz, was injured and had to pull out. I was the alternate. During interviews on the show I was asked where I was when the Ultimate Fighter Show called me at the last minute. My response was, "I was at the clubs when my phone rang." I told this story because I didn't want Liz to know I was at a hotel with Tarah.

I walked up and saluted. "That would be me, sir, reporting for duty." He informed me that we were in a hurry and needed to be on the road as soon as I got my suitcase. When my bag arrived he carried it to a van parked outside. We zoomed out of there and ended up at some big hotel/casino. As people came out to greet me, one of them spoke into a walkie-talkie.

"He's here. We are coming up now."

I was led into a room with a big desk. People scurried about; everyone was in a hurry. There were big cameras lying around and a huge stack of papers on the desk.

One of the guys shook my hand and asked me to have a seat. "Glad you made it, Mr. Jackson. How you feeling?" he asked.

"That's a lot of papers!" I said, ignoring the question.

"Don't worry. You don't have to read them all. I'll summarize it all for you," he replied while looking at his watch.

"Guys, we go live in five minutes!" he shouted. People began loading up camera gear and boom microphones.

"You made it just in time, Mr. Jackson. Basically, all this stack of papers says is that you agree to…." He explained in very short quick words that I was signing my life away.

"Great! I can't wait to sign!" I sarcastically replied.

"Guys, we are live in three minutes!" he shouted.

He handed me a pen and put his hand on the stack of papers. "Now, after you sign and date, I'll pull a sheet away. Then sign and date the next page, and I'll pull that sheet away, and so on. Get the picture?" he said.

"Got it!"

We began flying through the stack of papers faster than I could imagine. My signature didn't even look like a signature after a while. It looked more like a big "X." We were down to the last paper when he shouted in victory, "Done! Guys, we're on in thirty seconds!"

He looked at my bag and pointed toward the desk. "All right. Cell phones, laptops, anything that could be used for communication with the outside world must stay here."

I handed him my cell phone. "That's all I got," I said. He smiled and put his hand on my shoulder. "You ready man? You excited?" he asked, looking into my eyes.

"I am," I said with a big smile. I was a little bit drunk, but hey, who's to know, right?

"Rolling!" he shouted. The camera crew ran outside with their equipment and entered the lobby area. He looked at me and smiled. "Everyone will know your name after this show is over," he said as he opened the door and stepped aside.

I walked out and headed down the hall toward the cameras.

Destiny awaits! It's show time!

30 Meeting the Lifeguard

I could see other UFC fighters coming down the halls headed toward the lobbies. Cameras followed each one of us. The first fighter I recognized was Pete Spratt. Pete and I had a history.

The fighters climbed into two different vans, and we were whisked away to "The House." I sat quietly while everyone else talked, still buzzing from the vodka. What now? Would I be able to stay off the bottle?

Arriving at The House, we each picked our rooms. After situating myself, I met up with other fighters in the living room.

"Scorpion! I want you to know I'm a fan," George Rivera said to me as he held out his hand.

My jaw dropped. If anyone was a fan, it was me! I was one of the youngest guys on the show, and here I was looking at guys who'd fought in the UFC when I used to sit on my couch watching them on VHS! That's how long ago it was. I'd watched their fights and never imagined I would be talking to them, let alone hear them say that they were fans of mine.

Someone opened the cabinets in the kitchen, and at that moment my worst fears were realized. There was a fully stocked bar.

That night I lay in bed, troubled. The contract required that I wear a microphone necklace at all times, except when showering or training. The microphone wasn't the problem. The problem was that I couldn't sleep. I was missing my son and having serious alcohol withdrawals.

The next day they divided us into teams. I was the first one picked for the Blue Team, but the Gray Team ended up winning the coin toss, so they'd get to pick who would be the first fighter from our team. As long as they kept winning, they'd get to keep picking. I knew they would avoid picking me because I would be too much of a threat. I was too well rounded. I had strong stand up and wrestling, and a good Jiu-Jitsu game. Whoever picked me would be in for a fight!

They ended up selecting two very dangerous fighters first: Rich Clemente; then the following week Pete Spratt.

Rich had good stand up and a tight ground game. Pete Spratt had some of the best stand up in MMA, and on top of that he was in the best shape of anyone on the show. His ground game was good, but not at the level of the other fighters. Spratt had taken out Robbie Lawler with kicks in UFC 42 and had trained with some of the best Muy Thai trainers around.

Pete and I used to be rivals. We're both "strikers," and we knew that one day we'd eventually run into each other. But, on The Ultimate Fighter we became friends and training partners.

When the coaches came in, I was glad to see that Randy Coutoure was one of them. I immediately pulled him to one side and gave him my situation.

"I was called in at the last minute, and I'm out of shape, but I know I can win this thing. Will you help me train?" I asked.

He put his hand on his chin and considered everything I'd said. Finally, he looked around to see if the other fighters could hear; then he gave me a short speech. I got pumped! "Let's get you in shape," he said, as he grabbed the medicine ball and handed it to me.

After medicine ball drills, he hooked a rubber cable to my torso, and I pulled him back and forth across the room. We wrestled, and he helped me perfect my take downs.

Two weeks into the show, some fighters started complaining that being locked up in The House all the time was too much like prison. The producers finally relented and took us to the YMCA for a little break, though we were still not allowed to talk to anyone other than the show's fighters or producers.

At the pool we found out that George St. Pierre and I were the two fastest swimmers. We decided to race, and I beat him by an arm's length. My life-guarding years paid off.

Speaking of lifeguards, standing nearby, watching curiously, was a beautiful lifeguard who couldn't figure out why all the cameras were filming us. Some of the other fighters tried chatting her up, but she showed no interest, so I swam over and took a shot. We talked while the other fighters were wise-cracking.

"Control your hormones, Jeremy!" and "Watch out for the Scorpion!" the other fighters shouted.

After a while, the camera crew came over and gave me the "Look", as if to say, "Don't forget the rules: you can't talk to people outside the show." I looked at her and whispered, "I gotta go, but I'll come back in a little bit."

We were all heading toward the lockers to change so we could go play basketball. A man was changing next to me. "Excuse me, do you have a piece of paper and a pen?" I whispered.

"As a matter of fact, I just might," he said, as he reached into his locker and pulled out a pen and some paper. The other fighters saw me drawing a map and said I was crazy. I drew a map of The House and how to get there. You couldn't miss the place because of the stadium lights shining all around the property. I think I gave a meeting time of 11:00 p.m.

I walked out to the pool area and put the map down. I approached the pretty lifeguard and pointed to where I'd put the map. "There is a letter over there for you. It explains everything. It's from me," I said with a smile. She smiled back!

The letter introduced me and had my phone number at the bottom. On the back was a map of The House.

31 It Is What It Is

Later that night, all the fighters were sitting around the fireplace in the backyard of The House. For two weeks no one had ever sat around the fireplace;   now they all gathered there. In fifteen minutes the lifeguard would be meeting me at the back wall of The House, which was just a hop and a jump away from the fireplace.

The camera crews stayed with the fighters. In addition to the mobile cameras, there were stationary cameras inside and outside The House. Watching people sit on the toilet can be entertaining, I suppose.

I sat around the fireplace with the other fighters and did some plotting: how do I get everyone to go inside the house within fifteen minutes? As far as I knew, she could already be behind the wall waiting for me.

I could try standing up and saying, "All right, everybody inside! Let's go!" But then they would think I was either crazy or up to something. Even if it worked, a camera crew would stay with me, so I wrote a note and handed it to one of the fighters sitting next to me. It basically said that I was meeting the lifeguard in a few minutes and needed everyone inside. He smiled and whispered to another fighter.

A fighter sitting across the room noticed the whispering and wanted to know what was going on. "What's with all the secrets? What's the note say?"

The fighter sitting next to me stood and yawned. "Well, I'm really tired. I'm gonna call it a night," he said.

As soon as he walked away, the rest began to follow, but not all of them. A few remained and continued chatting. Crap! I whispered to another fighter and his eyes lit up. Now he, too, knew what the note said. He whispered that he would go in The House and start a big scene with another fighter, drawing the camera crew away.

He went in, and within thirty seconds the camera crew took off to see what all the commotion was. Even the rest of the fighters ran inside.

It worked! I was all alone now. I walked over, pretending to urinate in the trees and climbed the brick wall. I sat on it and realized it wasn't going to work. Beyond the brick wall was the complete darkness of open desert. She would have to be crazy to walk in that darkness.

I stayed for ten or fifteen minutes just in case she came. After a while, I called it a night and went back in the house. Before I walked in the back door, I looked up in the trees and on the roof of the house there were cameras everywhere.

I went into another fighter's room and noticed there was a handful of them kicking back, talking. They were the ones who had helped me create the diversion.

"So? What happened?" one of them said.

I felt stupid because she didn't even show up, but these guys didn't need to know that. I wanted them to think I was cool, so I told a lie. "Yeah, we hung out," I said, as I sat down and made myself comfortable. I saw that it entertained them, and they wanted to know more. We had been bored out of our minds for the past two weeks: no TV, Internet, cell phones, or girlfriends. We needed some entertainment, so I created a story, telling them that she and I had a great time. Then I went to bed.

Later that night, I was awakened by one of the producers and told to go downstairs into the living room. There on the couch was the same handful of fighters. They looked like little children in trouble.

"Sit down!" the producer grumbled as she pointed toward the couch. As soon as my butt hit the couch, she began grilling us. I felt like a little kid, and I'm sure the other guys did too.

This little woman, just a tick over five feet tall and barely 115 pounds, had a collection of the toughest, most powerful and dangerous men on the planet sitting in small puddles of their own pee. Even more terrifying was that I seemed to be the object of her anger.

"You know, you should be kicked off the show for this," she said, "but we are just going to fine you. I'll discuss it with the other producers." She turned and began to march off.

"Wait!" I said as I stood up and followed her toward the front door. She turned around and stared at me. "I never met up with her. Review the cameras in the trees! You know I never left the premises," I said in desperation.

She studied my eyes, and I knew I only had a couple of seconds before she walked away. Maybe I should show her the "Jeremy Jackson Hurt Puppy Dog Look." Actually, I better not, because it looked like she wanted to punch me in the face.

Before I could say anything, she turned around and walked out the front door.

The next day, we heard that training was canceled until further notice. Dana White and Randy Couture came to The House, and Dana gave a long speech. At the end of his speech he said something I'll never forget.

"It is what it is. Pack your bags, you're going home."

Now where had I heard that before? Maggie had written almost those identical words on my bedroom wall in 2002. "It is what it is. Pack your bags and leave."

When Dana walked out of the house, I could feel all the cameras zooming in on me. I felt like the whole world was focused on me.

What now? Do I chase Dana down and explain what happened the previous night? I'm innocent, right? Well, I did write a note to the lifeguard asking her to meet me behind the mansion, but she never showed up. If she had, I'm sure I would have left the premises. Technically, I was in the wrong.

Sitting there on that couch, I felt shame and regret. This was the closest I had ever been to reaching my goal of capturing the UFC title. I was so close!

While I desperately tried to explain that the lifeguard had never come, one of the producers took me to a back room; he didn't believe me. We sat down in front of a camera, and he told me they needed one last interview before I left. I was in deep thought. "I can't look stupid in front of the whole world, so I'll just go along with what I've already said." I stuck to my original story and was on an airplane out of town within an hour.

I felt that the producers could have dealt with this in private, but they had done it for ratings and drama. This was what I got for telling lies.

32 Living Like a Rock Star

Liz picked me up from the Burbank airport, and the second I got in the car we started arguing. I probably should have called Tarah instead, but Liz had control of my mind, and she was the first person I thought of when I left the show. We argued the whole way home about stupid stuff. Why couldn't we just get along? Pride! We both had a lot of pride. I was trying to change her into something she was not, and she was trying to change me into the man she wanted me to be. We needed to take another break from each other.

Around this time my manager called, inviting me to come live with him in San Diego. He had offered me a room before; I'd always declined, but this sounded like a good time to accept his offer. I needed to get away from Liz and get focused.

I packed my bags that same day and drove down to San Diego. When I arrived he showed me my room. "This will be your room. The 'War Machine,' John Koppenhaver, used to sleep here," he said.[20]

I began training at City Boxing and Undisputed: two great gyms in San Diego. At night I worked at a strip club. No, I wasn't stripping! I was a bouncer.

I don't know how, but I was able to train throughout the day, work at the strip club all night, all the while boozed up on vodka. One time Liz came down to visit and watch me train. I was grappling with Dominic Cruz and the War Machine. During a one-minute break I refreshed myself (drank more vodka) and went back on the mat to grapple some more. Dominic came up to me and whispered, "Scorpion, are you drinking?"[21]

---

20   The War Machine actually became, and still is, a good friend of mine. We had a lot in common. Both of us had a broken past and we craved attention from fans. Unfortunately, his behavior, like mine, led to prison.

21   After reflecting on this I realized that out of all the training partners I had during my four years of drunkenness, Dominic Cruz was the only one to call me on it during training. I remember how shocked he looked.

Caught! He could smell it coming out of my pores! He looked down and shook his head. I knew he was disappointed.

While I was showering, Dominic approached Liz and shared what was in his heart. "You know, Jeremy's a great fighter; he could be the UFC champ if he really wanted it. But he's throwing it all away. I could smell the alcohol on him today," he said.

"I don't get it either. I give him chance after chance, and he just continues down the same road of destruction," she answered.

I held my premiere party for The Ultimate Fighter 4 at the strip club. I was so drunk that I don't remember what happened. But I can tell you this: once the show aired, I got recognized everywhere I went. Fame! Now I was on my way!

When my manager and I went to nightclubs, people would surround me and want to take my picture. "You're Jeremy Jackson!" someone shouted. "Can we take a picture??" another blurted out.

My manager laughed and put his hand on my shoulder. "Get used to it, JJ! Lots of people watch The Ultimate Fighter. Enjoy it! You're a star now!"

And I did enjoy it, a little too much. It became like a drug to me. I walked into stores, and the owners would start giving me free clothes. I walked into restaurants and ate for free. I didn't have to wait in line at clubs anymore. Women threw themselves at me. I felt powerful!

Any time I needed to build my ego, I went to places where I knew I'd be recognized. I felt like a superstar when I attended MMA events. I would stroll by the MMA clothing booths because I knew they would stop me and give me free stuff. By the end of the night I'd be driving home with a huge box of new clothes. If I received this kind of treatment, then what do men like Tito Ortiz and Randy Courtoure get? What about rock stars or actors? I could only imagine.

Around this time I received a phone call from Las Vegas. I was hoping it was the UFC, but it wasn't. It was the lifeguard's boyfriend! He wanted to know why my phone number was in his girlfriend's cell phone.

Wow! At least I know she programmed my phone number into her phone! I had written my number on the map I gave her when I was on the show.

Her boyfriend was yelling at me, asking who I was, and how I knew his girlfriend. I told him I didn't know who his girlfriend was, and that I wasn't sure how she got my number. He continued shouting, so I did was I should have done two minutes earlier.

CLICK! I hung up on him, and ignored his calls.

2002. Left to right: Oscar, Bodi, and me.

2000. Training at my old boxing gym in Imperial, before I moved away to pursue my MMA career.
Photo courtesy Jacob Welch

My stepdad Robby, me, and my mom, doing a "photo shoot" during a prison visit in 2017.

Top: September 26, 2003. Nick Diaz trying to take me down. "UFC 44 Undisputed"

Right: Jeremy Jackson

Bottom: September 26, 2003. Nick Diaz and me after the fight

Photos this page courtesy Jeff Sherwood – Sherdog.com

33 Charity Events

Early one morning, my manager came into my room and shook me awake. I had worked at the strip club all night, then partied afterward.

"JJ!! UFC called," he trumpeted.

I opened one eye and looked at the clock. I'd only had two hours of sleep! And stop yelling!!

"I'm so tired," I mumbled.

"JJ, listen. UFC is doing a charity event, and they want to know if you're in. The first day will be at a juvenile prison, and the next day will be at Glendale College. The juvenile prison is the same place they filmed 'Grid Iron Gang.' At the college you'll hang out with three hundred kids who have cancer. You in or out?" he demanded.

I loved doing charity events and promotional tours. I loved making a difference in kids' lives. Seeing their smiles was priceless. When I visited Mom and Dad in my hometown, people would bring their kids to meet me. Heck! They would be waiting in the front yard when I pulled up! It was awesome!

"Yeah, yeah. I'm in. When is it?" I asked, as I closed my eyes and rolled under the covers.

"It's next week," my manager said on his way out, gently closing the door behind him.

I leaned over, grabbed the bottle of vodka on my night stand, and took a few gulps. The door opened again.

"And make sure the bottle stays here when you go. You need to be sober," he said; then quickly closed the door again.

I set the bottle down and lay back. As he walked down the stairs, he made sure to shout one more thing: "And you have training in one hour!!" he bellowed.

One hour?? But I've been working all night at the strip club! I can't keep training as hard as I do on only three hours of sleep. But what can I do? I must train. This is my life for now.

The day came, and I met the other UFC fighters who would be joining me for the charity events. I ignored my manager, making sure my vodka was close at hand. We arrived at the juvenile prison sometime on a Saturday morning and hung out with the kids all day. Everything was a blur to me, but I remember telling them to stay out of trouble.

"If you are going to fight, do it in the ring or a cage where there is a referee and it's safe. Guys, why fight on the street when you can fight in a sport and get paid for it?" I asked.

The other UFC fighters spoke about the hard life and how to say "No" to drugs.

When night came we went to a nice Mexican restaurant in LA. The owner was very excited to learn that he had a bunch of UFC fighters eating at his restaurant. He pushed a couple of tables together for us. Then he had all the waitresses leave their regular tables to wait on us, which naturally put a lot of pressure on the other waiters who had to serve more tables than they could handle.

The whole time, people were coming up to take pictures. One of the fighters was getting more attention than the rest of us. I was a little jealous, but I'm not going to complain. It did give me the motivation to try and make my name more famous than this 155 pound UFC fighter. But for the moment we felt like kings, sitting at our table while adoring people surrounded us.

Later that night we arrived at our hotel in downtown LA. It was a really nice place, but the best part was that the UFC picked up the tab. We checked into our rooms, and it was then that I found out who I'd be sharing a room with. It was one of the heavyweights!

"I'm going to the store. Be back in a bit." I announced.

"Wait! We're gonna go with you!" they answered. Great! I wanted to buy alcohol and didn't want them knowing about it. I had been drunk the whole time and was doing a good job hiding it.

We walked down the street to a nearby store, and I went straight for the liquor section while the others went to buy snacks. I set the vodka bottles in a plastic bag and hurried to the counter. Maybe I could make it back to the hotel before they saw me. But it never works out the way you plan, right?

They all finished getting what they wanted and stood behind me in line. I lifted the bag of bottles and set them on the counter.

Clunk! The sound of the heavy bottles hitting the counter was loud enough for them to hear.

"You know we are going to a nightclub tonight on the roof of our hotel, right? I'm sure there will be plenty of alcohol there," one of the offered.

"Oh, I didn't know we were going to a club. Well, this will be for after the club." I said.

When we got back to our rooms, I put the alcohol in the refrigerator - all but one, that is. My heavyweight roommate watched as I began to chug it down.

"Easy, easy! Breathe, bro!" he said, while he walked toward the bathroom.

I laughed and took a few more gulps. People were always telling me to take it easy.

"You drink that like it's water," he called from the bathroom.

I walked over to the window and admired the view. A guy could get used to living like this. Suddenly I got a text. It was a female fan I had taken pictures with when I was a special guest at a restaurant in Anaheim. She wanted to hang out. I texted her back to let her know it would have to be after the charity event the next day.

"You ready, Jay?" the heavyweight asked. "Oh yes, let's do this!" I said, as I set the bottle down and followed him out the door. A few of the other fighters met us in the hall, and we all walked up together.

We took the elevator to the roof, and people instantly recognized us. After ordering some drinks, I went over and joined my roommate who was standing with a group of people near the edge of the roof.

"Hey! You were on the Ultimate Fighter!" one of the women shouted.

"Yes, that's me." I confirmed.

She turned around and shouted to her friends, "See, I told you it was him!" They all came over and began talking about the show. "We thought you were going to win, but then you wanted that lifeguard," one of them said. She actually sounded a little sad, or was it jealousy?

They looked at my drink and saw that it was empty. "Can we get you another drink?" they asked.

"Sure." I answered. Then it hit me. Here I was surrounded by beautiful women, yet I felt so alone and empty. I had popularity, power, women, and everything else, but inside I was empty. I set my glass on the table and put my hands on the rail to look over the edge. It sure was a long drop. What if I just jumped off?

I could hear the women still talking to me, but I wasn't listening.

"Hello?" a woman said, while she waved her hand in front of my face, trying to get my attention. I looked at her and smiled. "Hey, I'm sorry. I was just thinking…." I pointed over the side of the building and was about to tell her the truth, but instead I said, "I was thinking what a beautiful view it is from way up here."

She laughed and looked out at the city. "Yes, it's all right I guess," she answered.

I looked over at one of the other UFC fighters and saw that he was taking pictures with people. One of them noticed I was looking that way and lifted his beer to say "Cheers!" Just then a woman handed me a drink, so I lifted my glass in his direction and smiled.

The women were still talking to me when my mind began to wander again. Is this all there is to life? There has to be something more, because this isn't life!

"Heellloo? You all right?" one of the women asked, as she put her hand on my shoulder.

"I should probably get going," I said.

"Wait! Where are you going?" she asked.

"I just gotta go."

"Can I come with you?" she asked.

"Actually, I need to be alone," I said, as I walked toward the exit. One of the other fighters made eye contact with me and held up his hands with a confused look on his face as if to say, "Where you goin'?"

I made my way back to my room and grabbed my bottle. After a few gulps I felt better. What was I looking for? I walked over and looked out the window. If only I knew what this "something" was that I was seeking. I was sure that if I found it, I'd be happy. I marched out of the room and took the elevator downstairs. As I was walking through the lobby, some fans stopped me to take a quick picture. They wanted to talk, but I told them I had to be somewhere. I walked down the street with a bottle of vodka in my hand. A cab driver was sitting on the hood of his car as I approached him.

"Just head that way," I pointed, as I jumped into the back seat.

We had been driving twenty or thirty minutes when I noticed we were in a very dangerous part of LA. "I'm not going any farther. It gets worse from here," he said, as he parked.

I paid him and began walking down the street. A police helicopter's spotlight searched for someone. A drug deal was happening in a dark alley nearby. I took another drink of the vodka. Where was I? How did I end up here?

My phone made a noise, signaling that the battery was dead; then it shut off. That's not good. I had been out all day and forgotten to charge it. Now what? I saw a pay phone nearby, but all my important phone numbers were in the phone that had just died. A pay phone would be useless!

As I was sitting there thinking, a car rolled up next to me. A black man rolled down the window and stared at me.

This is a bad part of town. He is probably going to kill me just because of my color, or maybe rob me. "You need a ride?" he asked.

I looked around and figured this may be my only chance. If he kills me, he kills me.

"Where you headed?" he asked. "I'm staying at a hotel downtown." I said.

"Get in, I'll take you," he offered.

"Really? That's like thirty minutes from here," I pointed out.

"That's OK, get in." Well, if he's going to kill me so be it. I jumped in, and we headed for the hotel. I thought for sure he was going to rob me. Who picks up a stranger at this time of night in this part of LA?

"What is a white boy like you doing in this part of town at night, dressed like you got money?" he asked.

Yep! Here it comes! He's going to rob me. I should just hand over my wallet now and save the hassle.

"You wouldn't believe me if I told you," I said, making eye contact.

"Try me."

"Well, I'm in town doing some charity work. I fight in the UFC," I said, trying to sound nonchalant.

"And how did you end up over here?"

"That's the part I really don't know," I said.

He smiled and scratched his face. "What is the UFC? Is that a football team or something?" he asked.

"You don't know what the UFC is? Two men fighting in a cage? Mixed Martial Arts?" I said in shock.

"I'm not familiar with it," he said. This guy must live on another planet. He reached over and opened the glove box. I knew it! Here it comes. He's going to pull out a gun!

But he shocked me when he pulled out a pamphlet.

"You ever thought about giving your life to Jesus Christ?" he asked. I took the pamphlet and read these words: Do you feel empty? Searching for the truth? Are you tired? Come to Jesus Christ and He will give you rest.

This guy's a Christian! That sure took a lot of pressure off. I felt safe again. I looked back at the flyer, but my eyes were too blurry from all the alcohol. I didn't know what to say. When we pulled up to the hotel, I tried to give him money for the ride, but he wouldn't take it.

"Nope! I won't take that," he said.

"But that was a long ride. Take it for the gas money," I implored.

"The Lord put it on my heart to pick you up, and I was willing to drive you any distance," he said. I was overcome with awe. I opened the door and just stood there for a second. You don't see kindness like this very often, at least not in THIS world! I leaned in to look at him and tried one more time.

"I sure do appreciate it. Are you sure I can't give you some gas money?"

"The Lord will provide. You just make sure you read that pamphlet, and we'll call it even," he said. I closed the door, and he drove off. I stood there holding the pamphlet, more than a little surprised at the kindness of a total stranger. I looked at the back of the pamphlet and read, "The truth will set you free."

34 A Day at Glendale College

I opened the door to my hotel room and found my roommate sleeping. I gently set my phone on the night stand, but the noise still woke him.

"You must have had a good time. Where did you go, man?" he asked.

I thought for a second, still in shock. My mind was playing back what had happened earlier. I kept wondering if there were other people in the car that picked me up, or if it was just the black guy and me.

"Jay? You all right?" My roommate jolted me back to reality.

"Yeah, I'm not exactly sure what happened tonight," I told him, while grabbing the vodka bottle and guzzling it. Then I lay down and replayed the evening over and over. Eventually I fell asleep.

As soon as I closed my eyes, my roommate got up to get ready for the next charity event. "Wake up, Jay! We need to get ready to go." he said.

Within thirty minutes we were on our way to Glendale College to hang out with three hundred kids suffering from cancer. Before we went on campus, I inhaled a water bottle full of vodka.

As we were walking around campus, the kids began to get excited and looked at us like we were superheroes. The place was packed with three hundred kids plus their families and volunteer helpers.

The children came running up to shake our hands. They ranged in age from infants to twelve years old. Some had little doctors' masks over their mouths and noses, so I asked one of the helpers about them. "Why do some of the kids have masks on?"

She looked forlornly at one of them. "Those are the ones who have only a few months to live," she replied.

My heart sank to my stomach. I looked at the other UFC fighters and watched their eyes well up. I walked over to one of the kids wearing a mask and held up my hand for a high five.

"Hey, little champion!" I said. "I'm glad to be here with you!" His eyes studied my face, and although the mask blocked his mouth, I knew he was smiling. He looked like a little angel.

The helpers started directing everyone to the gym so we could sign UFC hats, clothing, and posters for the kids. There were three tables put together with a handful of chairs for us. The lines of kids at the tables went all the way outside and wrapped around the building. The volunteer workers stood behind us, opening boxes of UFC gear; then handing them to us so we could autograph them. It went like clockwork. The kids stepped forward and were handed their free hats, shirts, or posters. They were so excited!

As soon as they received their autographed items, they scampered off to proudly model their prizes to their moms and dads. It felt so good to put a smile on their faces!

After about thirty minutes, a woman behind me chastised the kid for whom I was signing a shirt. "Hey! What are you doing in line?? This stuff is not for family members!" she shouted. She seemed angry.

I didn't understand, so I asked her what was wrong.

"We don't know how much UFC stuff there is. This is only supposed to be for the three hundred kids, not for their brothers and sisters too!" she said with an attitude.

I looked at the little guy in front of me as he dropped his five-year-old head in shame. He turned and started walking away; then I saw a name on the shirt I'd just signed for him.

"Alex?" I asked. He turned and had a shocked look on his face, wondering how I knew his name.

"Don't forget your T-shirt, champ!" I said.

His face lit up, and he ran and gave me a hug. I set the shirt on his shoulder, and he stared up at me with a huge smile. My roommate was sitting to my left, and I was sure he heard what happened because he signed a UFC hat and put it on Alex's head.

The woman behind us sounded really bitter. "If you guys run out of UFC stuff, it's your fault!" she warned.

"Look, it's not just the three hundred kids with cancer who are suffering, but the families, too. This event is for all of them," I pointed out.

My roommate saw the UFC secretary talking with some people and walked over to her. I saw her look my way; then make a phone call.

A few minutes later, Roomy reclaimed his chair. "The UFC secretary said not to worry about running out of items. They'll make sure everyone gets something," he said. I held out my fist and bumped it with his.

When we finally got to the end of the line, our hands were cramping. I noticed the volunteers setting up tables and preparing food.

"Looks like we're eating, Bunkee!" I said.

We split up and sat in different areas, so that we could all eat with different families. The bitter woman who had scolded Alex earlier sat down next to me.

"Hey, I'm sorry if I sounded mean earlier. I just couldn't stand the thought of some of the kids not getting anything," she said.

I understood her point and could hear in her voice that she cared about these kids. As we spoke, kids kept coming up to take pictures with me. We were still speaking, when I heard the announcement for everyone to head to the campus theater.

"Thank you for what you're doing," she said.

"I enjoy hanging out with these kids," I explained. We got up and headed for the theater.

The other UFC fighters and I were backstage while the seats were filling. The fighters came out one at a time to give a speech. I was almost last. I walked out, sat at the edge of the seat, and got comfortable.

"You know, I am so glad to be here," I began. "You may look at us like we're heroes, but in reality you're the real heroes. When the UFC called and asked if I wanted to come hang out with you guys, I got so excited I could hardly stand it!" I said, while scanning the crowd. Then my eyes locked with one of those who was wearing a mask. He was probably three or four years old, sitting directly in front of me. It was as if we were the only two in the room. He could have been my son. He could have been me when I was his age.

My mind went blank. I couldn't speak. Here I was drinking my life away, feeling miserable, empty, and not wanting to live. But this child would give anything just to have a few more years; when in reality, he probably had just a few months left.

I stood up, approached the other fighters, handed one of them the microphone, then walked alone to a corner of the room. I sat there thinking about what a hypocrite I was. I can't really describe what I was feeling. I just felt ashamed.

I heard an announcement for everyone to make their way to the football field. We split into groups, and the fighters gave everyone, including the families, a workout: sharing boxing and kickboxing skills.

I looked around and saw all the families laughing and having a good time. I wondered why I didn't do more charity work. It really felt good.

My phone buzzed, and I saw that I had a text. It was the fan I'd taken a picture with a few weeks before. She was waiting outside in the parking lot. The announcement came that the day was over, so we said goodbye to everyone. I hurried out to the parking lot and saw her standing by her car. She was stunning!

"Hey, how did it go?" she asked.

"It was amazing! I wish I did it more often," I exclaimed. Then I hopped in her car, and we spent the weekend together.

I was sitting in the kitchen eating breakfast, when my manager walked in with an armload of paperwork. He took a seat next to me and frowned at my "Breakfast of Champions"– a bowl of cereal and a side order of vodka.

"JJ, I've got some radio interviews lined up for you," he said, while pulling out his laptop.

"Sounds good," I responded, sipping on my side order.

He looked at the glass and said, "I need you to be sober for these interviews."

"When are they?" I asked.

"One is on Friday, and the other will be Saturday or Sunday. I'll have to double check and make sure," he said, almost apologetically.

"This weekend?" I asked.

"Yeah, why?"

"Well, Friday I have to be at a high school football game in my hometown. I'm donating money to the athletic department and promised to make an appearance. On top of that, Liz is coming on Saturday and leaving Sunday night," I said in frustration.

"OK, I'll reschedule the one on Friday, but why can't you just take Liz with you while you do your interviews on Saturday and Sunday?" he said, as he scanned his emails.

"Because all they want to talk about is the lifeguard incident. That'll make Liz mad, and then it will lead to a weekend of fighting," I explained unhappily.

"You guys'll probably fight the whole weekend anyway. Honestly, I don't know why you two are still together," he said with a laugh. I didn't blame Liz for not wanting to hear me talk about the lifeguard. But he was right. Liz and I fought all the time, about silly things.

"It's all part of the job, JJ. It's what people know you for. Now they simply see you as a player," he said with a grin.

"But I'm not a player!" I protested, while shoveling in a spoonful of cereal. At that exact moment, a stripper from the club where I worked sauntered through the kitchen and opened the door to leave. "Bye, Scorpion," she chimed. "I had a good time. Call me," she continued, in a singsong voice. Then she disappeared out the door with a very provocative twitch to her hips.

"And who's that?" he demanded.

"I dunno," I mumbled though my full mouth. "A stribber? Senabor? One of those 'S' words?" Talking is hard with a mouthful of cereal.

"JJ, do you see what I mean? You used to be known for your fighting skills, but now you are known as a 'man whore'!" he accused with a serious voice.

He was right. People used to talk about how quick my hands were, but now they only talked about me being some kind of player.

My phone buzzed, and I saw it was a text from Amber. Really?? Now?? She was a woman I had been conversing with by phone and email, but never met. My sister in Louisiana had given her my phone number a few weeks prior, and we spoke for about an hour a day. She lived in Louisiana near Sis.

The text said, "Can't wait to hang with you this weekend."

"Oh, no!!" I shouted.

"What is it?" my manager asked.

"I was supposed to catch a flight to Louisiana this weekend to hang out with Amber. She already bought the plane ticket!" I said, covering my face with my hands.

"JJ, you're a mess," he stated. Then he closed his laptop and put it in his bag.

"What do I do?" I pleaded.

"Hey, all I do is handle your fight business. Your women problems are not my job!" he asserted with a smile.

I sipped the rest of my vodka and put my dishes in the sink. "I gotta make some phone calls. I'll see you at the gym in a few hours," I said.

"One question before you go: a Spanish station wants to do an interview with you soon, but you gotta be fluent in Spanish because it's all in Spanish. You in or out?" he asked.

"In. Sounds good. Line it up," I answered.

"You speak Spanish, right?" he asked, skeptically. "Yep!" I answered, while looking for an energy drink in the refrigerator.

"No entiendes lo que digo? Verdad?" ("You don't understand what I'm saying, right?")

Of course I didn't understand a word he said, so I gave him one of the ten Spanish words I knew. "Si!" I proudly proclaimed. I figured that I had a fifty-fifty chance of getting the right answer. He began to write on a piece of paper, speaking out loud each word he wrote. "OK, doesn't understand any Spanish. Scratch that off the list," he declared.

I called Amber and told her I wouldn't be able to fly out to see her. She was heartbroken, but I had to cancel on her. I was trying to make things work with Liz and that wasn't easy!

Friday night came, and I had a good time visiting my old high school and meeting old friends. After they announced I was there, and the amount of my donation to the athletic department, I drove back to San Diego with Tiffany, my date for the night. Maybe my manager had a point with regard to my woman problems.

The next morning, I awakened to my phone vibrating. Liz was texting to let me know she was in town. Lying next to me was Tiffany, who had driven all the way from Camarillo just to be my date to the football game. From Camarillo to San Diego is about a three-hour drive, and now Liz was coming from Oxnard, which is about the same distance.

"Tiffany, you gotta go. I have to be somewhere, and I'm already late!" I said, more than a little worried.

She grabbed her belongings and drove the three and a half hours to get back home.

Liz showed up about twenty minutes after Tiffany left. Unfortunately, we began arguing within the first thirty minutes. She was not happy that I had interviews scheduled for the weekend.

"OK, look, I'll try and do it over the phone so we won't have to go to the studio," I tried.

Liz sat near me in my bedroom and listened to the telephone interview. Everything was going great until the interviewer asked a question that staggered me.

"So, Jeremy Jackson, everyone wants to know: why do you walk around with two cell phones?" he asked. The bottom fell out of my universe. Liz didn't know I had two cell phones. The phone I was holding almost fell out of my hands.

"T-Two cell phones?" I stuttered, stalling for time to think.

"Yeah, man, one time I was talking to you when you were a guest at the San Diego Sports Arena, and you had all these cell phones on you that you kept answering," he stated with a laugh

BUSTED!!

When I was around Liz, my phone would ring constantly from all the women I was dating, and Liz wouldn't allow me to turn the ringer off. She said I didn't need to turn it off since I had nothing to hide. So, I simply bought another phone and used it to talk with other women.

I turned my head slowly to look at Liz and saw her packing her bags. I started tap dancing, juggling this phone interview while trying to convince my girlfriend to stay. I covered the phone and whispered, "Liz, wait! I can explain."

"You pig!" she shouted. "I'm out of here!" She continued packing her stuff.

"You still there, Scorpion?" the interviewer asked. He had to know something was up. "Uh, yeah! I'm still here. Um, why do I have two cell phones? To look important I guess," I said hurriedly into the phone.

"I thought it was because you have so many women calling you," he said with a laugh. Obviously, this guy was trying to get me killed. This was not going well at all.

"Wait, Liz! Please don't go. Liz, stop!" I said, trying to cover the phone again.

"I don't know why I drove all the way down here for you! You haven't changed," she growled.

"Liz, let me finish this interview, and then I'll explain," I said from my knees.

"Fine, but make it quick," she said, glaring at me with her arms crossed, the way only a woman can.

"Scorpion? You there?" the voice in the phone innocently asked, wondering if I'd hung up.

"Oh, I'm still here. We must have a bad signal or something. OK, um, you asked me about the cell phones. Yeah, I just wanted to look cool. The night you saw me with two cell phones was the night my manager asked me to hold his phone. I don't have a bunch of women!" I scoffed. My story was even starting to make sense to me!

"Oh, c'mon Scorpion. You can be honest," he said.

No, I CAN'T!

"I am being honest! There is only one woman in my life," I answered, while looking lovingly into Liz's eyes, patented pouty lip protruding.

Five minutes later, the interview mercifully ended. I explained to Liz that I was holding my manager's cell phone when I was at an event in San Diego, so people naturally thought I had more than one phone. That wasn't the truth, of course, but she believed it and stayed for the weekend.

36 Ultimate Fighter Finale

One night, while I was sitting on my bed drinking a bottle of vodka, I received a text. Since I'd just finished doing another telephone radio interview, I thought it might be them calling back.

It was from my buddy, Pete Spratt. "The UFC called me. They want us to fight at the Ultimate Fighter 4 Finale. Have they called you yet?" his text read.

I was shocked. Pete and I had become good friends since the show, but we were both warriors; fighting was our job. We both put food on the table because of our world-class combat skills.

"What do you wanna do?" I texted back.

"Let's give them the best fight they have ever seen," Pete replied. As I was reading his text, the UFC called. Ultimately, Pete and I agreed to fight each other.

I immediately began training for the fight, but then my neck started bothering me: the old injury that continued to haunt me. I saw my chiropractor twice a week and even had my own private masseuse who worked on me at least three times a week. These helped; without them, I don't think I could have continued fighting.

A week before the fight, Liz called and said she was taking her kids to "Knights of the Round Table." She asked if I would join them. Naturally, I agreed.

I was trying to lose weight for the fight, but here I was eating all this food at Knights of the Round Table. The food was delicious, and I had a blast, but I just couldn't focus on the fight.

Afterward, I drove back to San Diego and found myself in a parking lot outside a Von's grocery store. I had bottles of vodka on the passenger seat next to me, and I was gulping them down one after another.

My manager called and said the UFC wanted me in Vegas the very next day! The UFC likes to fly their fighters out a week before events for interviews, photo shoots, and other reasons. Not a lot of people know this, but UFC fighters have to sign at least one hundred UFC posters sometime during that week. Your hand begins to cramp after forty!

So here I was a week before a huge fight, sitting in a parking lot drowning myself in vodka. My manager was still on the line.

"JJ? Did you hear me?" he asked excitedly.

"Hmm? Oh yes, I'm here. I'm leaving for Vegas tomorrow."

"Yes. You're flying out of San Diego. Ben will be going with you. I'll meet you there later in the week," he said.

Ben was a training partner and my roommate. "Sounds good," I told him, then took a big chug of vodka.

"JJ? Where are you?" he asked.

"Where am I?" I said, as I looked around the Von's parking lot. "I'm at the gym." I lied.

"I'm at the gym, too. I don't see you. You upstairs or downstairs?" he asked.

"No, I said I'm at Jim's," I said.

"Who's Jim?" he asked.

"Just a friend. We were getting ready to go for a run," I assured him.

"All right. Be at the airport tomorrow. I'll see you in a few days. Oh, and leave the vodka at home," he said, as if he could see me through the phone.

The next day, Ben and I landed in Vegas and checked into the Hard Rock Casino. I had a week until my fight, and my neck was locking up horribly on me. I called my masseuse to see if she could make it out to Vegas, but she couldn't. I tried a few chiropractors in the area, but they didn't help. In fact, they actually made it worse.

When we got back to the hotel and were standing in the elevator, someone stepped in, speaking with a hard New York accent.

"Scorpion! What up, my man?" he asked. It was Mark Dellagrotte[22], one of the coaches from The Ultimate Fighter show. He was a great Muay Thai kickboxing instructor who helped me with my stand up game on the show.

"How ya doing, man?" he asked.

---

22   He starred in the movie "Here Comes the Boom."

"I'm all right," I declared. "My neck is locking up on me, though. You wouldn't happen to know any good chiropractors in town, would ya?"

"As a matter of fact, I just happen to know a guy. I'll give him a call and set up an appointment for you. Don't worry about the cost. I'll cover it," he said.

Bing! The elevator let us know we were at our floor. "Thanks! I appreciate it!" I said, as I walked out of the elevator. "All right, take care my brotha!" he said, waving farewell. What a nice guy.

The night before the fight, my mom, sister, and little brother arrived at the hotel. Liz showed up a little later. We all went out and had dinner; then walked around the strip.

When Liz and I got back to the hotel, we lay in bed, and I mentioned how bad my neck was hurting. She tried massaging it, but it continued to lock up on me. Later that night, Ben and my manager came stumbling into the room with some girls.

Liz was not happy; she felt disrespected. "What's going on?" she demanded.

"I don't know. I think it's Ben and my manager," I answered.

They were all next to us on the other bed, laughing and drinking. It went on for hours! Eventually Liz snapped.

"Are you guys serious?? Jeremy has a big fight tomorrow, and he hasn't slept all night!" she shouted, as she looked at the digital clock. "It's almost morning! The sun is coming up! You guys are so disrespectful."

What did I expect? My manager and teammate knew I wasn't taking this fight seriously. Why would they? Since we all lived in the same house, they knew I hadn't stopped drinking. They saw all the vodka bottles in my room and the different women leaving at 6:00 nearly every morning. They knew I wasn't focused, so they were considering this fight as a free vacation to Vegas.

Within a few hours, my other manager walked in. This manager took care of my finances, while the other one set up my fights.

"You ready?" he asked. Liz looked at me and wanted me to tell him what had happened the night before. I stayed quiet; Liz stormed off into the bathroom and slammed the door.

"You look tired, Jeremy. Did you get enough sleep?" the newly-arrived manager asked.

"Yes, I'm all right," I answered, trying to sound chipper but failing miserably.

"They want us in the dressing room a few hours before the fight," he declared.

A little later, I was in the back getting taped up for the fight. I looked across the room and saw the coach from the Ultimate Fighter, the guy from the elevator, helping Pete Spratt warm up! He was cornering Pete! Great. Hopefully he won't tell Pete about my neck.

It was our turn to enter the cage. Once we entered, we stood looking across at each other. Pete walked to the center to tell me something.

"Let's give 'em the fight of the night!" he said; then we touched gloves and returned to our corners.

During the first round, I took him down and tried to submit him. I knew I could submit him, because I'd tapped him out during training. But during the fight, he kept escaping my submission attempts.

By the second round, a sharp pain was shooting down my back. The pain was so bad I was feeling light headed. My neck continued to lock up on me. How badly was I injured? What if I damage my neck for life? Is it worth it? I kept trying to take him down, but I had absolutely no neck strength.

As I was holding a single leg on him, he began to push on the back of my head. The pain worsened. I had to make a choice. I did something that I'll regret to this day: I tapped out. Deep down inside I knew I could have finished the fight. I could have given Pete the fight he was looking for: the fight of the night. But everything happening in my life was just too much: the pain in my neck, the pain in my heart, and my restless mind. I was tired, emotionally tired.[23]

The fight was over.

---

23   What was I fighting for now? Was it all worth it? What's the point of building my name if all it does is create more emptiness. I didn't want to fight Pete Spratt. He was my friend. Only a bottle of vodka, pain killers, and a warm bath sounded good. Or a twenty-year-nap. All I knew was that I did not want to be in that octagon, even if it was one of the biggest arenas on earth, with screaming fans shouting my name. Sure, I could hear them, but their shouts were eclipsed by the turmoil in my heart.

37 Riding in the Beast

After my fight with Pete, I ended up in the hospital with a neck brace. It was during this time that Liz and I discussed living arrangements. We decided that maybe we should move back in together.

"Haven't we lived apart long enough? Let's get a place in San Diego. I'll stop drinking and turn my life around," I said.

"San Diego? I like my job. Why don't you come back to Oxnard?" she countered.

So, I packed up all my things in one day and moved back in with her. That same week, two men contacted me with an offer. They were opening a gym in Ventura and asked me if I would like to partner with them. I would own ten percent. It was actually a nice-looking gym that had everything: boxing ring, octagon cage, weight room, wrestling mats, and rock climbing.

It was an offer I couldn't refuse. We advertised and even built a fight team. But there was one problem: my life was still spinning out of control. I trained hard during the day and drank vodka like it was water. At night, I was out clubbing.

Needless to say, Liz and I started fighting again, and because of this I would sleep inside the cage at the gym. One night Tim, my business partner, brought a handful of people from the nightclub where he had been partying. I was asleep in the cage when I heard what sounded like a party getting started.

I grabbed the bottle of vodka that I always kept next to me and walked through the crowd.

"Come on, party with us!' one of the women called to me.

"I have a fight coming up, and I need some sleep!" I retorted.

I didn't have a fight set up at the time, but I was waiting to hear back from the UFC. I was hoping for another opportunity to put my skills on display. The pain in my neck was still bad, but by then I'd been introduced to a new kind of pain killer called "Roxy." This stuff was amazing! It allowed me to train in spite of the pain. But it was also very addicting.

The partiers watched as I walked toward the exit. "You're getting ready for a fight, and yet you're drinking vodka?" one of them asked, with a laugh.

"I said I needed to sleep. This," I said as I held up the bottle, "helps me sleep."

Outside was the gym's promotional van. I crawled in the back hoping to get some rest. As I was lying there staring at the roof, my phone went off.

"Are you awake?" the text read. It was Rachel, another woman I was dating on the side.

"I can't sleep," I texted back.

Fifteen minutes later she was lying next to me in the van. "Another restless night?' she asked.

"I hate it when I can't sleep."

"Here, try some of these." She handed me some pills, and I fell asleep in under thirty minutes.

We woke to a loud street bike roaring outside the gym. My business partner, Tim, was peeling around on his motorcycle all over the parking lot. He was riding that thing like he had a death wish.

"What time is it?" I asked Rachel. "3 a.m.," she answered.

I took a few gulps of vodka and stepped out of the van. Rachel was following behind me, when Tim saw us and parked his bike. "Scorpion? Hey, you wanna go for a ride in The Beast?" he shouted, as he pointed toward his old beat-up Bronco that was about a foot higher than when it came off the showroom floor.

I'd heard horror stories of his off-roading escapades. "Well, I…I…" I began to stammer, when he interrupted.

"You can bring your girl!" he said, while walking toward the Bronco.

I looked at Rachel, and she shrugged her shoulders as if to say, "Why not?"

She climbed in and sat in the back seat. I took the front. "You might want to buckle up, Scorpion!" Tim said, with an evil grin on his face. Actually, he looked a lot like the devil at that moment.

I took a few more gulps of vodka right before he jammed the pedal straight to the floor. We flew full speed from parking lot to parking lot, jumping curbs. We then went off-roading to the freeway. He was going as fast as that Bronco could go! He aimed straight for a hill that led over some train tracks.

I took another swig of vodka and looked at Tim. He was still staring at me with that big grin. He wasn't even watching where he was going. I thought for sure we were going to crash, but I didn't care.

He continued full speed toward the hill. I glanced at Rachel to see how she was doing. The poor girl looked like she'd seen a ghost.

Tim was still staring at me with his stupid smile as the Bronco climbed the hill. Next thing I knew, we were airborne.

I looked outside my window and couldn't believe we were actually flying through the air over the train tracks. It seemed like we were in the air forever. Then I heard Tim begin to sing.

"Chitty chitty bang bang, chitty chitty bang bang, I love you!"

I turned to look at him, and he was still staring at me as he sang, not watching the road. Suddenly, the wheels touched the ground, and we began to bounce all over the place, almost flipping over. Somehow we didn't flip, and the Bronco held together. Tim made a sharp turn and aimed the Bronco toward the hill again.

"Round two, Scorpion!" Tim said, while staring at me. Before I could tell him to keep his eyes on the road, the Bronco peeled out and we were going full speed toward the hill. That's when I decided to chug the rest of the vodka. I looked at Tim, and of course he was still looking at me, not watching the road. It was like he wanted to see my reaction

"Don't be scared, Scorpion!" he shouted, as we began to climb the hill again. I looked back at Rachel as the wheels left the ground, and she was pale as a ghost. Her eyes were wide with terror. As we flew through the air, I turned to look at Tim. He was still staring at me with that silly grin. The wheels came crashing down, and we bounced a few times, almost flipping.

We must have jumped that hill ten times. Finally, we drove back to the gym.

"Jeremy? Wake up," Rachel whispered, as she shook me.

Where was I? I looked around and noticed that I was in the back of the van. Rachel was lying beside me.

"I need some coffee," I said, as I sat up and climbed out of the van.

I couldn't remember what happened that night. As I walked past the Bronco, I noticed the front of it was trashed.

"What happened to the Bronco?" I asked.

"You don't remember? Last night we went off-roading with Tim," she said, as we walked into the gym.

Opening my locker, I grabbed a bottle of vodka and took a few drinks. "How about that cup of coffee?" I asked.

"Jeremy, are you OK?" Rachel asked.

Why are people always asking me if I'm OK? It's perfectly normal to keep bottles of vodka all over the place, isn't it? I kept bottles in my lockers, in my car, at my house, and at my friends' and girlfriends' houses.

"I'm fine, Rachel," I said, as I took a few more drinks.

"I'll go get you some energy drinks and coffee," she said. If I didn't have energy drinks or coffee, I would be too sleepy from the vodka. I needed an upper so I could stay awake and train all day.

After training, I went back to my locker and took some more pain killers. My neck was hurting. As I was chewing the pills, Mark, one of my other business partners, walked in.

"Wanna go riding?" he asked. He wanted to take the street bikes and head down the coast.

"Let's do it!" I cheered. "Here!" he said, handing me a helmet.

There were two street bikes parked in front of the gym. I hopped on one and peeled out, not thinking much about what was in front of me.

SMACK! I hit something solid; then felt myself rolling on the ground. I stood up as quickly as I could, to play it off like nothing happened. I saw the bike lying in front of a tricked-out truck.

"What happened?" I asked Mark. He stood in shock for a second and then shook his head.

"Well, before I could get my helmet on, you took off full speed and hit that parked truck head on. You rolled a few times; then bounced up like nothing happened," he explained.

"I feel OK," I said as I checked myself for any serious or lasting damage. Later that day, my ribs began to bruise up, and my shoulder was killing me. Of course, the worst pain was in my neck, but I was used to pain and it wasn't going to stop me – as long as I stayed drunk and had pain killers handy.

If I'd had pain killers in my system during the Pete Spratt fight, then I probably would've survived and won. But the UFC does drug tests, and I didn't want to get fined and suspended. Fighting was my career, and I needed to pay the bills. Fighters could be suspended anywhere from six months to five years. Fines are usually thousands of dollars. It's not worth getting caught.

38 My Last MMA Fight

In January 2007, the inevitable finally happened. My fight manager called to tell me that the UFC cut me. This meant I'd be fighting in the smaller shows until I could prove myself again. My manager, always on the ball, had a fight lined up for me the second he found out that I'd been cut from the UFC.

The event was Total Combat, and it would be held at a casino in Yuma, Arizona.[24] It was right next door to where I'd grown up.

"Who do you have for opponents?" I asked my manager.

"I have a few guys who want to fight you, but there is one who has been bugging me for a while now. He is actually from your hometown," he said with a laugh.

From my hometown? There were only a few fighters from my hometown at this time, and they were all close friends of mine. None of them would be asking to fight me.

"Who is he? I asked.

"Hector Carillo." The name sounded very familiar. It took me a few seconds to put a face to the name. When I made it to the UFC in 2003, there was a guy from my hometown who was always running his mouth about me, saying he could beat me. At that point in my life, I was full of pride and believed in using my fists to solve problems. So, without a moment's hesitation, I told my manager that I wanted a piece of Carillo. This would be my chance to silence his trash talk, or this would be Carillo's opportunity to prove all the stuff he had been saying.

The <u>Ventura County Star</u> found out about my upcoming fight and contacted me about doing a big story about me.[25] The reporter told me that he'd be following me everywhere until I had my fight. I didn't like this at all because I didn't want him to know about my drinking.

---

24   Total Combat 19; March 31, 2007

25   "How Mixed Martial Arts Made and Changed A Man – A Fighter's Fight." Zeke Barlow. Sunday, April 15, 2007. www.vcstar.com

I did my best to hide it from him. I even bought gallons of vodka and filled up large containers of empty water bottles, so he would think I was drinking water. I trained like an animal and was in the best shape of my life. I honestly don't know how I was able to get in such great shape with all the booze in my system, but I did. Every five minutes during training, the bell would ring and I would squirt vodka in my mouth.

The day of the fight, I received a phone call from my masseuse. She told me that Liz was really sick and couldn't make it to the fight. She had food poisoning and was in the hospital. I had to make a choice. Do I cancel my fight or continue? Once I spoke to Liz on the phone, I knew what I had to do.

"Finish what you went there to do. Fight and win," she instructed. Any man on the planet, hearing those words from his woman, will either succeed or die trying.

That night I walked away with a win; Hector walked away with a broken arm. Do I still have hard feelings? No way! I have a lot of respect for anyone who steps into the cage with me. It takes a lot to enter the Octagon. Hector's a warrior and a strong wrestler.

During the after-party, I did a photo shoot, with some models, for an energy drink company while friends, teammates, and assorted admirers watched. As soon as that shoot was done, other people stepped up to take pictures with me. That was when "the feeling" came back.

It was the same feeling I'd had during the charity event at Glendale College in 2006. It was the same feeling I'd had when I was on the roof at a club in LA. I felt empty inside: empty and lost. But I'd quickly changed this feeling by chugging down a few more shots of alcohol with my friends. This was how I numbed my emptiness and pain.

When the club closed, a nice motor home was waiting to pick me up. My partner owned it; it had been our transportation to the fight. Everyone piled into the motor home until it was completely full.

Driving down a back road in the middle of the desert, swerving all over, isn't fun. The driver was my business partner, who was probably more drunk than I was. Fittingly, the song "Living on a Prayer" by Bon-Jovi was blasting on the speakers.

Everyone was singing along and having a blast, while I sat in a corner booth looking at the desert darkness. It was that feeling coming back: emptiness! I knew we could crash at any moment, but I didn't care. I had all these people around me; yet I still felt like the loneliest person on the planet.

This was how I felt after every fight. One second I was being swarmed by people who wanted to take a picture with me, or have me sign something for them: a shirt, a body part, whatever; staring at me as if I was the center of the universe. Then I'd wake up in the morning, and it would all be gone.

If I could get that UFC title, I knew I would be happy.

39 Oxnard Civic Center

I was invited to be a special guest at some local MMA fights that were being held at the Oxnard Civic Center. Liz, as women will do, was taking forever to get ready. I hate arriving late anywhere, but instead of arguing, I decided to go to the bedroom and enjoy some soothing music.

I was listening to a song my older brother and I used to listen to when we were kids, "Stand By Me." I had the player on "repeat" and was perusing old pictures of Oscar and me hanging out.

How could I ever move on? My heart began to break all over again. Tears ran down my face.

At that moment, Liz walked in the room and looked at me. "I'm not going anywhere with you if you're going to be sad! Are you going to be in this mood at the fights?" she demanded.

"Really, Liz?? Here I am hurting, and this is how you want to treat me??" I asked, incredulously.

"Quit being a baby!" she scolded, while digging for boots in the closet. I walked over to the nightstand and grabbed a vodka bottle, pouring what was left into an empty Jack-in-the-Box cup.

"You ready?" I demanded, while taking a few gulps.

"Yes, but we aren't taking my car," she declared.

This turned into a big argument.[26] I didn't like driving my car to special events. A Toyota Echo wasn't the coolest car in the world for a man to be driving. Besides, I hadn't paid my registration for a few years and didn't have insurance.[27]

---

26   As I reflect on the arguments Liz and I had, I try to put myself in her shoes. She was with a destructive man who only cared about himself. I didn't need to say anything to make her angry. All I had to do was to continue screwing up.

27   By this time, I was beginning to think I was above the law. I quit paying my insurance and registration, using the money for alcohol. All the attention I was getting was going to my head, and I began to think I could do whatever I wanted and get away with it.

After ten minutes of arguing, we finally decided to take my car. I didn't want to be late, but when I looked at my watch I noticed that we already were.

"Liz, let's go! I'm late!" I shouted.

During the drive, all we did was shout at each other. It was only a matter of time before it, as usual, turned physical. We argued over the dumbest things. Within five minutes, she slapped me on the side of my head.

"You do that again, and I am going to take you back to the house and leave you there!" I threatened.

"Of course you will! That's what you want! You want to spend time with your groupies!" she yelled back. She was really picking up steam. "And you can't do that with your girlfriend there, can you?? That's why you want to take me home and leave me! You pig!" she screamed, while slapping me again.

"No, it's because you keep hitting me," I clarified. And yes, it would be weird to hang out with my groupies in front of you!

Before I could say any more, a few more slaps landed upside my head. "That's it!" I bellowed, as I turned down a dirt road.

"You're a cheater!" she yelled, adding fuel to the fire.

I parked the car in the middle of a dirt field and screamed, "Get out of my car!"

"What?? I'm not getting out!" she retorted.

"I said, 'GET OUT OF MY CAR!'" I yelled, in a tone that would have made most men run for the hills.

"I ain't going nowhere!" she exclaimed.

I don't blame her for not getting out, because we were in the middle of nowhere and it could have been dangerous. But I had too much alcohol in my system, along with a heart full of pride. And, I was tired of getting slapped. "OUT!" I demanded.

"You can't take a little slap from a girl," she accused. "And you call yourself a UFC Fighter?" By now she was giggling. That's right, poke the bear!

Actually, she did hit hard for a little lady, and the fact that I'd shown her how to fight didn't help. She hit harder than some of my training partners. Note to self: never teach your girlfriend, lover, or wife how to throw a punch!

I turned off the ignition and got out. Looking around, I spotted a big wooden log. I picked it up and slammed the hood of the car with it, leaving a huge dent. That'll teach her! Did I mention I was furious and not thinking clearly?

"GET OUT OF MY CAR!" I repeated, for the third time.

She had a calm look on her face, as if to say, "It's not my car you're trashing." This angered me even more, so I threw the log at the front driver-side window, and it made a huge hole in my windshield. Amazingly, she still had a calm look on her face as I wrestled the log out of the window.

"You done? We're gonna be late, moron!" she calmly pointed out.

"Keep your hands to yourself, and don't hit me!" I shouted through the hole in the window.

"Don't be a wimp!" she shouted back.

"Liz! I'm telling you!" I said, as I watched her put on some lipstick. Putting on lipstick?? Why isn't she scared?

When I got back in the car, I noticed all the damage done to the windshield.

"Man!" I said.

"This is what you do when you drink, idiot!" she said, while putting her lipstick back into her purse.

"Shut up! Don't talk to me until after the event!" I shouted. Overall, she won. I came in second, and my Echo was a distant third.

Obviously, I had to stick my head out the side window to drive. I probably looked like Ace Ventura driving down the road.

I pulled into the parking lot and found a spot farthest from the event. I didn't want people seeing my car.

"Drunk!" Liz said in a low voice, as she watched me down a cup of vodka.

"What did you say?" I growled.

"I said, 'Come on, we are late!'" she said, as she began to walk toward the building.

"I heard what you called me!" I said.

"Then why did you ask?" she purred.

We sat in the front row watching the fights, and I continued drinking throughout the event. It was almost time for them to announce my name, to let the crowd know that I was there. This is the time for the special guests to walk into the cage, smile, and wave.

"You're disgusting, Loser!" Liz said under her breath, as she sat next to me watching me drink my life away. At that moment, they called my name over the loud speakers.

"Don't be jealous, Liz! I'll be back. Watch my drink!" I said, as I stood up and fixed my shirt.

"I'm not watching anything for you, you drunk!" she tried to yell, over the cheering.

"It's MY name they're calling out there, not yours!" I reminded her. "Drunk!" she mumbled.

As I made my way toward the cage, I realized I could hardly walk. I was so drunk that I almost passed out.

"Here he is! The Scorpion, Jeremy Jackson!" the announcer hollered. My name echoed through the arena. I remember crawling into the cage because I was too drunk to walk. I climbed to my feet once I reached the center; then shook hands with the other special guests and waved to the fans.

Liz was sitting in the front row with her arms crossed, and I could read her lips. "Drunk," she said silently. I took my eyes off her and looked back to the screaming fans.

Then it all went blank – completely – absolutely blank.

"Hello?" my mom said, as she answered the phone at 3 a.m.

"Mama?" I said, sitting in my car in the middle of some unfamiliar city.

"Jeremy? Are you OK?" she asked.

"I don't know where I am!" I said, with more than a little fear in my voice.

"Where are you? Can you see any stores or signs nearby?" she asked, with concern.

"Mama, I'm so lost. I've made a mess of my life. I don't even know how I got here." I looked around to see if I could spot any freeway signs.

"Jeremy, just sleep it off. Stay in your car and don't drive anywhere until you sober up, OK?" she said.

"I'll sleep it off," I said, as I hung up the phone. And then I screamed at the top of my lungs.

I felt so lonely and empty inside. With each day that passed, I felt like I was losing more control of my life.

One day, as I was sitting in the office at the gym, one of my business partners walked in. He looked frustrated and unhappy about something.

"Let's talk," he said, closing the door behind him.

"What's up?" I asked, as I leaned back in my chair.

"Look man, you fought in the UFC, right? You were on the Ultimate Fighter TV show. You're famous!" He continued, "Why can't you call some of your friends and see if they'll come out to the gym and do a seminar or something? Maybe do some autographs?"

"Well, I never really thought about it," I replied.

"Might as well take advantage, right?" he said with a smile.

"I guess I could call some of them. But I gotta be honest with you: these guys are busy trying to make a living. A lot of them simply don't have time, and plenty of them have managers who keep them booked for the entire year," I explained.

"Let's try this, Jeremy," he offered. "You get 'em here, and I'll make sure they get paid." He paused a moment, then went on, "Maybe they can do a seminar and sign autographs. I'll pay for the plane tickets, hotel stays, transportation, and their time. What do you think?"

As a response, I picked up my cell phone and started thumbing buttons. Sure enough, a lot of them had fights coming up, or had to attend events as special guests. They said they would've come if they weren't already booked.

My partner slammed his fist on the desk and said, "Aren't these people your boys?" he asked. "They won't miss one event for you?"

"I'm sure they would if I asked them to, but I wouldn't want them to change their schedules just for me," I replied.

"Jeremy, this is business! They understand business. Call 'em up and get one of 'em here!" he demanded.

Business is business, so I called Shonie "Mr. International" Carter, who lived in Chicago. After I fought Shonie in 2003, we became good friends.

"Scorpion!" a cheerful voice answered on the other end of the line.

"Shonie? Hey, it's me again. Look, I know you gotta be at a big event soon, but I really need a favor. Is there any way you can get here? I'll make sure you are well paid." I said.

It was quiet for a moment, and I knew he was thinking it over. "All right," he finally said. "I'll come to your gym."

"Thanks, Shonie! I really appreciate it," I said gratefully. My partner was listening, and he made a fist pump, as if to say, "YES!"

"Shonie, I'll have my people contact you and take care of the plane tickets and hotel," I said, before hanging up.

We picked Shonie up at the airport and brought him to our gym. My partner sponsored a grappling tournament the next day. The following day would be Shonie's seminar.

For the grappling tournament, I stood in our cage and announced the rules to all competitors. I wore dark sunglasses to hide my eyes. I was pretty drugged up on Ecstasy, OxyContin, Norcos, and several kinds of steroids. All that was mixed with energy drinks and vodka. My hands were shaking so violently that I couldn't control them. It couldn't be nerves, because I had done stuff like this many times. My body was simply overloaded with chemicals.

I set the microphone on the floor, because as long as I held it up to my mouth, people could see my hand shaking out of control. "I don't need the microphone," I said, raising my voice. "I can be heard without it!"

Afterward, I walked around meeting people and taking pictures with fans. While I posed for a photo, I could literally feel my heart pounding throughout my body. I felt like my head was going to explode. I desperately needed to get my shaky body under control, so I made my way toward the motor home that was parked behind the gym.

As I headed toward the back door, more fans gathered around, asking for photos with me. I couldn't even smile because my facial muscles were completely out of control. I needed to get to the safety of the motor home immediately.

Shonie spotted me from across the room and hustled to my rescue. I wasn't sure if he knew what was happening, but I think he knew I was trying to get away from the crowd, so he walked up and started singing. The crowd began to flock around him, giving me a chance to slip away.

Sitting inside the motor home were some of my students. Some of these guys are now fighting in the UFC, but at this time they were just starting out. They were kicking back, resting before their submission matches. They were excited to see me and thought maybe I'd come in to give them a pep talk or something, so they just sat quietly and stared at me.

"Hey guys! How ya feeling? Nervous?" I asked. They all nodded in unison.

"Well, if it makes you feel any better, I get nervous before each fight. It's normal," I answered. Even as I spoke I could feel my body shaking. I needed to lie down for a little while. I felt like my heart was working way too hard.

"See ya in a bit," I said, as I stumbled toward the back of the motor home. While I slept, I could hear Shonie's voice on the speakers announcing the event. Was I dreaming? At that moment my business partner walked in with a beer in his hand.

"Scorpion? What are you doing in here? You need to be out there meeting people and taking pictures! Everyone is looking for you," he exclaimed.

"Is that Shonie I hear on the microphone?" I asked.

"Yeah, I asked Shonie to be the announcer," he said with a laugh.

I walked out of the motor home, and made my way back into the gym. I noticed Liz and her mom sitting in the front row, and there was an empty seat next to them. "Jeremy, are you going to leave us here alone all day, or are you going to sit with us?" Liz asked.

I was so drunk and high that I had forgotten that my girlfriend was even there. I was such a mess!

I sat down next to Liz and asked if she and her mom were enjoying the matches. They said the only thing entertaining was Shonie on the microphone.

After the event we took Shonie to some of the local clubs. At one of the bars we ran into another UFC fighter who'd been on a different season of The Ultimate Fighter than I had. This guy was a friend who was known for getting violent when he drank. Sitting next to him was one of the competitors, who had competed earlier in the day. He was also a huge UFC fan. He was excited to be hanging out with three UFC fighters.

Shonie was standing in front of the jukebox trying to find a good song, while I was ordering some drinks. The other UFC fighter was sitting at the bar, when the fan began to ask him questions. "What's it like to fight in front of so many people? What is your favorite submission hold? Can you beat Tito Ortiz?" His questions were becoming annoying.

Before he could finish his next question, the UFC fighter picked him up and slammed him to the floor. He had his knee on the guy's belly and began landing right hands to his face. I ran over and tried to pull the fighter off of him, but he pushed me, and I went flying across the room. My back smacked into the wall next to the jukebox. Shonie made eye contact with me; then focused back on the jukebox to try and find the perfect song.

I ran back over, and this time I was able to pull the fighter off of the fan. I told the fighter to go outside and walk it off. Then I reached down helped the fan stand up.

"Come on, you can hang out with Shonie and me," I said.

"Can I take a picture with you guys?" he asked. "Sure, but we gotta get out of here before the fighter comes back. I know a bar that's not as quiet. We can kick back there," I assured him.

"Wow! That was so cool! I just got beat down by a pro fighter!" he said proudly.

The next day was the seminar, and only a few people showed up. I called my business partner and asked him where everyone was. After talking with him, I found out he didn't advertise the seminar.

"How are people supposed to know about it?" I asked in frustration.

"I didn't think about that," he answered.

Shonie taught the seminar anyway. During the demonstrations, I was holding my son and trying to make him laugh, while my girlfriend stood next to me watching the seminar. Tarah, my son's mother, was ten feet away talking with my mom. What Liz heard my mom say caused her to explode.

"She won't let Jeremy talk to us. He can't even come near us!" Mom said in a low voice to Tarah.

Liz began cussing at my mom and ran at her to take a swing. I set my son down and caught Liz in my arms. "Let's go! Outside! We're leaving!" I said, as I escorted her out the back door.

Before I left, I told my business partner to take care of Shonie and make sure he paid him.

Later that day, I drove to my partner's house to pick Shonie up and take him to LAX. When I pulled up, I saw Shonie driving down the street in a little dune buggy. There was a quad parked in my partner's driveway, so I hopped on it and followed Shone down the street. We rode around for a few hours before I took him to the airport.

As we waited for his flight in a local coffee shop, I asked Shonie if he got paid. "Not really," he replied. Shonie is too humble to ask for anything, even if it's owed to him. Good thing I asked him! I felt bad, because I knew he lost a lot of money coming to my gym for the weekend. I let him know that I would take care of it.

I called my partner and asked him what was going on, and he said Shonie got to keep what he made from the seminar. "Only a few people showed up to that seminar because you didn't advertise it!" I hotly accused. "If you had advertised, the place would have been packed. Not only is Shonie my friend, but he is well respected by other fighters. If you screw him over, you'll tarnish my name, and my word will mean nothing. You said you would take care of him if I got him here, so do it!"

He agreed and sent Shonie a check.

41 The Fight That Never Happened

Sometime around September or October of 2007, I hired a new fight manager who also became my new boxing coach. This guy was probably the best manager I had ever had. He worked hard to get me sponsors and set up fights. And if that wasn't enough, he was an excellent boxing trainer. He and I became good friends.

He called me one night to let me know that Strikeforce wanted me to fight Cung Le in November. The winner of the fight would fight Frank Shamrock the beginning of 2008. I almost dropped the phone! Shamrock's a legend!

Would I have enough time to get in shape to fight Cung Le? I was at a physical level where I could fight successfully in a lower-level event against a B-level fighter, even when handicapped by alcohol, but I would have to be on my A game to fight someone of Le's caliber. I asked my manager if he thought I had enough time to get ready. He assured me, "You'll be ready."

He called the promoter and let him know that I agreed to fight Cung Le. We began training immediately. We studied Cung Le's fights and came up with a game plan. We would beat him the same way I beat Shonie Carter in 2003. Both Le and Shonie were good at throws, so if a fighter clinched with him, there was a good chance that fighter was getting tossed. Le also had good striking ability. Overall, his stand-up game was lethal, but I knew I had the upper hand at boxing.

Le was great at keeping a good distance from his opponents so he could eat them up with his powerful kicks. If his opponent tried to take him down, Le simply threw him. So, the game plan was to get in and make him box; then get out of his kicking range.

In order to beat Cung Le, I had to get in and make him box, but I couldn't just rush in. It's not that easy. I would have to get past his kicks. If I stayed still, his kicks would do some serious damage. If I backed up, he would follow up with more kicks. The only choice I had was to go forward, but I would have to time his kicks. As soon as he would lift his leg to kick, I would have to close the distance and land my punches. If I wasn't able to close the distance fast enough, it would be devastating. If I ran into his kicks, it would be like getting hit by a Mack truck.

So, I was going to try and force Cung Le to trade punches with me, while smothering his kicks. I trained six to eight hours every day. I was heavy into steroids at this time, and it was pretty obvious. I was hurting my training partners at the gym; I was too strong. I had to find fighters at my level: someone who could push me and challenge me.

I began training at Big John's gym in Valencia, California, and at Eddie Bravo's in Hollywood. By the end of October, I was in awesome shape. As my manager/trainer had promised, I was ready for Cung Le.

On Halloween, I was trick-or-treating with Liz and her kids. Halfway through the night, I had to stop and get back to training. I dropped Liz and the kids off at home and went to the gym to train with my coach. We trained for a few hours; then turned in.

That same week, I received a phone call from my manager. Cung Le didn't want to fight me! He canceled the fight, opting instead to fight Sammy Morgan. I was shocked!

We tried to figure out what happened, but the only thing we could think of was that Le was looking for a good fight before he fought Shamrock, but didn't want to fight someone who had a good chance of beating him. I'm sure he'd heard what kind of shape I was in; that's never hard to figure out. Anyone could have gone to Big John's or Eddie Bravo's gyms and watched me train.

With no fights lined up, I sank deeper into depression. I was losing my motivation to fight. I was losing that "Eye of the Tiger." I felt like a boat without a rudder.

I completely lost control.

42 Hulk Syndrome

It was the end of 2007, and I experienced a horrible sleepless night. You may be thinking, "Big deal! I've had sleepless nights!" This wasn't normal. A girlfriend gave it an appropriate name: the "Hulk Syndrome."

Liz and I were in our apartment in Oxnard, lying in bed asleep. Suddenly, I was awakened by some strange burst of energy. My heart was beating with so much force I thought it was going to explode out of my chest. My eyes were tired, but my body was ready to take a lap around the world. My muscles kept flexing, and I was clenching my teeth.

"Liz, something's wrong, I feel weird and can't sleep," I whispered.

"I don't care. Don't keep me awake. I have to work tomorrow!" she growled.

This had happened before; I'd kept it from her, but tonight was like no other! I looked at the clock: it was only 11 p.m. I needed to get some sleep because I had to train the next day.

What could be causing this? I had been drinking vodka nonstop for the last few years. Plus, I had pain killers and all kinds of different steroids in my system. At first, I thought it was just a serious case of Restless Leg Syndrome, but this wasn't limited to my legs: it was my entire body, including my head. I was flexing, but I couldn't stay still. I had a feeling flowing inside me that was unfamiliar, and I didn't like it one bit. I didn't like being scared.

The only thing that seemed to help was to exercise, so I jumped out of bed and began working out on the floor. I did a hundred pushups straight, followed by a hundred squats. It took away the feeling for about twenty seconds, but then it came back, twice as strong. I felt like I was turning into The Hulk. I began by flexing my muscles as hard as I could; then I shadow boxed and did Mountain Climbers: on all fours, you lift one knee to your chest while stretching the other leg backwards, then alternate with the other leg.

"Shut the f*** up, Jeremy! I'm trying to sleep! What the hell is wrong with you?" Liz shouted.

"I'm sorry, but I can't sleep. I'll go in the living room," I said, as I walked out of the bedroom. I tried watching TV, but it didn't help. I jumped on the floor and repped out 200 pushups. Hopping back to my feet, I began to shadow box and throw some kicks.

Maybe I needed some alcohol? It had been a few hours since my last drink; I walked into the kitchen, grabbed a bottle of vodka, and gulped down as much as I could.

"What's happening?" I asked myself. Jumping back on the floor, I continued exercising.

"Jeremy, there are some sleeping pills in the medicine cabinet," Liz shouted from the bedroom. I went straight to the cabinet and found some little pink pills.

"How many do I take?" I hollered. "I don't know, maybe one or two," she said. I threw about four in my mouth, and washed them down with vodka.

"Thanks, Babe," I shouted.

"Now shut up and quit making all that noise!" she demanded. An hour later, my eyes were closing, but I couldn't stop doing pushups and shadow boxing.

"Shut up!" Liz yelled. I walked into the bedroom with tears trickling down my face.

"Liz, what's happening to me?" I begged. "I can't sleep or stay still. Help me! I want to sleep but I can't. I'm soooo tired."

"Go outside or something. You are keeping me up!" she exploded. I decided to take her advice and went outside. It was freezing cold. I stood there breathing in the icy air, while my body continued to flex like The Hulk.

What's happening to me?

I could barely keep my eyes open, but my body was full of energy, so I started jogging slowly down the street. Every time I passed a stop sign, I'd pick up the pace. Eventually, I was running so fast that my eyes were having trouble staying open, but no matter how tired my eyes were, I still couldn't sleep. I simply couldn't hold my body still.

I ran like Forrest Gump! Finally, I fell asleep, but while running at a fast pace. I expected to pass out, but I didn't. I woke up and was still running, but on a different street. I continued running and fell asleep again, waking up somewhere else. I began to realize the danger of this. What if I was hit by a car?

I knew I had to burn off this energy or I wouldn't be able to sleep. As my muscles continued to flex with all their might, I felt I had to try one last thing. I was going to sprint back home as fast as I could.

Without a second thought, I took off running the fastest I had ever run. Block after block, I sprinted down the road. This was going to work; it had to work.

I was running so fast I could have passed cars on the street, had there been any. My plan was going so well, but I fell asleep again. When I woke up, I was still going full speed, but at least I was closer to home. Every few feet, I'd slap myself so I wouldn't fall asleep again. I must 'ave looked like a mad man. Eventually, I made it home. Even though I felt like I could run another twenty miles, I jumped into the shower, still feeling like I was going to fall asleep. I dried off and went into the living room. The clock said 3:30 a.m. I had to be at the gym by 6 a.m.

I jumped on the floor and started doing pushups until I finally fell asleep. I woke up face down on the living room floor with Liz kissing my cheek.

"Good morning, Ugly. I have to go to work. I love you. Don't you have to be at the gym by 6 o'clock?" she asked. I moved my body and knew the Hulk Syndrome was leaving.

"What happened last night?" I asked as I rolled over. She opened the door to leave and said, "I don't know, but you were really annoying me. Love you! Bye!"

I had nights like this more often, and the only way I was able to fall asleep was to drink vodka until I passed out.

43 Domestic Violence

There had been signs of domestic violence in my relationship with Liz in 2005 and 2006, but it wasn't until 2007 that it began to escalate. I no longer felt that Liz wanted to be with me. When I threatened to leave, she no longer begged me to stay. I could sense she was tired of giving me chance after chance, but I wasn't even trying to turn my life around. She wanted a stable man who would love, trust, and respect her: someone who would help out around the house and ask her how her day went at work.

I didn't know how to give her any of this, and even if I did, I was too self-centered to do it. Because of my insecurities and lack of emotional control, I became very controlling and refused to let the relationship end. I tried using several tactics to control her, but none of them worked. No matter how scary my threats were, she told me she wasn't afraid. Even when it turned to physical abuse, she returned what I dished out. Each week, I felt like I was losing her more and more.

We'd fight and then I'd buy her flowers to make up, promising to be a better man. Sure, a piece of her may have wanted it to work, but I could tell she was emotionally and physically tired of trying.

Though I hate to admit it, I was becoming a monster. I could tell you what a wonderful person I was, but I'd be lying. It is shameful to think of who I was during those dark years of my life, but it needs to be said. I was not some kind-hearted man who loved and respected women.

I always told my friends and family about how mean Liz was to me, but I left out that I was ten times worse. I wanted them to think I was the victim, but all this ends today. By the year 2007, I had become a domestic abuser, a stalker, and an angry, jealous, callous man.[28]

---

28   Some of my friends didn't want me to include this chapter because it makes me look bad. But this chapter needed to be included for several reasons: first, to shine a light on domestic violence because it is happening all over the country and most of it doesn't even get reported. Second, I wanted people to know I was not the nice guy everyone assumed I was. And third, it would only be fair to Liz for people to know the truth about my actions.

In front of my students, clients, family, teammates, and coworkers, I pretended to be a good person, but I was far from it. Only those within my inner circle got a glimpse of my dark side. I can't tell you how many times Liz had to call one of my friends to come and get me because of my destructive behavior.[29]

It wasn't uncommon for Thomas to receive a phone call from Liz. "Thomas, you gotta come get him. He's acting crazy again, and I don't know what to do!" Liz would plead.

There was rage building within me, and all I could do was suppress it with vodka, pain killers, Ecstasy, and steroids; this was only making the problem worse. Here's the best way I can describe what I was feeling. In the movie "Blood Sport," Frank Dux gets some kind of substance thrown into his eyes in the finals, which blurs his vision. Frank could not see his opponent clearly and it causes him to scream at the top of his lungs in anger. For those who have seen the movie, you can hear the anger and desperation in his scream. I understand that scream, because it was the same scream coming out of my heart all the time. I could not see clearly because of all the poison I had in my system. I was physically, emotionally, and mentally exhausted.

I was depressed and I didn't even realize it. If I lost Liz, I felt like I'd be more alone than I already was. So the relationship continued, but it wasn't getting any better. It was becoming a very dangerous situation.

---

29   I usually found out the next day what exactly happened the day before. Liz would say, "You make these crazy faces and you start breaking everything."

44 Mental Hospital

I woke up staring at the midnight sky. I had no idea where I was or how I got there. All I knew was that I was completely drunk, outdoors, and in what seemed to me to be the middle of nowhere. I looked to my left and noticed a bridge about thirty feet over my head. Then I turned to the right and saw complete darkness. I was lying on a hard surface. Some gremlin had put a large rock under my back. I lay there trying to remember how I got there, but I couldn't remember a thing.

As time passed, I looked to my favorite part of the sky; there they were, my three bright friends: Orion's Belt and the Big Dipper. You couldn't miss them!

Some familiar questions came to mind: Who am I? What am I doing here? You might think those were silly questions, because I knew my name was Jeremy Jackson and I competed in MMA, but who was I really? Why was my life a mess?

My eyes were fixed on Orion's Belt. Ancient people had looked at those same stars for generations past. As I was deep in thought, a bright light shone in my eyes. I could hear police radios as more lights entered my sphere of vision.

"I see him! He's alive!" someone shouted from above. "That's at least a thirty-foot fall. How did he survive that?" another shouted.

What were they talking about?

They made their way down and put me on a stretcher. As they were carrying me out of the empty river bed, I looked back and saw the boulder I'd been lying on; it was about the size of a kitchen stove. I closed my eyes.

A few minutes later, I woke up in an ambulance. I noticed they were cutting my clothes off and inserting a catheter. When they saw my eyes opening, they began asking questions: "You okay, buddy? Do you know your name? Do you know what happened to you? Can you feel your legs?"

I heard someone whisper, "I think it's the guy from the Ultimate Fighter." Before they asked the next question, my eyes closed again, and when I woke up I was in the hospital.

"What's wrong with you, Jeremy?" a familiar voice accused. "You have issues." I opened my eyes and saw Liz standing by my bed.

"Liz, what's going on?" I asked.

"You jumped off a bridge, you idiot!" she exclaimed as she walked behind some curtains.

"I didn't jump off a bridge!" I responded, with more than a little attitude. I could hear her talking to someone behind the curtains, but who were they? I tried listening in, but the voices were too low. A doctor walked into the room and picked up a clipboard hanging from the end of my bed.

"You are lucky to be alive, Mr. Jackson," he said.

"I didn't jump off of any bridge, Doc, if that's what you're thinking," I said with frustration.

While the doctor and I were talking, a sheriff walked into the room – not a good sign!

"Well, you feelin' all right?" the sheriff asked.

"I'm OK. I can walk," I answered. Another sheriff walked in, pushing a wheelchair.

"Why don't you have a seat in this chair," the first sheriff said, "and then we're going to take you to see another doctor."

"I just saw the doctor," I said, as I pointed at the man in the white coat. "He's right there!" The doctor looked at the sheriff; then walked out of the room.

"Yes, that was the doctor, but we need to take you over to a special doctor, and he'll authorize your discharge," the sheriff said.

"I don't understand," I answered.

"Look, the faster we do this, the quicker we can get you out of here, OK?" the sheriff explained. I obediently sat in the wheelchair, and he wheeled me out. I noticed a handful of sheriffs standing outside the room, and as he pushed me through the hallways, the sheriffs followed.

A few minutes later, we went out a back door and headed toward another building that had a sign above the door: Psychiatric Care.

"What's this?" I asked. "Just talk with this doctor, and you'll be done in no time," the sheriff said, as he opened the door and wheeled me in. I was taken into a small room where a woman was sitting behind a desk. She looked at all the sheriffs standing behind me; then turned to me with a look of confusion. One of the sheriffs called her out of the room to speak with her in private, but I could still hear them.

"Why so many sheriffs?" she asked. "He's just one man."

"He's a UFC fighter," he warned her in a low voice. Their voices got quieter, and I could no longer hear what they were saying. After about three minutes of whispering, the sheriffs left me alone with the woman. There was a very large man in hospital scrubs standing behind me.

"Mr. Jackson, you have to stay with us tonight," she said. "Then you'll see the doctor tomorrow."

What?? I was tricked! Those sheriffs knew that I wouldn't be going home.

"I'm not staying here!" I declared.

"Look, we know who you are. This guy behind you is going to take you to your room. If you don't cooperate with us, we'll have to strap you down. Trust me," she said, "you don't want that. Are we going to have any problems?"

I glanced at the big man behind me and instantly knew I could easily take him. His size didn't intimidate me at all. It would be over in two seconds. Pride began burning within me. I wanted to show them what I was capable of and that I didn't take threats lightly, but what would hurting this guy get me? I wanted to go home, so I cooperated. I figured that once I saw the doctor I would be released.

They took my clothes and put me in a medical outfit. I stayed in a little room with a small bed. I lay in bed wondering what was going on. Everything was a blur, but one thing was for sure: I was a screwed-up mess.

The next morning, they lined us up for pills. I didn't want the pills because they might make me really tired. I wanted to be alert around all these crazy people. But I couldn't refuse, since I was told they were mandatory. Crazy people were all around, poking me with their fingers.

"Are you my friend?" one of them asked. "Sure, why not?" I replied.

One spilled food on the floor; then she began eating the spilled food with her spoon. "Amelia, don't eat that!" a nurse shouted. Amelia looked under the table and found some old gum to chew. I was about to throw up. Was this hell?

My best friend, Thomas, called the hospital and tried to convince them to let me go, but the doctor said he needed to talk with me before making any decisions. "He's suicidal," the doctor told Thomas.

"Who, Jeremy? The guy loves himself too much. He is stuck on himself," Thomas replied.

"Stuck on himself?" the doctor asked.

"Jeremy's always admiring himself in the mirror," Thomas said, laughing. "He's totally stuck on himself."

After speaking with Thomas, the doctor called me into his office. "So, why don't you tell me what happened last night?" he began. Leaning back, he made himself comfortable. Then he folded his arms across his chest and stared at me. I tried to dig into my thoughts, but I couldn't remember what had happened the night before. The only thing I knew was that I'd waked up under a bridge, so I made up a story.

"Well," I started, "I was walking near a bridge and a bum came up and pushed me off!" The doctor sat bolt upright in his chair and put his hands on the desk. "A bum pushed you off a bridge?" he repeated, staring into my eyes.

"That's right," I confidently asserted. "A bum."

"Where did this bum come from?" he asked. "How am I supposed to know?" I replied in frustration. "I'm telling you what I know, man. Some bum pushed me!"

"Interesting," he said, as he began writing things down on a notepad.

"Why is that interesting? And what are you writing?" I demanded.

"Well, because a witness was driving over the bridge and saw a man jump off. In fact," he continued, "a few witnesses reported the same thing." Doc leaned back in his chair.

"That is interesting," I noted.

"Yes, indeed it is," he said, removing his reading glasses and setting them on the desk.

"Doctor, I'm telling you," I persisted. "That bum pushed me. I don't know what else to tell you." I leaned back in my chair and crossed my legs.

"You know what's even more interesting?" he asked with a grin.

"What's that?"

This guy knew something, but he wasn't telling me. How much did he know about me, I wondered?

"You had an older brother who died when he fell off a bridge after a car accident, right?" he asked. My heart sank to the pit of my stomach. I didn't want to talk about that.

"Um," I stammered, "I did have an older brother. You're correct."

"Coincidence?" he asked.

"I told you a bum pushed me off!" I blurted.

We sat and stared at each other for about ten seconds, and I knew he was studying me.

"All right then," he finally concluded. "I can see that you're going to stick to your story, but I'm going to release you anyway. I spoke to your friend earlier, and he told me that you're too in love with yourself to commit suicide. That's good enough for me. I'm not saying I buy your 'bum' theory, but bye and have a good day, Mr. Jackson."

Thomas was outside waiting for me. "Vulch!" he shouted. (Vulch was a nickname he'd given me a while back. He said I was the Scorpion in the ring, but when I partied, he called me The Vulch, since when I walked into a club I didn't leave any women for anyone else.)

"Hey Thomas, thanks for helping me out," I said as I jumped into his truck. "I owe you one." Thomas was always there when I needed him.

As we were driving, I asked him, "Do you know what happened to me last night? I don't remember anything."

He looked at me and then back at the road. "Vulch, you were outta control last night. You, Chris, and I were out clubbing, and around midnight you became the 'Sculch.' There was no stopping you. We were afraid to take your keys because we didn't know if you would get us in a submission hold or something. You took off in your car with your lights off, and we thought for sure you weren't going to make it," he told me. (Chris had given me the nickname "Sculch" a few months back. It was a combination of "Scorpion" and "Vulture." When I lost control, my friends called me "Sculch.")

That would explain how I ended up under the bridge. Although people say I jumped, I don't think so. I think I walked down there and passed out.

But, who knows?

45 Guardian

After that night, a friend of mine became my bodyguard. He weighed 260 pounds and was not fat. This guy was a strong wrestler, who also helped me prepare for my fights. He became known as the "Guardian."

When I went to clubs, he stood near me and kept an eye on me. He drank only coffee and energy drinks. He wasn't there to protect me from others; he was there to protect me from myself. Once I got to a certain point in my drinking, the "Skulch" stage, my mind would go blank, and I would wake up the next day having no memory of where I was or what I'd done.

As I entered the Skulch stage at clubs, I was no longer fun to be around, nor was I a good wing man. One time an old friend had a big fight coming up on Pay-Per-View,[30] and he asked me to watch his house while he fought. Former boxing champion Fernando Vargas was a very successful boxer, and this made a lot of people from his home town jealous. He didn't like leaving his house alone while he was fighting, because haters would try and mess with his stuff. He had surrounded his house with security cameras, one every few feet.

I invited Guardian to come with me, and we watched Fernando fight from his home movie theater. As I was watching the fight, Guardian suddenly was gone. I didn't want him to miss the rest of the fight, so I went looking for him. I found him staring at the security camera monitors.

"You all right, Guardian?" I asked.

"Hold on, Scorpion," he said, as he ran out of the back door with his finger in his ear, like he was a secret agent or something. He didn't have an earpiece. What's wrong with him?

I watched the monitors and saw him stop on the front lawn. There was no one out there. He put his finger in his ear again, as if he was receiving a message from a NASA satellite; then he disappeared from one monitor and suddenly appeared on another. What was he doing?

The back door opened, and he came running in, out of breath.

---

30   November 23, 2007; Fernando Vargas fought Ricardo Mayorga

"Did you get him?" I asked teasingly. "No, he got away!" he answered, trying to catch his breath.

I was watching the cameras the entire time, and I didn't see anything. Only he saw whatever it was.

The next night, I was clubbing and brought Guardian with me. As I sat at the bar, he stood behind me with his arms crossed and biceps flexing. Occasionally, he would put his finger to his ear, as I had seen him do the night before. I thought it was kind of funny. My friends thought it was weird and made me look stupid. They said I should get rid of him; I probably should have.

Two months, later I found out he was texting my girlfriend Liz and giving her information about my night life. She knew details that no one else could have known except for Guardian.

One day, I received a text message from Guardian, but it was intended for Liz. I was curious, so I looked through her phone. Just as I suspected: he was throwing me under the bus and also flirting with her. As I read each message, it was obvious that he had a crush on Liz. He was betraying me.

The next day, I called him into my office. We stood there chest to chest, and I stared into his eyes. Even though I hadn't said a word, my look said it all. I was a little nervous because he is a big dude with a lot of strength, but I knew I was a better fighter than he was, and I had confidence in my skills. In training, I'd taken him every time we faced off, despite his superior strength.

I looked him in the eyes and told him how I felt about him texting my girlfriend. Of course, he denied everything. After telling him that I'd seen the text messages, I told him it would be best if he left before it got ugly. "You need to go," I said angrily. "There's no referee here to break us up. You know what I'm capable of!"

When he walked out, I felt a little pain in my heart. He was a close friend and a good training partner. We had spent a lot of hours training and bleeding together, but he had betrayed me, and I could no longer trust him.

46 God Drawing Me in

A few weeks later, Liz and I moved out of our apartment and into a nice little home two or three blocks away. Though it seemed like a good idea at the time, it turned out to be a disaster since it put a lot more stress on our relationship. I hadn't fought in nine months, and the gym I owned wasn't bringing in any money. I made a little bit of money doing private lessons, but most of my earnings went to bills and booze.

One day, after a man from the carpet store finished installing our carpet, he spoke with us in the driveway about Jesus Christ. He preached to us for about an hour, and neither of us spoke until he was done. At first I didn't want to hear it, but something told me that I needed to listen. It felt like my heart was burning inside.

There was something unique about him. It was like he had peace in his life; but how could he have peace of mind in this world? It seemed as if he had everything he needed; he was content. The man said he had Jesus and that was all he desired. How was that possible?

After he walked away, Liz and I looked at each other and said, "That sure came out of nowhere!" As we walked inside our new home to check out the carpet, we continued talking about how nice it had been to hear him share his experiences with God.

"I needed to hear that," I said to Liz. "So did I," she replied, looking at me. "It was perfect timing."

I can't tell you how many times I've run into situations like this, and at the most random times, too. I would meet someone who would just start talking about Jesus. There were times I would be coming out of a nightclub, and someone would hand me a flyer, telling me all about Jesus.

That Sunday, we decided to attend church. Neither of us could remember the last time we'd gone to church. When you can't remember, it's been too long.

The next day, I was sitting at a local gym talking with the owner. I was trying to rent some space so I could open another studio. As we discussed business, he suddenly began talking to me about God! He invited me to come and listen to him preach at a local park in Camarillo. I told him I would think about it and let him know.

Later that week, I went to spend time with my two-year-old son. While I was holding him, I asked Tarah if she would like to go with me to the nearby park and listen to some guy preach.

"Won't Liz be mad?" Tarah asked.

"Liz and I are having problems right now," I replied.

"Did she throw you out again?" she asked, pouring me some iced tea. "I don't understand why you keep going back to her, Jeremy.'

"Me either. Anyway, you wanna go or not?" I asked. "Sure. I'll drive," she offered.

We drove to the park and saw the guy preaching to a group of people. We sat in the parking lot with our windows rolled up, not really knowing what to do. "OK, are we just going to sit here, or what?" Tarah asked.

I took a few gulps of vodka from my Jack-in-the Box cup and stared at the crowd.

"Jeremy? Hello? Tell me again why we came here?" she asked in frustration. As I stared out of the tinted windows, I could hear my son singing a very familiar song. "Twinkle, twinkle, little star, how I wonder what you are...." he sang.

Wham! That song flooded me with tons of memories! I sang that song when I was a kid; in fact, it was the first song I remember singing.

"Jeremy?" Tarah repeated.

"Um...just drive," I directed, as I watched the preacher, who had a Bible in his hand.

"What? I thought we were going!" she said.

"No, I changed my mind. Just drive," I said, while taking another sip of vodka. When she began to drive away, my son started singing the "ABC" song. "I don't get you, Jeremy," Tarah accused, as she drove from the park.

I'm not sure why I changed my mind. I'd been drinking and felt guilty. Also, I didn't want the preacher putting me on blast, telling the crowd who I was. I just don't know. One thing I do know looking back, is that God was calling me. Did I answer His call? No! I ran each time, just like Jonah in the Bible. God was using people to get my attention, or sometimes a simple tug in my heart, but I tried to block His voice by staying busy and drowning myself in vodka.

In the beginning of 2008, my drinking jumped to a new level. Many said I was trying to drink myself to death. I drank vodka all day and well into the night. I drank it like water. Even though I usually fell asleep around 4 a.m., I still didn't stop drinking. How is that possible? Well, while I was sleeping I would grab a bottle of vodka, which I kept on a night stand next to my bed, and chug as much as I could; then fall back to sleep. When I awoke at 5:45 a.m., I would chug some more.

Around this time, I began to get horrible headaches. I was taking Ecstasy, Oxycontin, Norcos, and stacking different kinds of steroids. Sometimes I felt like my heart was going to blow right out of my chest. My ankles and wrists began to swell to frightening dimensions. I was subjecting my body to abuse.

I was invited to be a special guest at a club in Oceanside, California. I had to be on a plane to Pennsylvania the next day, to attend an event where I was invited to be the guest host and speak on camera.

As usual, I brought my best friend, Thomas, with me. And, of course, we partied all night. By 5 a.m., I'd just begun to close my eyes when I realized I had to be at LAX by 6:15 a.m.

"Thomas!" I blurted out. But Thomas didn't move. He had just passed out.

"Thomas!!" I repeated.

"Yeah? What?" he answered with a cranky voice.

"Dude, we gotta be at LAX!"

"Don't worry, the plane never leaves on time," Thomas gently explained. "As long as we get there fifteen minutes early, we'll be all right."

I kept trying to convince him to get up, but he was out. Sleep sounded better anyway. I was exhausted.

At 5:30 a.m., the promoter on the East Coast called me to see how everything was going. I did all I could to get out of the event, but the promoter wouldn't budge. He had already advertised on TV, radio, and posters that I was going to be a special guest at the event. Plus, he'd already given me some "up front" money.

After hanging up with the promoter, I told Thomas we needed to go. I don't remember how we got to LAX, but we were too late. Our plane had left.

The promoter was not happy when I gave him the news. Even if I caught the next flight, it wouldn't get me there in time. I let him know that I would give back the front money.

A few hours later, we arrived back in Ventura. I went to hang out with a woman I was dating. We parked on an empty street, and she watched as I chugged a bottle of vodka.

"What's wrong, Jeremy?" she asked, with concern in her voice. I took another drink and stared out of the side window of the car. "I'm not real sure, Joselyn. I feel empty. That's the best way I can explain it," I answered.

"What can I do?" she asked, putting her hand on my shoulder. Looking down the street, I saw a father playing with his son. I was drinking my life away, while I saw my two-year-old son only occasionally.

"I hate myself," I said. "I hate this world. I just don't wanna live anymore." I took another sip of vodka. "Can I tell you something, Joselyn?"

"You can tell me anything, and it will stay between us. I promise."

"When a crowd surrounds me and wants my picture or autograph, I feel important. But deep down inside I know these people could care less about me. They see a person who was on TV, and they want to take a picture for bragging rights. The sad thing is, I don't care. I still want to feel important. All these people stare at me like I'm someone special, even though I'm not," I tried to explain.

Joselyn put her hand on my face and said, "Jeremy, you ARE special."

"No, Joselyn! Don't give me that! About a year ago I was a guest in LA, and I hung out with all these kids who had cancer. These kids wanted to live, and I wanted to die. What's wrong with me?" I said, as I finished the vodka.

"I wish I could help you," she said.

"Take me to my friend's house. I need to be alone," I said, as I pulled out another bottle.

Sure, I had a lot of people around me throughout my career, but I never wanted people to know what I was really feeling. Anytime I felt vulnerable, lost, afraid, alone, or hurt, I'd pick up a bottle of vodka and chug until I was numb, or I'd throw painkillers in my mouth.

There were a few times I'd start to open up to someone, but when I began to feel vulnerable it was time to get away. I'd hop in the car and drive so I could be alone. How was I going to fill this vacuum in my heart? I filled it with whatever I could: alcohol, drugs, sex, and attention from fans.

I didn't know how to connect with people. I didn't know how to talk about my feelings. Something was happening in my heart, and I didn't want others to know, because I didn't want anyone to think I was weak; it was this secret that was fueling my crazy lifestyle.

Later that day, Joselyn dropped me off at my friend's house.

"Hey, Sculch!" Chris said to me. Chris let me stay at his house when I didn't want to sleep at the gym.

"Can I crash here?" I asked.

"Mi casa es su casa, amigo," he said, while playing his guitar.

That night, I found myself alone on the couch. Chris was out clubbing. I pulled all the vodka bottles out of my bag and set them on the coffee table in front of me. I also pulled out more than fifty sleeping pills that a doctor had prescribed the week before. I told the doctor I couldn't sleep, so she prescribed some medication, warning me not to take more than two or three pills at a time.

As I sat there on the couch, I took all fifty pills; then I grabbed some Oxycontin, Ecstasy, more than fifty ibuprofen, and threw them in my mouth. I walked over to the liquor cabinet and took out some large vodka bottles.

I chugged the first bottle and tossed it on the couch. Picking up the second bottle, I walked outside and sat on the porch, waiting for death to deliver me from my pain. I had so much in my system that I thought for sure that would be my last night on earth. I sat there drinking the vodka, waiting to die.

Looking up at the stars, I was hoping to see Orion's Belt, but it was too foggy. I felt myself begin to shiver and wondered how much longer until I was dead. Will it hurt? What happens after death? These questions were floating in my mind; then it all went blank.

"Vulch?" said a voice from a distant dream. "Vulch?" it repeated.

I opened my eyes and realized I was face up on my friend's couch. Chris was looking down at me in shock. "What happened??" he asked, as he looked around the room.

I sat up. Everywhere I looked, I saw vomit. It looked like I must have run from room to room, layering vomit everywhere. The couch looked the worst.

"I don't know what happened," I said, as I scanned the room. "I promise I'll clean it all up. Hey, not to change the subject, but I gotta be at the gym at 6 a.m. to train. You wanna work out with me?"

"You feelin' OK to work out, Sculch?" he asked.

"Not really, but I need to," I answered.

Chris had a crazy look on his face as he stared at me. He saw where my life was headed, and it didn't look good. He had no idea what he could do to help.

But God did, because He had other plans for me.

48 Saying Goodbye to Joselyn

Somewhere around this time, Joselyn started to fall for me. She wanted a relationship; what she didn't know was that I was still seeing Liz and had just started dating a woman named Stephanie. I didn't know how to be faithful. Lying was like breathing to me.

I couldn't juggle another relationship. I was already paranoid that Liz would find out what a cheater I was. She slept with a knife under the side of her bed and said she would use it on me if she ever found out I was cheating: she wouldn't tell me, she would just lop off my private part while I slept. I didn't think she was kidding.

I had to do a lot of lying so I wouldn't get caught. I lied so much that I didn't know what reality was. I'd be crazy to think that I could juggle another relationship while I trained six to eight hours a day, taught MMA classes, trained clients, and made guest appearances. What stressed me out most was the possibility of Liz and Stephanie finding out about each other; adding Joselyn would be unbearable.

The first thing I was going to do was break things off with Joselyn. I invited her out for drinks and told her it would be best if we stopped seeing each other. I thought she handled it pretty well until we got in her car to leave. While she drove, I sat in the passenger seat looking out the window. It was quiet, and I was pondering how well she'd taken the news. Suddenly, the car began to speed up. We were on a little side street that had a speed limit of 20 miles per hour; we were tripling that at 60.

I slowly turned. Joselyn was staring at me; not at the road. "Jeremy, why?" she asked. "Why are you doing this?"

"Joselyn, watch where you're going! Pay attention to the road!" I exclaimed.

But she continued looking at me. "Why? Why, Jeremy?" she cried.

"Joselyn, I don't care if I die, but I don't want anything to happen to you. Now stop this car!" I demanded. We were all over the road as the car continued to accelerate.

"Why, Jeremy?" she asked again.

"Look Joselyn, I don't deserve you. You're too good a woman. I'm a mess. You don't want to be with a guy like me. I'm doing you a favor! Now pull over!" I shouted.

"Please, Jeremy, I can help you!" she said, tears rolling down her cheeks.

"You want to help me? You can start by stopping this car!" I said, while holding on to the dashboard. "Think of your daughters!"

The car slowed, and we turned down another street. "POLE!" I yelled, but she continued staring at me.

BAM!! The car crashed into the pole, and we came to a complete stop. A police car was driving by, and the officer saw the whole thing. He turned his spotlight on us and was about to pull over; suddenly, a car flew by, racing down the street at over 100 mph.

The cop looked confused, but finally backed up and went after the other car.

"Joselyn, listen. I'm not the man you want to spend the rest of your life with. Trust me," I said, putting my hand on her shoulder.

"So this is it?" she cried. "I'm afraid it is." I replied. "Take me to my friend's house, and you can stay there until you sober up."

It was tough saying goodbye to Joselyn. Not only was she beautiful, but she was kind and gentle. She could have had any guy in the world. Why she wanted me is a mystery.

After breaking off with Joselyn, I was still stressed out. I worried about Liz and Stephanie finding out about each other. I knew it was only a matter of time until my unfaithfulness would be revealed. I had to break it off with one of them.

Though I cared about Liz, our relationship wasn't healthy. I was tired of fighting with her. I made up my mind and chose to end it with her. Stephanie was who I wanted. She would lie in bed at night while I sat on the floor, and listen while I shared what was in my heart. The problem was I thought I was sharing everything that was in my heart, but I wasn't. I was only able to share what was in the shallow end, because I had never probed my heart's depths. The liquor, drugs, licentious lifestyle, and my career never gave me time to reflect. I was trying to forget my past, not remember it.

But could I handle being with only one woman? I was sure willing to give it a try.

49 Reality Sucks

Liz and I were always in an on-again, off-again, relationship. Since we were always breaking up, then getting back together, it became a game to me. I also had mixed emotions about her, so I was confused. On the one hand, I loved her, but on the other, I hated her. How was that possible? I know she must have felt the same about me, especially during my drunken rages which seemed to be happening more often. During those times, I'd call her a whore[31] and accuse her of cheating. Looking back, I believe she was faithful throughout the three years we were seeing each other.

When we both agreed to end things for good, it really felt like the end. The way she looked at me was not the same. I noticed fear in her eyes. Fear? Liz was a woman who feared nothing, so this was something new.

As I drove away from her house for the last time, I tried to understand why she was afraid.[32] Reflecting on anything was not a normal thing for me, because I never wanted to remember the past: my childhood, Oscar's death, or even what happened the night before. I lived for the present.

I grabbed a bottle of vodka that sat on the passenger seat and chugged as much as I could. The past would remain drowned forever in the endless

---

31   When I was a teenager, someone I looked up to tried to give me some advice, to prepare me for the world. "All women are whores," he began. "What about Mom? She's a woman," I asked. "She's a whore. They all are. Every woman on this planet is a whore, and they will rip your heart out without thinking twice." My teenage mind could not wrap my head around the thought of all women being such evil creatures. But I looked up to this man and believed every word. He was my hero. I didn't realize at the time that this would mold me into seeing women as enemies, to be used for my pleasure only. They became objects with no feelings of their own.

32   I was very intoxicated that last night, and I could hardly stay awake. With several kinds of steroids in my system, as well as painkillers, Ecstasy, and over a gallon of vodka, I made a shameful choice that I will forever regret. I'm not blaming the substances, but my poor choice in using them.

sea of vodka I consumed. I would never have to face reality as long as I had it, but this was about to change.

Two days after Liz and I separated, I was arrested. Stephanie and I were at a movie theater in Ventura when two men with bulletproof vests and assault rifles ordered me to the ground. Liz had pressed charges against me.

I was taken to the Oxnard Police Station; as I began to sober up, they read me my rights and told me what Liz had charged me with.

Rape. It was a horrible word that made me twitch every time I heard it. Why would Liz make up such a lie? Or was she telling the truth? Was I capable of such a thing?

I had been drunk for four years straight, and it felt like I was waking up from a long nightmare. My life seemed as if it had been on cruise control. Drinking nonstop every day gave me the chance to escape reality, but now that I was sober, reality was showing its ugly face. I hated reality! My reality was a world filled with unfaithful people who would take any opportunity to rip my heart out.

Turning on the news reveals the real world: some guy shooting up a mall, or a theater, or a school. This sick world is becoming worse each day. This is reality. People are entertained by watching Jerry Springer, Maury, Steve Wilkos, Cops, Cheaters, The Young and the Restless, and countless others. These popular shows concentrate on people's problems. I watched them, too. This is life! We live for seventy or eighty years, and then we die. Many don't live that long. People are dying daily of cancer, in accidents, starving to death, or murder. After working eight to ten hours a day, most come home and turn on the television or get online. The next day is a repeat, and the day after that.

I watched movies, wishing I was the main character. I started a MySpace page, and put everything that I could on there, hoping others would check me out. On weekends, I went to bars or clubs until the next sporting event or concert. I stressed about money, about bills, about everything.

You never know if someone you love is going to be ripped from you by death. You never know if you'll have your job tomorrow. Your house could float away in a storm or be destroyed by a tornado. If you live in Florida, your house might fall into a sink hole and vanish. California is expecting a massive earthquake. If you live in the mountains, you could be washed away by a mudslide or lose your home to fire.

My chances of having some serious health problems are high. This is life? There has to be something more. What is the meaning of it all? How many celebrities have overdosed? How many have committed suicide? How many are drug addicts or alcoholics? These stars have it all, and yet are desperately unhappy, trying to escape reality – just like the rest of us.

For four years I drank to escape this truth: the world is falling apart. All we can do is find something to distract us so that we don't have to face the facts. Some turn to alcohol, drugs, or sex to escape reality. Others turn to video games, movies, sports, sleep, or crime. And, sadly, some take their own lives.

I sat in a small cell at the Oxnard Jail freezing my butt off. I had on shorts, a thin T-shirt and sandals. I was so cold that I took the toilet paper roll and wrapped myself up like a mummy. The look on the guard's face when he saw me was priceless. The only part of me that was visible was my eyes.

Reality sucks!

What was I supposed to do? Sit there and stare at the wall all day? Where was my vodka? I needed my phone so I could take a picture of myself and post it. At least let me watch Jerry Springer!

Then it hit me: what about my son? What about the things that mattered? What about my family? My little brother needed me. The last time I spoke with him was a few weeks prior to my arrest. I remember him sitting on my couch, staring at the floor. I walked over and sat next to him.

"What's up?" I asked him.

"Why is it so difficult? Everything was fine until 2004! He was my best friend, Jeremy!" he said, as he broke down crying.

"Bodi, don't you think I hurt? Look at me! My career was on track until Oscar died in 2004," I said as I stood up, holding a large bottle of vodka. "My heart aches every day. If you only knew how many times I've tried suicide. Look, it's just you and me now, but we have each other."

Here I was a few weeks later, sitting in jail facing a life sentence. I would never again be there for my little brother.

Reality was really beginning to sink in.

"Reality is that which, when you stop believing in it, doesn't go away."
Philip K. Dick

50 Meet My Biggest Fan

Later that night, I was transferred to the Ventura County Jail. I was crammed in a small cell with ten or more men. These are the tanks they put you in during the booking process. During booking, they take your fingerprints, take your picture and ask personal questions. You spend a day or two in these small rooms, waiting for a bed to open upstairs.

Since there was no room in this small tank, I had to sit next to the toilet. I was listening to everyone's conversations and was amazed to hear each guy claiming to be innocent. I didn't believe any of them.

"Do I know you?" one of the guys in the tank asked me.

"I doubt it," I answered.

"No, I know you from somewhere, too," another said.

"Well, I don't know you," I said, with an attitude.

It got very quiet after that awkward exchange, and everyone was beginning to lie back and get some rest. We had to sleep in one position all night because there was no room to move around.

I found a spot where I could "spoon" the toilet and try to get some sleep. This was a bad idea. When someone had to use the toilet, they would have to step over others to get to where I was. I would wake up and try to move a little, but it wasn't far enough away because I felt urine splash on my arm. My first thought was to get up and give the guy a beating, but I was too tired and struggled to keep my eyes open.

Sometime the next day, I was escorted upstairs and put in a cell the size of a small closet. There was hardly any room in the cell, most of which was taken up by the two beds hanging from the wall. One bed was above the other, and a small metal desk was connected to the back wall. There was a man lying face down on the bottom bunk. His arms were down by his sides, and he appeared to be dead.

CLANG! The door slammed shut behind me, and I thought for sure the man would wake up, but he didn't even move. Was he dead or what? This can't be good! I'm in here with a dead body. When I got closer, I could hear him breathing. I didn't have to worry about that anymore.

I looked at the top bunk and wondered how I was supposed to climb up there. I saw no ladder or step, so I stepped on the desk and used it to jump up. What do I do now? It was a weird feeling having no cell phone, computer, TV, friends, keys, Chapstick and my bottle of vodka. I was craving alcohol.

What does a person do when he has absolutely nothing? I didn't have any other choice but to stare into space and daydream. I tried closing my eyes, but I couldn't because I was getting the shakes without alcohol. A little bit later the door opened, and I climbed down off the bunk to see what was going on. The man who was lying face down finally turned his head and looked at me.

"Oh, hey! What's up? How long have you been here?" he said, as he sat up on the bed.

"Um, a few hours," I answered. I watched drool drip from his chin and hit the floor. His mouth was wide open as he stared at me with a blank look.

"Are you OK?" I asked.

"Hmmm? Oh, I'm on meds. They are some good meds. Want some?" he said.

Well, I do want some pills, but not if they are going to make me look like this guy! I don't want to start drooling on myself. "I'm OK," I said.

He stood up and walked out the door. "It's chow time," he mumbled.

I followed him out, and we grabbed some food trays from a tray slot in the wall; then walked back to the cell. "This is supposed to be food?" I asked. It was disgusting, but I forced myself to eat it.

He finished eating his meal in thirty seconds; then passed out on his bed. I climbed up on my bunk after finishing my meal and noticed that I was shaking again. I couldn't stop thinking about alcohol. There was nothing I could do to get my mind off drinking. I tried exercising, but it didn't help. I couldn't sleep; all I could do was shake.

A week passed, and I began to have dark circles under my eyes. I wasn't sleeping, and I couldn't hold down any food. My "celly" slept all day, every day, and only woke to eat and use the toilet. I wondered if I should have taken him up on his offer and taken some of his meds so I could sleep.

The door opened, and a guard was standing there. "Jackson? You're moving to another cell," he said with a loud voice. I followed him out and looked back to say bye to my celly, but he was face down and didn't even know I had left. The guard was escorting me down the hall, and we came up to another section.

"You fought in the UFC, didn't you?" the guard asked.

"Yes, sir," I answered.

"You're a good fighter. Man, I hate to see you in here!" We stood in front of a metal door and waited for the guard in the tower to push a button and open it. All I could do was stare at the floor because I was ashamed.

C'mon, door! Open already!

As soon as the door opened, I could hear someone in one of the cells shouting a name I knew very well. "Scorpion! Scorpion!" the voice shouted.

Who was shouting? A crazy fan? An old friend? Who could it be? My eyes focused, and I immediately recognized his face.

"Jerry?" I said, as my jaw dropped. A few months earlier, I had met a guy at the gym I owned. He wanted private lessons. I gave him my card and told him to call me sometime. Later that day, I was having a meal with Thomas at a Greek restaurant where Stephanie worked, when my phone rang.

"Hello?" I said.

"Scorpion?" a voice replied.

"This is he," I answered, and took a sip of my drink.

"You busy?"

"Who is this?" I asked.

"Jerry Norwal from your gym. Would you like to make some quick cash? You think you can come over to my pad and train me for an hour? I'll make it worth your time," he said.

I covered the phone and whispered to Thomas, "I gotta go train this guy for an hour. Wanna go with me?"

Thomas stood up and said, "Let's roll!" and then took one more bite of his meal.

We drove in Thomas' car and followed the directions that Jerry had given over the phone. It was a house about fifty yards from the beach. There he was, Jerry Norwal, standing in front of his house. He was a clean-shaven heavyset man with short blonde hair. He reminded me of the comedian Chris Farley.

"Scorpion! I can't believe you came! This is so awesome! Let me show you my crib!"

As he led us toward the house, Thomas leaned over and whispered in my ear, "I think your boy is drunk." I couldn't tell because I was drunk myself. I had just finished a bottle of vodka before Thomas and I met for lunch.

Jerry led us through his house, which turned into a weird tour. The more he spoke, the more evident it was that he was either drunk or high. "We are going to work out in the garage. It's my gym," he said, displaying a cocky attitude.

We walked into the garage and interrupted two older men lifting weights.

"Dad, this is the Scorpion, Jeremy Jackson. I need the garage because he's going to train me," Jerry said. The two older men looked at me with eyes that said, "Who?"

His dad answered, "Jerry, you are going to have to wait. Bill and I are using the garage right now."

Jerry became furious and shouted, "We are in the presence of a legend! You guys are embarrassing me in front of him. I need the garage, Dad!"

Let's get one thing clear. I was far from being a legend. I was only popular with a certain crowd. I was a small name compared to other UFC fighters, but it felt good being called a legend, even by a drunk guy who didn't know what he was saying.

His dad looked at me and said, "You guys know he's drunk, right?"

This made Jerry explode with cuss words as he turned bright red. Most of what Jerry was saying didn't make sense. He turned to look at me and grabbed my wrist. "Follow me. I'll pay you in advance for your time," Jerry said, as he led me into his room. Thomas followed right behind with a big grin on his face.

As Jerry was digging in a box next to his bed, I looked around the room and noticed he had my fight pictures on the walls. I looked at Thomas, who looked at me with big eyes and a wide smile. Thomas had seen me sign plenty of autographs and pose for photos with fans, since he was my right-hand man, but he hadn't seen a fan this hard core before.

Jerry found what he was looking for and slapped it into my hand. It was a wad of one-dollar bills. "Let's train!" Jerry said, as he walked out of his room and headed back to the garage. I looked at Thomas, and he shrugged his shoulders. I was about to tell him something when we heard loud shouting coming from the garage. Things were really beginning to get weird.

Thomas and I walked into the garage and saw Jerry arguing with his dad.

I did what I could to calm the situation down. "Hey Jerry! How about we go work out on the beach?" I said, as I put my hand on Jerry's shoulder.

He thought for a second and then walked out the front door, shouting more profanity at his dad. I guess he liked the idea of training on the beach. He led the way and never looked back.

"What a weird day," I told Thomas, as we walked side by side.

"Well, it's about to get a lot more weird!" he said with a laugh. I looked in the direction Thomas was staring, just in time to see Jerry make a sharp right turn and then walk straight into someone's house.

"What do we do?" I asked Thomas.

"Let's bounce! He won't even realize you're gone. Tomorrow he won't remember anything," he said.

"No, I can't leave yet. He already paid me. I'm on the clock," I said, holding up the wad of ones. Thomas and I were standing outside the house Jerry had entered, wondering if we should follow him. We could hear Jerry moving things around in the house and shouting.

"Yep! Right here! This is the spot, Scorpion! We can train right here," Jerry shouted.

"I'm going to get him out," I said. "Right behind you," said Thomas. We walked in and followed the noise.

"Actually, I found a better spot, Scorpion! Right here! Yep! This is it, Scorpion! Scorpion!! Where are you??" Jerry shouted from what sounded like the backyard.

"I think he's in the backyard," Thomas said. The shouting was getting louder, until finally we saw Jerry. He was shadow boxing, punching the air like he was in a championship fight.

"Jerry, let's go to the beach and work out. This isn't our house!" I protested.

"What? I own this block! I'm filthy rich!" Jerry shouted, as he threw a few more kicks, followed by punches.

"What are you guys doing in my house?" a man said as he stood behind us, holding a plastic grocery bag in each hand.

It looked like he just returned from the store, which would explain why the door was unlocked. The store was down the street, and he knew he would only be gone for a few minutes. He wasn't a big man: average guy, maybe in his mid-forties.

"Look, I know what this looks like, but we were trying to get him out of your house," I said, as I pointed toward Jerry. The man looked over our shoulders and saw Jerry punching and kicking the air with all his might.

"Jerry?" the man said.

"You know him?" I asked.

"Unfortunately. He lives down the street," the man answered.

All three of us watched in amazement as Jerry was swinging, missing, and falling to the ground. He would get back up, breathing heavily, and swing some more. Thomas began to laugh, which caused me to laugh as well. We both looked at the owner of the house and noticed that he didn't share our mirth. We both stopped laughing abruptly.

"Please get him out of my house," the man said, as he walked into the other room to put his bags down. Thomas and I walked closer to Jerry and tried to convince him to follow us outside.

"Come on, Jerry, we're going to do a big UFC workout on the beach!" I coaxed. Thomas and I turned around to act as if we were heading for the ocean. I looked back, hoping Jerry was following. Suddenly, he marched past me, heading out the front door and passing Thomas as well. I walked over to the owner of the house as he stood in the living room.

"I hope he didn't break anything," I said. As I was still speaking, I could hear Jerry wheezing again. His shoes were stomping the concrete. We walked outside and noticed Thomas had fired Jerry up.

"Jab! Jab! Hook! Uppercut! Kick! Make the Scorpion proud!" Thomas shouted, as he clapped his hands. He looked at me with a big grin and began to laugh.

"It's been an hour and his lesson is almost finished, so he's getting his money's worth!" Thomas exclaimed. While Thomas was still speaking, a police car pulled up in front of the driveway.

"This should be interesting," the homeowner said.

The police officer stepped out of his car and walked toward Jerry, watching as he swung and kicked. "You wanna tell me what's going on?" the officer asked Jerry.

"He is just finishing a private lesson," Thomas said.

"Private lesson?" the officer asked.

"Private lesson with the Scorpion!" Jerry shouted, as he continued punching the air. The officer looked at Thomas and then looked back at Jerry.

"Have you had anything to drink today, Mr. Norwal?" asked the officer.

"Maybe!" shouted Jerry.

"You wanna stop all that so I can talk to you?" the officer asked, with increasing frustration.

"Not really!" Jerry said, as he was bobbing and weaving, dodging invisible punches.

"You know I can arrest you for being drunk in public?" responded the officer.

"No you can't, b****!" Jerry shouted. The officer's face changed; he walked toward Jerry, who began to walk slowly toward the owner's house, looking over his shoulder. The officer was closing fast, so Jerry picked up his pace. He didn't make it very far because the officer pulled out his Tazer and fired, hitting Jerry directly on his butt. Jerry looked toward the sky as he fell to his knees, squealing like a little girl. The officer cuffed him; then escorted him to the patrol car.

"When's the next lesson, Scorpion?" Jerry asked. I looked at Thomas in amazement. How do I answer that? It didn't matter at that point, because he was already in the patrol car.

"Definitely a strange day. That's the last time I go to someone's house to train him," I told Thomas.

"Usually people pay for entertainment, but you were entertained … and got paid for it!" Thomas replied.

We watched as Jerry was driven off, the back of his head visible in the patrol car.

We had always wondered what happened to Jerry after that day, and here he was sitting in jail all this time! "Scorpion!" he shouted, as I was walking up the stairs to the second floor. When I entered my new cell, I could still hear Jerry shouting, "That's the Scorpion! He's my trainer! He's here to give me my next lesson!"

Great! He remembers.

My celly was a white man in his late thirties. "You someone famous?" he asked, as I climbed to the top bunk.

"Far from it. That guy down there is on some heavy meds," I replied.

I sat there on the top bunk staring at the ceiling, and I didn't speak another word.

51 The Words That Touched My Heart

Later that night, a guard stood at the door of my cell to let me know I was being moved, again.

"Jackson, you're being transferred to Todd Road Jail," he said. My door opened, and he escorted me down the stairs, passing through many doors and into a long hallway.

"You look familiar. Do I know you?" the guard asked. "I don't think so," I replied.

"Wait a minute! Weren't you on The Ultimate Fighter?" he asked. I looked around to see if anyone else might have heard. The last thing I needed was for the other inmates to find out who I was and want to challenge me.

"Yes sir, I'm Jeremy Jackson," I said in a low voice.

"I knew it! What the heck you doing in here?" he asked.

"Well, that is a long story. I'd rather not talk about it," I said, while looking at the floor. We took the elevator to the bottom level, and I was in the booking area again. A door opened, and I was put in a tank with several other inmates.

"Scorpion!" someone excitedly said. I knew the voice, but I didn't want to believe it. I turned, and sure enough, there was Jerry Norwal leaning against the wall.

"Hey, Jerry! You been in this jail this whole time?" I asked. He launched into a long story about how the DA was trying to give him five years in prison.

"Five years? For what? You didn't do anything!" I exclaimed.

"Terrorist threats," he answered.

"Terrorist threats?" I replied.

"Yeah, my dad said I threatened him," he said, while putting his head down. A voice came out of nowhere as soon as Jerry made that last statement.

"That's the system for ya! Lock ya up as long as possible for somethin' petty!" the voice continued. I looked around at the other men in the cell to see who was speaking, but everyone was just sitting there listening. The toilet flushed from behind a three-and-a-half foot wall, but I didn't see anyone behind it. I heard water running in the sink, but still didn't see anyone.

Then a little man walked out from behind the wall while drying his hands off with a paper towel. He was a "little person" and was probably in his early thirties. He had tattoos on his neck, arms and hands. His head was shaved and he spoke like a thug, standing about three and a half feet tall. It looked like he was wearing skis because his shoes were too big for him. The jail didn't have shoes that fit him, so they gave him normal-sized shoes and clothes. His hands barely peeked out below his sleeves, even though he kept rolling his sleeves up.

I sympathize with people who have disadvantages, because I know what it feels like. As I looked at this little man standing in front of me, wearing clothes and shoes too big for him, I felt compassion for him.

He was looking up at me with a funny look on his face. "Hey Homie, do I know you from somewhere? Where do I know you from?" he asked, as he pointed up at me.

"He's the Scorpion! He knocked out Nick Diaz!" Jerry interjected.

"Thanks a lot, Jerry," I wryly replied. The little man continued to stare at me for a few seconds with his mouth open. He then climbed up on the bench next to me and stood on it to get a closer look.

"Yeah! I think I saw you fight on TV! You're a bad dude. You got some hands on you, boy! None of my homies are going to believe this. I'm standing next to the Scorpion!" the little man said.

Everyone in the tank started talking at the same time about my career. One was talking about a front-page newspaper article he had read about me. Another said he was hoping I had won The Ultimate Fighter show in 2005. Jerry was rambling about how he gets private lessons from me.

The guard walked by to see what all the commotion was. When he looked at me, I just shrugged my shoulders as if to say, "I have no idea what's going on."

The guard walked away, as everyone kept trying to talk over each other. A man with a short gray beard, who looked to be in his fifties, was sitting quietly in the corner. He spoke words I'll never forget.

"The Lord said, 'Come to me, all you who are weary and burdened, and I will give you rest.' Matthew 11:28," the man said. I'd heard those words before, but this time I felt them touch my heart.

Everyone was quiet, not knowing how to respond. Jerry looked at the man with hatred in his eyes. Jerry didn't want to hear anything about Jesus or God.

The old man looked into my eyes, and said, "Life is empty and meaningless without Jesus Christ." For once in my life, I wanted to know more about Jesus. I wanted to hear more about the Bible. It all felt so pure!

"Jesus Christ is our hope and our peace," the old man said. I wanted him to continue speaking, but I was afraid to look weak in front of the other guys. I was drawn to the words and could feel a strong pull within my soul; I had a reputation to uphold: I was the Scorpion!

While I pondered what he said, the little man stood on the bench next to me, touching my cauliflower ear.

"Does it hurt?" he asked, as he squeezed it. "No, I have no feeling in my ear," I answered.

Cauliflower ear is what you get from years of wrestling or cage fighting. Your ears swell up and eventually harden. The little man was fascinated with mine, trying to see how hard he could squeeze it. "Does that hurt?" he asked, as he squeezed harder.

I shook my head. "No," I said. "How about that?" he asked, bending it back and forth. "No pain," I answered.

"Jackson, Gonzalez, Norwal, Dixon, Murphy, Delgado, and Torres!" a guard shouted from in front of the door. "Get in two lines. Let's go! I don't have all day."

Everyone scrambled to get in two lines. Any time an inmate is transported outside a jail or prison, he is shackled by the ankles and wrists; then handcuffed to another inmate. Jerry stood right next to me, hoping we would end up getting handcuffed to each other; he was pushed aside by the little man.

"Out of my way! I'm going to be handcuffed to a celebrity! Move over!" the little man said, as he shoved Jerry out of the way.

He looked up at me with a big smile, and I smiled back. I glanced ahead and noticed the inmates in front of me were being handcuffed to each other. I didn't mind being handcuffed to a little person, but how was I going to be able to walk? I would have to lean all the way to my left. How would I look? I would probably look silly! I have to protect my image!

We stepped forward, and the guard cuffed the little man's right wrist to my left wrist. We made our way through the booking area, walking in front of all the tanks full of inmates. I could hear everyone laughing, watching me trying to walk while leaning over. I was beginning to feel stupid, until I looked down and saw my cuff mate looking up at me with a big smile and a sparkle in his eye. He was walking like he was the coolest guy on the planet. From that moment, I didn't care anymore what people thought. It felt good knowing I was putting a smile on his face. He thought I was a celebrity!

We arrived at the van and were waiting to climb in, when I looked down and saw the little man pull his hand out of his handcuff.[33] His hand was so small that not even the handcuffs fit him.

He smiled and slid his hand back. It was obvious that he was showing off. All I could do was smile as we climbed into the back of the van. As soon as we sat down, he pulled his hand out of the cuff and relaxed for the drive.

Less than half an hour later, we arrived at Todd Road Jail. The little man put his hand back into the cuff, and we were escorted inside. Once there, they took the cuffs off all the inmates and put us into a section that had sixteen cells: eight on the bottom and eight on the second floor.

My cell door opened, and as I walked in, I saw a man lying face down on the lower bunk. I recognized him right away: he was my first celly from Ventura County Jail.

I clapped my hands as loud as I could, and it woke him up. He turned and looked at me, and I noticed he was drooling again. His eyes focused and he recognized me. "Oh, hey! How long have you been here?" he asked.

"I just stepped into the cell," I answered.

He sat up, and drool began to drip from his mouth to the floor. I determined not to walk around the cell too much. That was nasty!

---

33   "Little man" died in prison in 2015.

"I can't feel my mouth," he said, while touching his lips. "I can see that," I smiled.

"These meds are strong, but good," he said with a grin. "Whatever you say," I said, climbing up on the top bunk.

Most of the inmates I saw looked just like this guy. They walked around like zombies, drooling, and showing no emotion. Everyone was on some kind of meds. This was how they did their time. They stayed tranquilized.

I was tempted to get my hands on some of those pills so I didn't have to face reality, but I didn't want to walk around drooling. What I really craved was alcohol.

52 I Move in With the Old Man

The next day, our cell door opened; it was our time to shower or use the phone. This is known as "day room time." I went straight to the phone and tried to call Stephanie, but I wasn't able to get through, so I went to the second floor to take a shower.

While showering, I looked around the day room to see who was out of their cells. I noticed the old man with the short gray beard, sitting alone reading the Bible. Everyone else was staring at me and whispering.

Were they planning to stab me; waiting for me to drop the soap? My knowledge of jails was limited to what I had seen in movies!

I felt uncomfortable, so I dried off and walked to a table that was near the old man. I could hear him reading Scriptures. I wanted to hear more, so I sat across the table from him.

"Oh, hello there!" the old man said. I began to open my mouth to ask him a question, when suddenly I was interrupted by some guys with tattoos all over their faces.

"You a UFC fighter?" one of them asked. Great! These guys are going to jump me. Which one should I knock out first?

"Yeah, why? What's up?" I responded. He reached into a paper bag, and I prepared myself. If he pulled out a "shank," I was going to lay him out with a left hook; then knock out his buddies standing behind him.

"Can you sign this for my kid?" he asked, as he handed me a piece of paper with some nice artwork on it. I felt like an idiot! This guy just wanted an autograph. I needed to relax.

"Sure, I can do that," I said, while taking the paper from him. The other inmates standing around began to ask for autographs, as well, and soon the guard in the tower noticed the commotion. I saw him pick up the phone and make a call. "They will probably send me to The Hole because I'm causing a scene," I worried.

I looked at the old man with the gray beard and noticed he was trying to read his Bible, and I realized I was disturbing him. "I'm kinda tired. I'll see you guys later," I said, as I stood up to make my way back to my cell.

As I walked, I was thinking about how I wanted to talk with the old man, but it didn't happen. But, eventually, the time would come.

Later that day, I heard my last name over the loudspeaker. My cell door opened, and I walked down the stairs to the main door. The door opened, and a guard escorted me to a room where two guards were sitting at a desk. The guard who was with me stepped out and closed the door behind him.

"We know who you are. We are just checking on you. Anyone recognize you yet?" one of them asked.

"Yes, a few have," I said, looking down at the floor. Suddenly, I thought of something. Why don't I ask the guards to move me in with the old man?

"Hey, would it be possible to put me in with the old man who is a few cells down from me?" I asked.

"The old man? Why do you want him as a celly? Is your celly giving you problems?" he wondered. "No, no. it's not that. It's just that this old man is the only one who treats me like a normal person," I said.

"I'm sure we can move you in with him, but we gotta be honest with you. The 'higher-ups' want to put you in segregated housing," another said.

"What is that? Sounds like isolation. Did I do something wrong?" I asked.

"It is isolation. They don't want you training other inmates. Also, they don't want you choking out an inmate or killing someone," he replied. The door opened behind me, and a guard stuck his head in.

"Hey guys, it's chow time. I gotta get him back," he said.

"We are going to see what we can do about moving you in with the old man. But we don't know how long you will be in there, because you are probably being moved to segregation," said the guard who was sitting behind the desk.

I thanked them for their time and stood up to walk out. "Jackson?" one of them called.

I stopped and turned around to look at him. "What was it like to fight on TV?" he asked.

I looked off into the corner of the room, remembering the feeling I had the first time I was invited to fight in the UFC: walking down the hallway of Mandalay Bay and entering the Octagon, with the bright lights and screaming fans.

"Well, it was like a dream," I said, then turned around and walked away.

When I arrived back at my cell, my celly was face down, sleeping as usual. He turned over and looked at me when the door closed behind me. "How long was I out?" he asked.

"Dude, I just walked in. I don't know. It's chow time right now, so get ready," I said.

After eating, a guard told me I would be moving a few cells down. I was very happy to hear this. I was finally going to be able to talk with the old man.

I noticed the old man's celly was carrying his stuff out of his cell, and he didn't look happy. I grabbed my mattress, which resembled a yoga mat, and carried it to my new cell.

I walked in and, sure enough, he was reading his Bible. "Oh, hello!" he said.

"Yep, it's me!" I replied. I set my mattress on the top bunk and climbed up. I looked around and noticed he had papers taped to the walls. One said, "Jesus is our hope!" and another said, "Look to Jesus!"

He noticed I was staring at the Bible he was holding. "Do you have a Bible?" he asked.

"Um, no sir. I don't have one," I answered.

"No need to call me sir. My name is Harold," he said.

"It's Jeremy," I said, while shaking his hand.

"Well, we are going to have to get you a Bible," he exclaimed "Yes, sir," I replied. "I'd like to get a Bible," realizing he was staring at me with a serious look. "I mean, yes Harold, I'd like a Bible," I said with a smile.

He filled out a form for me and got it ready to send out through the mail. "This is so you can get a Bible," he said.

"Harold, you think you can read some words out of the Bible to me?" I asked.

"Absolutely!" he answered. He grabbed his Bible and began to read.

Now, when I was little, I went to church every Sunday but never paid attention. I was either sleeping on the pew or playing with toys. I went to church as a teenager, but I was too caught up in passing notes to the girls sitting in the next row. I went to church as an adult sometimes, but I was usually daydreaming or texting.

As Harold was reading the Scriptures, I felt a sense of peace. I didn't understand it. All I knew was that I felt something good and pure. It was like the words were from another world.

"The LORD of hosts is with us; the God of Jacob is our fortress." Psalm 42:7

"The officers answered, 'No one ever spoke like this Man!'" John 7:46

Though I had heard these words countless times in church, it was like I was hearing them for the first time. That night as I lay in bed trying to sleep, I was pondering the words Harold had read to me, but I was distracted by my craving for alcohol. I had the shakes. I shook until I fell asleep.

53 Suicide by Hanging

The next morning, the guards told me to get ready because I'd be moving to a different section. The guards I had spoken with the day before warned me this might happen. I was being moved to isolation. I had no choice. I was being moved for the purpose of safety, both for the institution and other inmates.

I said goodbye to Harold and we parted ways. When I walked into the segregation section, I noticed a different mood. It was quiet. There were faces looking out of the cells, watching me. These guys looked like the troublemakers of the jail: men who needed to be segregated from the rest of the population because they were dangerous. Stone-cold faces stared at me, devoid of expression.

My cell door opened; I stepped in, setting my yoga mat on the metal frame. I felt my cell phone vibrating in my pants pocket, but when I reached for it I realized I didn't have my cell anymore. My mind was playing tricks on me.

"I need a drink," I said to myself.

I stared at the wall for a few hours, wondering if maybe I was just having a nightmare and needed to wake up. I lay on my bed shaking. I couldn't tell if it was hot or cold in the cell.

Looking up, I noticed an inmate standing at my door. It was his one-hour day room time.

"'Sup, Blood? I want you to know I'm a fan," he said.

"Cool! Nice to meet you, bro," I answered.

"Here, I just made this. Don't trip. It's on me. You don't owe me anything," he said, while sliding a bag full of juice through the side of my door. I could smell the alcohol. I poured some in a cup and swallowed it down; then followed it with another cup, and another, until it was gone.

"Take it easy, Blood! Check it out. I'll teach you how to make your own alcohol, so you can have it whenever you want it," he said. Make my own alcohol? Good! I can stay drunk the whole time.

He turned around to see if the tower was watching him and said, "You like pills?"

Do I??!! "I sure do!" I said excitedly. As long as they don't make me drool, simple painkillers will do.

He explained to me what lies I needed to tell the doctor in order to get medication; then he taught me how to make my own alcohol. I did my best from that day forward to stay drunk and high.

A few weeks passed, and I felt like I was slowly dying inside. I felt empty and trapped in a dark hole. I climbed up on the metal desk in my cell and looked out the tiny window, hoping I might see something that would take my mind off of myself. The window was about four inches tall and twenty inches wide. It had some kind of sticky stuff on the outside of it to prevent inmates from seeing out. Why have a window if you can't see out of it?

I tried to find a spot clear enough so I might be able to see the stars. All I could see were a few stars and bright lights on the tops of the buildings. My eyes focused on three particular stars: yes, Orion's Belt! My mind flashed back to the first time I saw those three stars when I was a kid, sitting on the floorboard of my dad's Chevy truck.

I climbed off the desk and sat on the bed. Where did my life go wrong? Once I was that little boy looking up at those three stars, wondering if one day I could reach them. I never thought I'd be sitting in a jail cell.

It was September 10, 2008, the anniversary of my brother's death. This was the day I would leave this world for good. Around 2 p.m. I took well over a hundred pills, including Tylenol and aspirin. I took a dull plastic container and began to carve into my wrist, placing a rolled up towel in my mouth to clench because the pain was excruciating. I pressed back and forth until I saw blood, but I wasn't able to cut the vein because the plastic was too thick and dull. I had to go to Plan B.

I grabbed my sheet and tied it around my neck. As I was tying the other end to the bookshelf, there was a knock at the door. An inmate I'd never met before was standing there. It was his day room time, and he wanted to show me some books that were on the book cart.

"Hey, what's up?" I said, with the sheet still around my neck and the other end around the bookshelf. I unwrapped it from the shelf and walked to the door.

"Everything all right, Homie?" he asked.

"Oh, I was just about to work out," I replied.

"You working out your neck or what? Is that a scarf you are wearing?" he asked, with a chuckle.

"Something like that. Look, I'm kinda busy. Can you come back tomorrow?" I said.

I'm kinda busy trying to kill myself! Can you come back tomorrow when I'm dead?

He ignored everything I was saying and began to pull books off the cart to show me. "How about this one? This is a good book, Homie," he said.

"OK, sounds good! I'll take it! Just put in in front of the door, and I'll get it when my door opens," I replied, too quickly.

"Oh, this is a good book, too!" he said.

"OK, I'll take that one, too. Just put it by the door!" I said in a hurry. I was trying to get rid of this guy so I could hang myself. He obviously planned on spending his entire day room time in front of my door. I was going to have to wait until late night when everyone would be inside their cells.

I took the sheet off my neck and pretended to be interested in the books he showed me. When he finally left, I sat on my bed and couldn't believe how close I was to hanging myself. Within twelve hours I would try again, but this time I was determined to succeed!

I spent the rest of the day vomiting in the toilet. Maybe it was the thought that today was my last night on this planet. Would I go to heaven or hell? Did they even exist? What if I became a ghost that wandered the Earth for eternity? What was on the other side of death?

10:30 p.m. It was time to finish the job. The guard had just done his check, which would give me at least thirty or forty minutes. Everyone is locked in a cell, and no more doors will open for the rest of the night. The lights were already turned down low, and it was dead quiet. I said a quick prayer as I prepared to put the sheet around my neck, "God, I'm scared. Please don't send me to hell."

I tied the sheet around the top of the door this time, since it was much higher than the bookshelf. I slipped my head through the loop I had made and let all my weight drop so that the sheet tightened around my neck. It felt like a boa constrictor was around my neck.

THIS IS IT!! It was really happening! I was about to see what was behind that mysterious gate called "Death." At first, I felt like I was high, because there was no oxygen going to my brain.

Then, the horrible part: I tried to breathe in, but couldn't. What have I done? No matter how hard I tried to breathe, I couldn't. The only thing I could do was convulse and hope it didn't last too long.

Suddenly, a voice on the intercom echoed through the building. "Lock it down for movement," the voice said. Movement? At this time? They only called for movement when an inmate was in the day room and he needed to be locked in his cell before another inmate could be brought to medical, court, attorney visit, or a regular visit.

Strength entered my body, and I was able to put my feet down and stand up. I tried taking the sheet off my neck, but it was too tight. I kept trying and eventually was able to get my fingers between the sheet and my neck. I quickly pulled it off and threw it under the bed.

I looked out my cell door window to see what the movement was, but the lights were still off, and it was dead quiet. In fact, the guard in the tower looked like he was asleep. I didn't understand what was happening. I should be dead right now. Maybe I am dead and don't know it. I pinched myself to make sure.

"Ouch!" I cried. I'm definitely alive! But who said to lock it down for movement? I heard it clear as day. I sat on my bed in shock for a few minutes. Then, I was overwhelmed with emotion because, for once, I was actually glad to be alive. I wanted to live! "I'm alive!" I said, over and over again.

I took a real hard look at what my life had become. It had been such a blur. It seemed like yesterday I was four or five years old, sitting on the floorboard of my dad's Chevy, staring up at the stars in awe. I had dreams of becoming a star. What happened? One thing was clear to me: I was tired. I was tired of being a drunk; tired of being a bad father to my son; tired of being a screw-up. I was emotionally and physically drained.

But was it possible to change? Some men can change, but was it possible for this man to change? When I looked at my reflection in the metal sink, all I saw was a loser, a man who didn't have the strength to pursue change. I didn't believe in myself. I didn't know how to change. Where do I start? I wished there was a sign saying, "Walk this way."

I flipped through my Bible, and it spoke about doing everything through God's power. How do I do that? It didn't make any sense to me.

I climbed up on the desk and looked toward the stars. "God, somehow I believe it was you who saved me tonight. Every time I have tried taking my life, You have saved me. Obviously it isn't my time to go. I am addicted to alcohol and pills, and I am so tired of living like this. I sure have made a mess of my life. I have a two-year-old son out there, whom I have neglected because of alcohol. I think I am going to need Your help to change. God, if You are real, give me the strength to turn my life around. I don't want to be a drunk anymore. Please help me! Amen."

54 God, Where Are You?

The next day, the inmate who taught me how to make alcohol slipped a bag full of Pruno under my door. "Scorpion! I gotta go to court right now, and I don't have time to drink this. Drink it for me. I don't want to leave it in my cell," he said in a hurry, then ran off.

I took it and set it on the floor in front of my door, then sat on my bed. "I'll drink this last bag; then I'll quit," I promised myself. "But if I can't quit today, I'll never be able to quit! Today has to be the day!"

"God, give me strength," I said, as I picked up the bag and poured the liquid down the toilet.

I knew this was not going to be easy. "Today has to be the day!" I argued. I washed out the bag and threw it away when I had day room. That same day, I quit taking pills.

When night came around, I couldn't sleep. I was shaking all night and craving alcohol. It got so bad that I took the mattress and threw it on the floor, spending the rest of the night there. This became my nightly routine. During the day, the alcohol maker came to my door and tried to share his hatch with me. I told him I didn't drink anymore, but he slid it under my door anyway. I poured it into the sink as he cursed me.

"What the #*#*? You're *and#*$!*# wasting it!" he shouted.

"I told you I don't drink anymore," I said. He walked away from my cell, cussing and calling me names.

By November 2008, I had been sober for two months. It was a battle each day, but I was holding strong. I tried reading my Bible during the day, and at night I shook until I fell asleep. I felt like I was battling this addiction all alone. I felt lonely and empty. Was God going to help me? Will it ever get easier?

"God, where are You? I can't do this alone. I need Your help. Are You going to help me?" I asked, while looking up at the ceiling. As soon as the last word left my lips, guards stood at the door. The door opened and they escorted me down a long hall.

"What's going on?" I asked. No one said a word. They led me into a room where more guards were waiting. Some had bulletproof vests on the outsides of their clothing, and they looked like they were part of a SWAT team.

"Is someone going to tell me what's going on?" I asked again. They put me up against the wall and chained my wrist to my waist; then attached the chain to my ankles. Rushing me to the back of the jail, they opened the back door. A van was surrounded by unmarked cars and men holding military-style weapons. The side door of the van swung open, and I was shoved inside, then chained to the floor. The van door slammed shut, and we zoomed out of the driveway. The unmarked cars were ahead of and behind the van.

About five minutes later, motorcycle cops showed up and blocked off the intersections, so we did not have to slow down or stop. Two guards sat directly behind me in the back seat.

"Are you guys escorting the President of the United States?" I asked, sarcastically.

"Shut up!" one of them shouted.

What next? A bag over my head? This was kidnapping! Crazy things went through my mind. I thought they were going to take me somewhere and shoot me, maybe selling my organs on the black market. Then I saw the Ventura County Jail in the distance. Why were they taking me from Todd Road Jail to Ventura Main Jail in the middle of the night?

They pulled up to a gate, and it slowly opened. Men carrying weapons jumped out of the unmarked cars and followed the van down a ramp that led underground. We were in a tunnel leading directly under the jail. The van came to a stop, and the door swung open. I was unbolted from the floor and whisked into the jail. As I walked, the chains cut into my ankles.

I went through a door, followed by another door, and many other doors. I finally saw a sign that read, "Segregation." I was led down a long hallway through another door. Sitting at a desk, a guard looked at me and said, "Welcome to the Dungeon."

As I looked around, I realized why they called it the Dungeon. This place was toward the bottom of the jail, isolated from everyone. As they led me to a door toward the back, it opened and I stepped in. A few feet in front of me were two cell doors. The one on the left opened, and I walked in. It was dark and gloomy, different from my previous cells.

The door closed behind me, and the tray slot opened. "Let's get these chains off of you," the guard said. I leaned against the door, and he reached through to remove the chains.

"Why am I here?" I asked.

"I don't know. Our orders were to put you in the Dungeon," he replied.

"Am I being punished for something? Did I do something wrong?" I asked.

"No, you're not being punished. What makes you say that?" he answered.

I looked at the cell behind me and held out my hand. "Well, sir, this looks like a place where you put the worst of the worst. Isn't the Dungeon for troublemakers?" I asked.

"Look, Jackson, you're not being punished. You are gonna be all right," he said, as he closed the tray slot and walked away.

I turned around and scrutinized my new cell, which reminded me of a small closet. What caught my attention the most was the emptiness. I sat on my bed and bowed my head.

"God, I feel so alone right now. Where are You? Why does it seem like You continue to punish me? Haven't I been through enough already? I want my life back. I'm tired of being in here! I haven't had a drink of alcohol or taken any pills in over two months, and this is my reward? God, help me! Tell me what to do. I am lost and don't know where to go from here," I prayed.

The tray slot opened, and the guard dropped a bag containing my property onto the floor. I opened it and saw my Bible and a few papers. My eyes were drawn to the Bible. I took it out of the bag and sat on my bed.

"You all right over there, neighbor?" A voice came out of nowhere. I scanned the cell to try and find an opening in the wall, but there was none.

"Yeah, I'm all right. Where are you?" I asked, as I continued to look around.

"I'm right here, by the toilet," he said. By the toilet was a vent with tiny holes in it. I looked through and could see the shape of a face on the other side. "My name is Mario," he said.

"I'm Jeremy. How long you been down here?" I asked. "Too long!" he replied with a laugh.

We talked for many hours, getting to know one another. My butt was falling asleep, but I didn't care. It was nice to talk to someone. There was something different about him. He reminded me of a younger version of Harold. He didn't cuss or speak about perverted things. This guy had peace and was full of joy! How is that possible when he's sitting in a dungeon at the bottom of a jail?

"Your last name is Jackson?" he asked. "Yes, how do you know that?" I replied.

"I heard the guard say your last name. I'm gonna call you JJ," he said. I didn't mind, because my friends have always called me JJ.

"You read the Bible, JJ?" he asked.

"I try to, but it's a difficult book to understand," I said.

"Well, the Bible is a spiritual book. You can't just read it like any other book. You gotta ask God to give you understanding. The carnal man cannot understand spiritual things. Are you a Christian?" he asked.

"I am. I've been a Christian all my life," I answered.

"Really?" he questioned. "When did you receive Christ as your Lord and Savior?"

I thought for a second, and wasn't sure if I had ever received Christ as my Lord and Savior. My mom was a Christian, so I assumed I was born a Christian. "I don't remember," I answered. "I've gone to church since I was a kid."

"Going to church doesn't make you a Christian. If I sat in a garage my whole life, would that make me a car?" he asked.

"I believe in God," I said in frustration.

"Even the devil believes in God," he replied. I was getting more frustrated. I thought believing in God was enough to get anyone into heaven.

"Why should God let you into heaven?" Mario asked.

"Because I have a good heart. I'm not a bad person," I countered. He took me through the commandments, and I realized I had broken all of them.

"If you broke one, you broke them all and are worthy of eternal punishment," he explained.

"What?? Then nobody is going to heaven!" I said, raising my voice.

"Exactly, JJ! 'For all have sinned and fall short of the glory of God.' Only God is good. There is only one way to heaven, and that is through Jesus Christ," he continued.

I knew a little about Jesus from all the years of Sunday School and church. He died on a cross a long time ago. When? I didn't know. "Jesus died for everyone's sins, right? And after He died God chose Him to be His Son," I said.

"Jesus has ALWAYS been the Son of God. He came from heaven and entered our world. 'The Word became flesh and dwelt among us.' His mission was to die for our sins," he explained.

I thought Jesus was just some guy who angered the Roman soldiers, and so they crucified Him. I thought He had failed His mission. I didn't know it was His mission to die. And even more, He came from heaven!

"JJ, I think you should spend some time reading the Scriptures and talking to God. 'Make your calling and election sure,'" he suggested. I was speechless! I needed to search through the Bible to see if this guy was telling the truth. I needed to see it for myself.

"Mario, I think I'm going to call it a night," I said.

"All right, JJ! Goodnight!" he replied.

I lay down on my bed and stared at the ceiling, wondering if I was a real Christian. Was I born again? Have I been fooling myself all these years, thinking that I was on good terms with God? My body began to shake, and I knew I was craving alcohol. I tried to block the cravings, but it wasn't easy.

Eventually, I fell asleep.

55 Born Again

The next morning, my neighbor woke me up by speaking into the vent.

"'Arise, shine, for your Light has come! The people who walked in darkness have seen a great Light. Those who dwelt in the shadow of death, upon them a Light has shined!'" he exclaimed.

"What time is it?" I asked.

"Today is a blessed day, JJ," he said with excitement.

"It is? Why is that?" I asked, as I rolled out of bed to use the restroom.

"Because the Lord has risen!" he shouted.

"That's nice," I sarcastically replied. I could hear him still talking as he walked away from the vent. "The Lord has risen, JJ. He has risen," he said, again and again.

"Well, all right then. Someone is excited," I replied. I could hear the guard serving the food trays down the hall; it was chow time.

"Hey, Mario! Was that something out of the Bible you said earlier? You know, arise, shine, all that?" I asked.

He came back to the vent and said, "Yes, it's Isaiah, chapters 9 and 60." "Interesting," I said.

The food showed up, and we grabbed our trays and ate.

Later that day, he called again from the vent. "JJ, you mind if I read you today's Psalm and Proverb?" "Sure, go ahead," I said, as I sat by the vent.

After reading them to me, he taught me how I could read the Psalms and Proverbs each day. He called it the "Potter's Wheel."

"You know, the last thing someone taught me was how to make alcohol," I told him.

"Well, this is way better than alcohol. Alcohol not only ruins lives, but it destroys minds. The Word of God will transform your life by renewing your mind," he said.

I knew all too well how alcohol could destroy a person's life. "I need my mind cleaned out. I have filled it with a lot of junk," I said.

"The Lord will take care of that, JJ," he promised.

Around 8:00 that evening an older Asian man walked into our section and sat in front of Mario's door. I heard Mario talking to him, but I couldn't make it out. Suddenly, it was quiet and I could hear Mario's footsteps in his cell.

"JJ, you want to talk with a chaplain?" he asked through the vent.

"Sure, why not," I replied.

The tall Asian man picked up his chair and sat in front of my door. A guard walked over and opened the tray slot so the chaplain and I could talk. He introduced himself, then asked if he could pray for me. After he prayed, he opened his Bible and began to share it. The more he read, the more I realized I was still a lost sinner. All my life, I thought I was a Christian because I went to church and believed there was a God. I didn't know Jesus. I knew about Him, but I didn't know Him. I had no personal relationship with Him.

I thought about where I would have been if I had succeeded in hanging myself a few months earlier. I'd be in hell! It gave me chills. The chaplain finished his sermon, prayed again; then said goodbye. I called Mario to the vent and let him know I needed some time alone to pray.

"I'll talk to you in a little bit, JJ," he agreed.

I fell to my knees and looked toward the back window. "Oh God, all my life I thought I was a Christian. I was so blinded by Satan. I confess, I am a lost sinner, and I need a Savior," I said, as I put my face to the floor. My eyes filled with tears. "I don't know how all this works, but I believe Jesus died for me, and I receive Him now. I give You my life. Do as You please. I'll follow You wherever you lead me."

It felt like a hundred pounds was lifted off my back. I had peace and joy. I felt free, even though I was locked in a dungeon. In fact, I went to bed that night and didn't have any desire for alcohol or pills. The shakes were gone, and I slept like a baby.

I had finally found the answer to the question Robert Ferguson had asked me back in 2000: what is the meaning of life? It is to live for the glory of God and to enjoy Him forever. That was the answer. We were created for God. Our minds will be restless until we find rest in Him.

Things were beginning to make sense. I even saw the world differently. My goals and desires began to change. I had a strong zeal to become more like Jesus Christ. I could feel the love of God pouring into my heart.

I used to think God was somewhere beyond our galaxy. If I prayed, I felt like I was leaving a message, hoping He would hear it someday. But God is not far from us! He pays attention to everything we do, and He knows all our thoughts.

I used to think He created the Earth, wound it up, set it in motion; then took off for a vacation to a faraway galaxy. But now I know He is a personal God and desires for us to know Him. He is a God who cares; a God who was willing to die for us. And mostly, He is the only TRUE God.

I couldn't set the Bible down. I read verse after verse, chapter after chapter. I began to memorize large sections of the Bible. I quoted until I fell asleep, quoted it in my sleep, and woke up quoting it. I filled my mind with the Word of God.

This became my normal routine each day.

56 The Beginning of My Transformation

Two weeks later, Stephanie began to notice the change in me. Reading the Bible all day, every day, was changing the way I saw the world; the way I saw God, and the way I saw myself. It was changing the way I saw everything.

I called Stephanie from the phone in the day room and she told me, "Jeremy, you have definitely changed a lot these past couple of weeks. Now, if you quit cussing, I wouldn't even recognize you," she said.

She was right. I still had a filthy vocabulary. I couldn't say one sentence without using at least two curse words. I had been talking like that since I was a teenager. Cussing is what helped me overcome my stuttering. If I quit cussing, my stuttering returned.

But the filthy language had to go. How could I pray to God with the same mouth that spewed filthy language? The Bible commands us not to let filthy language come out of our mouths:

"Let no corrupting talk come out of your mouths, but only such as is good for building up, as fits the occasion, that it may give grace to those who hear." Ephesians 4:29

"Let there be no filthiness nor foolish talk nor crude joking, which are out of place, but instead let there be thanksgiving." Ephesians 5:4

We are to honor God with our mouths. The cussing had to go.

"All right, Stephanie. I'm going to ask God to clean out my mouth and remove all bad language. It may take months, or even years, but I will quit cussing," I declared.

I prayed over the phone, so she could hear what prayer sounded like. "God, I want to stop cussing. In your Word it says we are not to use filthy language. It seems impossible for me to stop, because I have depended on it for so long, but I know You will help me. I ask this in Jesus' name."

The next day I woke up to eat breakfast, grabbing my tray from the slot, and sitting at the desk. "Hey, JJ! Your food taste like soap?" Mario shouted.

"I don't know, I haven't tasted it yet!" I replied. I took my first bite and, sure enough, it tasted like soap. "Yep!" I shouted back. I tried the rest of the meal, and everything was soapy.

"They must not have rinsed the trays well enough!" Mario shouted. We let the guard know when he picked up the trays, but it didn't help. We had the same problem for lunch and dinner. There was even soap in our milk. This went on for about seven days. We spent a lot of time at the toilet because the soap upset our stomachs.

Then I remembered my prayer to God a week before. I had asked him to clean out my mouth and remove my cussing. I realized I hadn't cussed all week. Did I think it was the soap that helped me quit cussing? No way! I believe it was the power of God. All the soap did was remind me of my plea.

Stephanie continued to watch me change. I had quit cussing, drinking alcohol, taking pills. All of these had been replaced by love, joy, and peace. "I don't understand, Jeremy. How are you doing this? You are a different person. Why couldn't you have been this man when you were out here?" Stephanie said to me one day on the phone.

"I can't explain it. All I can say is that God is the one who is changing me. I have a purpose now," I answered.

"How is it that you are locked up, but you are happy and free? I'm free out here, but I'm miserable, and in a dark hole that I can't climb out of," she said.

"Stephanie, give your life to God," I replied. Stephanie didn't believe in God and lived a lascivious lifestyle. My extravagances are what led me to her. She wasn't ready to give her life to God; in fact, she had plans that night to go out and get drunk at the clubs.

As I sat in my cell later that day reading the Bible, I could hear screaming coming from a cell next to me. In my section there were only two cells: mine, and on my left was Mario's. The screaming was coming from the cell on my right, which was in a different section.

"Leave me alone, Satan! Get away from me!" a voice was shouting. Mario ran to the vent to ask me if I could hear it. "JJ, who is that??" Mario asked.

"I don't know. Someone is screaming that Satan is getting him," I said. It gave me the chills, because this grown man sounded terrified.

Mario and I prayed for him and called it a night. I lay in bed, tossing and turning, unable to sleep. This guy continued screaming and kicking the walls throughout the night. I laid there, eyes open, until the sun came up.

The next few nights were repeats: he screamed and banged the walls. "Leave me alone, Satan! Get away!"

But, one day something different happened. He began to sing a song: a song I had heard before.

"Take me to the place I loooovvveee, take me all the way, I don't want to ever feeeeel like I did that day!" he sang. He sang the song over and over.

"Maybe he is going to kill himself," Mario said from the vent. While he was still speaking, the guard walked in and asked me if I wanted to go to the day room.

"Yes, sir," I said, as I walked to the tray slot so he could cuff me. I turned around and stuck my hands through the slot. After he cuffed my wrists, the door opened, and he led me the short distance to the day room.

When I returned to my cell an hour later, I noticed an eerie silence. "How long has it been this quiet?" I asked Mario. "When did he stop singing?"

"Right after you went to day room," was his reply. "I hope he isn't dead," I answered.

The guard was bringing the food trays around, and he came to the guy's cell. I could hear the guard ask, "Do you want your tray or not?" Then I heard running feet on concrete, keys jingling, and more people ran down the hall.

The guy hanged himself and was pronounced dead. I sat there thinking how, without God's mercy, that could have been me.

A few days later, Stephanie came to visit me. I could have a thirty-minute visit through a Plexiglas® window while shackled. As I sat across from her, she looked so lost and broken.

"What's wrong?" I asked.

"I don't know, Jeremy. I feel so lost, and I realize I've felt this way my entire life. I just didn't know it until now. I'm in a dark hole, and I can't get out of it," she said, as tears began to run down her cheeks.

"Stephanie, God is real. He is the one changing my life," I told her.

"Then why won't He bring you home?" she asked.

"He wants me to trust Him. He will get me out when the time is right; it will be in His time, not mine," I said.

"Tell me what to do!" she said, as she began to sob. "I'm lost! I'm empty! Help me!"

The guard opened the door behind me and let me know my time was up. I looked her in the eyes and told her how to find true peace. "Give your life to Jesus," I said, as I stood up to leave.

I looked back as I was walking out, and saw her staring at the glass in deep thought, weighing what I had said.

The next day, I called Stephanie from day room and she was excited. "I did it!" she shouted into the phone.

"Did what?"

"I gave my life to Jesus!" she exclaimed. I could hear the happiness in her voice. I was the first one she told. She hadn't told her family because she wasn't sure of their reactions. Her family was Roman Catholic and baptized her as a baby. They assumed she was already saved, even though she hated anything to do with God.

From that day, we read the Bible together over the phone when I had day room, and we prayed together at visits. Little by little her life began to change. She was cussing less and no longer went to clubs to get drunk. It was awesome to witness her transformation.

Not long after this, I received a letter from Jerry Norwal. He had been released. I wrote him back and shared the Gospel with him, telling him how God was changing my life. He wrote me a letter, trying to convince me that biblical Christianity was a lie. He even ordered a book for me that bashed anything to do with God. Another book showed up later called *Why I'm Not a Christian.*

Jerry was a free man now, but was he really free? I wrote him back, sharing some Scriptures with him. He wrote back and quoted some old philosophers, saying how happy he was. He said he didn't need God; God was for weak people.

I sent him one more letter and let him know that I would pray for him; he never wrote back. Jerry committed suicide in a hotel room. I was told he took a bunch of pills and then slit his wrists.

57 Feeling Human

Something happens to the mind after a person is incarcerated. I can't give you the scientific explanation, but I know something happens. I believe the brain goes through a transformation, as a defense mechanism, to prevent a person from going crazy. It's even worse for someone in The Hole. After 23 hours of solitude, with one hour out of the cell to shower or use the phone, the world around you begins to shrink.

One day, while I was sitting at my concrete desk writing, I noticed the letters on the page were moving, as if they were floating on water. I looked at the wall in front of me, and I was surprised to see that it was undulating, as water when disturbed by a rock being thrown into it. It wasn't just the wall in front of me: it was all four walls and even the metal door.

What was happening? I knew I wasn't sick because I didn't have a high temperature. There was something happening in my brain, but I couldn't explain it. Waking up in The Hole every morning, I was aware of the changes, both in my body and my brain, but I didn't want to accept them.

After experiencing this for a week or more, I had to tell my neighbor, Mario.

"Mario?" I called through the vent.

"What's up, JJ?" he answered.

"What I'm about to tell you might seem crazy!"

"Tell me," he replied.

"For the past week, the walls have been moving, and…." I began, but he interrupted me.

"It's normal," he responded quietly.

"What?" I was puzzled.

"I went through the same thing. Everyone does, some more than others. JJ, a lot of these guys have been in and out of jail since they were teenagers and don't even notice it. But someone like you, who fought in big arenas, will feel the change more. Your world was big, but now it is small – a tiny cell. I can't imagine what your brain is experiencing right now," he explained.

What he was saying made sense, but I was more than a little afraid. Would this change be permanent? Could I lose my mind? It was a lot to worry about, but what could I do? I could only cling to God and trust that He would protect me.

Mario shared a few more things about incarceration that he had learned. He explained to me that after a few years "inside," most inmates become institutionalized and give up. They feel helpless and allow themselves to just become numbers.

After about four years, an inmate's girlfriend or wife moves on. Somewhere between five and ten years, family and friends quit writing or answering calls; even the visits stop.[34]

Then he said, "JJ, it is around the ten-year mark that an inmate becomes depressed and stops caring about the outside world. As far as he is concerned, his whole world is his cell. He becomes bitter and angry, complaining the second he wakes up in the morning."

Dazed, I stared at the wall in front of me. Before I could say anything, Mario continued, "But your true friends and family will stay with you, even past ten years. Be thankful for them, because they are the rare ones."

Incarceration changes a man, period. He may not admit it because of pride, or maybe it was subtle enough that he didn't notice it, but the change does occur. I noticed I had a difficult time looking into others' eyes, because anytime I was cuffed up and taken out of my cell, I had to face the wall when I wasn't in motion. I was never allowed to look at the guards. I struggled taking long steps, because the chains prevented me.

These things I noticed right away, but it took more time to recognize the psychological impacts. After being subjected to deprivations for a long time, the mind will cope any way it can to preserve sanity.

The only interaction I had was a phone call with Stephanie during day room time. Other than that, I could only hope that a normal human being, like Mario, would be my neighbor so that we could have a decent conversation.[35] The only touch from another human was from the guards, who slapped the cold cuffs on my wrists and ankles, and the belly chain around my waist.[36] Sadly, I looked forward to these two minutes because they made me feel human. I longed for the touch of another person.[37]

---

34   This part scared me. I know many inmates who haven't heard from their families since the 1970s.

35   Many inmates are infantile. It's like talking to a 13-year-old in an adult body.

36   I have scars on my ankles today from the chains.

37   I was arrested in June 2008, but it wasn't until the summer of 2012 that I would receive my first hug; it came from Stephanie at a prison in Corcoran, California.

58 Werrrrrrmy

The guard walked into our section, and I heard him talking to Mario. Mario was getting moved out of segregation housing and back into the regular population. We said our goodbyes through the vent, and they took him away.

A few hours later, an older man was put into Mario's old cell. Within minutes, I discovered he had mental problems. He kicked the door all day and screamed all night. I couldn't get any sleep, so each day I waited until day room time and used my hour to rest. This routine continued for about three weeks until he was moved.

A short stocky man in his mid-forties became my new neighbor. This guy was even crazier than the last. He would start off talking real low to himself; then get louder and louder until it was a full scream.

"My mom makes the best sweet potato pie! Shut up! SHUT UP! I'LL KILL YOU! YOU KILLED THAT SWEET POTATO PIE!" he shouted. He collected books from the book cart; then tore the pages out and crumbled them up. One day, the guard came around to do his checks, stopping at Hampton's door. An ocean of wadded-up paper, four feet deep, covered the floor.

The guard knocked on the door. "Hampton?" the guard shouted, with no response. "Hampton?" he tried again.

Suddenly, a head popped up out of the center of all the papers. "What in the world have you done?" the guard demanded. Hampton's head disappeared again, like a hippopotamus submerging in a river. The guard picked up his radio and called for assistance. More guards appeared, as well as nurses and a senior officer.

"Where is he?" one of the guards asked.

"He's in that pile somewhere," the first guard responded.

They eventually convinced Hampton to cuff up and then took him to the day room so they could clean out his cell. This became Hampton's daily routine: tearing pages out of books and building a playpen.

"Jackson!" a guard called over the loudspeaker in my cell. "Pack your things. You're moving to a different cell." Shuffling inmates is a common thing in county jails. They don't want you to get too comfortable. I was put into a cell down the hall, closer to the guard desk. It was the same design as my last section: just two cells side by side.

My new neighbor, Dave, was a very intelligent man. He had a lot of knowledge about computers, law, and science. I asked him if he would like to read the Bible with me, and he agreed. After two days of this, he showed me his true colors.

"Jeremy, your bed is against my wall, and my bed is against your wall," he said.

"OK, what's your point?" I asked.

"So while you're a few feet away from me, lying on your bed reading your Bible, I'm over here flogging the dolphin all day," he exclaimed.

"Why would you tell me that?? What's wrong with you?" I angrily replied. Now I had that image of him in my head while I sat on my bed reading my Bible and praying. He kept trying to talk dirty to me in the vent, but I ignored him. Then he began shouting a distorted version of my name.

"Weeeeeerrrrrmy! Weeeerrrrmmmy! Weeeeeeeeeerrrrrmmmmmmy!" he shouted, rolling his Rs. At first I ignored him, but after a few hours it began to get to me. I couldn't read, write or pray. I couldn't even think straight. He sat next to the vent all day, repeating the same thing.

"W e r r r r ,   w e r r r r r r ,   w e r r r r m y !   W e r r r r m y ! Werrrrrrraaaaaammmmmmeeeee!" he shouted.

It sounded like he was starting a motorcycle or something. I felt like I was going crazy. My lack of response seemed to make it worse. This guy was out of his mind! He seemed to get a thrill out of torturing me.

Later that day, he found out what my charges were and began calling me a rapist over and over. That did it! I snapped and ran to the vent. "You better hope our doors never open at the same time! You will find out what I'm capable of! I'll make you eat your words!" I shouted.

"Ha!! I knew it! You're not a Christian. It was all a fake. See, I bring out the animal in you! That's right! Get mad! Let the tiger out! C'mon, Weerrrmy!" he shouted with laughter.

I stumbled back and fell to my knees, as tears filled my eyes. Looking up, I prayed quietly, "Lord, I am sorry I snapped. I felt like I was losing my mind. I'm sorry I misrepresented You. Give me more strength." While I was praying, I could hear Dave yelling in the vent. "Werrrmy, Werrrmy, Werrrmy, Werrrmy! Rapist!" he shouted. I continued to pray, "Lord, help me. This is too much for me to handle. I want to teach this guy a lesson, but something tells me You are allowing this in my life for a purpose. I won't ask You to remove it, but give me the strength to endure it."

"Werrmy! I know you hear me, Werrmy!' he shouted into the vent.

As I sat there listening all day, I was learning something about myself. My whole life, my heart had been full of pride, and I believe God was removing it from me. I had used my fighting skills to teach people a lesson if they disrespected me. If they crossed the line, I made sure they didn't cross it again.

What would happen if Dave's door accidentally opened at the same time mine did? It was known to happen. Sometimes the guards made mistakes, and sometimes they did it intentionally because they wanted to see a fight.

God was showing me what was in my heart. I wanted to break every bone in Dave's body so he would never bully anyone again. But, then it hit me: who am I to teach this guy a lesson?

In the Bible, in II Samuel, chapter 9, King David was traveling with his mighty men, when a man came out cursing him and throwing rocks at him. One of his men said, "Why should this dead dog curse the lord my king? Let me go over and cut off his head!" But David said to leave him alone, because he believed the Lord God was allowing it for a reason.

I realized that I shouldn't do something just because I could. Instead, I should do what is right. I also recognized that not only did I have a bad temper[38]; I also had a lot of pride. I thanked God for showing this to me and asked Him to help me deal with it.

"'O death, where is your sting?' I'll tell you where it is NOT, and that is in the hands of Jeremy "The Scorpion" Jackson. For that man is dead and in Christ."
– Christian brother Joshua Iraheta; September 19, 2012, Corcoran, California

---

38   Though I was realizing I had a bad temper, it wouldn't be until 2011 - at my first prison - that I tried to get it under control.

59 Déjà Vu

On October 6, 2009, I called Stephanie from the day room phone, hoping to do a Bible study with her. She sounded like she had been crying when she answered.

"Jeremy, you need to call your mom! It's about your brother Bodi!" she said, her voice shaking.

"Bodi? What's going on with Bodi?" I asked. Bodi was the only brother I had left.

"Jeremy, he's dead," she said in a low voice.

My heart sank to my stomach, while my mind flashed back to the day I received the phone call about my older brother's death in 2004. It was déjà vu. I felt all alone, abandoned. What now? Was this real? Maybe this was all a nightmare??

A guard standing outside the door asked me to cuff up so that the chaplain could come in and talk with me. I told Stephanie I had to go and hung up the phone. After the guard put the handcuffs on me, he let the chaplain in, and we sat at the table.

He broke the news to me; it was confirmed! It was really happening! Tears were running down my cheeks as the chaplain tried to comfort me with the right words.

The hardest part was calling my mom. I could hear the pain in her voice as she spoke. She wanted me to be at the funeral, and I told her I would do everything in my power to be there.

I didn't realize how difficult it would be to get permission from the judge.

My attorney set up a hearing that week. A friend of mine who was a well-respected parole officer spoke at the hearing, offering to take me to the funeral under his watch, with extra security along. I would remain in chains.

The female judge sat deep in thought, while my mom sat in the front row of the courtroom crying out my name. "Jeremy! The only son I have left!"

My step-dad tried to calm her, and I did my best to contain myself, as I was overcome with emotion. The D.A. walked up to the judge and said, "This man is dangerous. You can't let him out, even if he is in chains."

My attorney also approached the judge and pleaded for mercy. The judge looked down at the desk while she pondered everything she had heard. She looked up and saw my mom crying, and I heard her groan in frustration. Her eyes locked with mine as the D.A. got in the last word.

"You can't let this man out."

"Mr. Jackson, I want to help you, but I can't." the judge finally decided. "I'm sorry, I just can't."

Each word hit me like a hammer, and I tried to control myself. I wanted to kick the cage door off its hinges and give my mom a hug. It had been a year and a half since I had hugged her.

"Let's go," the guard said, leading me away. I could hear my mom calling for her only remaining son, as I walked through the back door.

"Jeremy! Jeremy, my son!" she cried. The door closed behind me, and my heart broke.

This was a big test for me. When my older brother died in 2004, I had turned to alcohol to deal with the pain. How would I respond to my younger brother's death? Would I again numb the pain with alcohol and pills?

Romans 8:28 says that all things happen for a reason, and I did what I should have done in 2004. I turned to God instead of drugs and alcohol. God is in control of the universe; nothing happens outside of His will. Alcohol and drugs had messed up my life once. I wasn't about to go down that road again, not now, not ever.

My brother's death came as a shock to all of us. He was healthy, he was in shape, and he was even going to church. But I do know that he had a lot of pain in his heart. He really missed our older brother, so to deal with the pain he bought some heroin and snorted it. When my mom went into his room the next morning to wake him up, she found him dead.

He had overdosed at the age of 23.

60 The Board Up

One night while I was lying in bed, I heard the guards going from cell to cell, commanding the inmates to take their mattresses off the door. This is known as "boarding up," a protest by inmates that prevents authorities from seeing into the cell. Another protest is a hunger strike, where an inmate refuses to eat. That actually made some sense to me, because it eventually gets the attention of the media or the ACLU, but I considered boarding up a waste of time.

Boarding up is what the inmates chose to do this night; they were protesting the corruption among the guards. In the cell next to me were two gang members, who already had their mattresses pressed against the door.

"Scorpion! Join us! These cops are corrupt! You are one of us! It's us against them!" my neighbors shouted.

By this time, everyone in the Dungeon had figured out who I was and were hoping to recruit me. "Call me Jeremy!" I told them. "I'm not the Scorpion and I'm not joining you guys! You are on your own."

I could hear the inmates down the hall banging on the walls and yelling my name. "Scorpion! You with us??"

Suddenly, a group of guards walked up to my door wearing combat gear and gas masks. They had helmets on and padding all over their bodies. I smiled. "Jackson, do you wish to cooperate? If you don't comply we will have to use force!" came a shout from behind one of the masks.

"Don't surrender, Scorpion! Fight with us!" the inmates shouted from down the hall. A small piece of me did want to rebel, but I was a Christian now. I represented God. We are to submit to authority.

"Jackson? Do you comply?" I heard again. "Yes sir, I wish to comply!" I replied.

They opened the tray slot, and I turned around to stick my hands through so they could cuff me. They brought me down the hall and put me in a small room. From there, I watched the cell extractions.

Flash grenades, pepper spray, screaming; then I would hear, "Pull!" The guards would pull a long rope, and an inmate would come sliding out on his belly, hogtied, gliding on the floor like it was ice. His eyes would make contact with mine as he slid past. Sadness is the best description I can give for what I saw on each face.

Just a few minutes before, he had felt like a warrior, but now he felt helpless. One by one, the guards drug them out on their bellies. It went on for hours into the night. Empty pepper-spray cans were starting to pile up on a table nearby. A few guards took off their masks and drank some water, while others took their places. The Dungeon was swarming with guards. They were everywhere.

After it was all over, the guards came to cuff me so they could take me back to my cell. One of the guards said something to me that made me smile.

"You know, we were upstairs when we heard the Dungeon was boarding up. The first thing we thought was 'Jeremy Jackson is down there!' To be honest, we didn't know how we would handle you," one of the guards said to me.

"You don't have to worry about me rebelling," I replied.

"Thank you for cooperating. You really are a model inmate," he said.

My cell door opened and everything was gone: my mattress, sheets, clothing, Bible, notepad and my journal. I didn't want them to have my journal! I had written a lot of personal things in it.

"Where's my stuff?" I asked.

"It's standard procedure. We have to take everyone's stuff. Nobody can have his mattress for a number of days. It's part of the punishment," the guard told me.

"But I didn't board up! I cooperated with you guys! Why do I get punished?"

"Jackson, I'll see what I can do. I need to talk with the captain since I can't do anything without his permission. Hopefully I can get back to you by tomorrow," he said.

I turned around and looked at my empty cell. I don't remember what I was wearing at that moment, but I know it wasn't much. I lay down on the bare cement block and curled into a ball. It was cold, and I couldn't sleep.

"God, I don't understand what is happening, but I want You to know that I trust You," I prayed.

Eventually, I fell asleep on the cold concrete and dreamed that I was walking through the hallways of the Arrowhead Pond in Anaheim, California. I was walking toward the beer and food window, with someone walking on my left.

"I think the next fight started," a female voice said to me. I looked to see who was speaking, and I saw that it was Liz. It wasn't just a dream I was having; that night had happened. It was an old memory from 2006. I could control neither my words nor my movements; I just went along for the ride, watching everything unfold.

I watched as we went up to the window and bought some food and drinks. We were walking back down the hallway, when a fan in his late twenties stood right in front of us.

"You're that guy!' he shouted. I knew he recognized me from The Ultimate Fighter, but he couldn't remember my name. He had obviously had too much to drink. He turned around and signaled his friends.

"Hey guys! You ain't gonna believe this! It's the dude from The Ultimate Fighter! The guy who hooked up with the lifeguard!" he shouted to his friends.

I looked at Liz, and her face was bright red. She was humiliated! Here she was standing next to her man, who was known for being a "player" on a TV show.

"Hold on! Can I get a picture with you?" the fan asked, as he pulled out his phone.

Liz was shoved to the side by the fans, and I could hear her calling to me. "Jeremy, let's go! Jeremy!" she shouted. The fan kept announcing to the people around him, "Yeah, it's the guy who hooked up with the lifeguard!"

"I didn't hook up with the lifeguard!" I protested.

"Jeremy, come on! Let's get out of here!" Liz yelled again, as she tried to make her way back through the crowd.

It was all becoming clear: I was so focused on myself that I didn't even consider her feelings. I woke up and noticed tears on my pillow. I had been crying in my sleep. I stood up and fell to my knees, totally exhausted.

"Oh LORD God, what a monster I was," I said as I sobbed. "I had no idea how selfish I was. All I cared about was alcohol, fame and sex. I know it was You who brought this memory as I slept tonight. You wanted me to see the man I used to be, and I see it, Lord. You saved me from this, and You are changing me. Thank You for having mercy on me. Thank You," I said, as I lay prostrate on the floor.

I reflected on my life. Oh, the kindness of God to show me my faults.

I have learned that sometimes God speaks to us in our dreams, as He did to His servant Job in Job chapter 33. He speaks to us during the day, but we may not listen. He speaks to us through His Word, and Psalm 19:1-4 tells us He even speaks through His creation.

61 Volunteer Chaplains

Every Sunday, a group of volunteer chaplains would visit my section, and a different group would come each Monday evening. Also, an old training buddy sent a volunteer from his church at least once a week to spend some time with me through the glass window. What a blessing these men were to my walk! They invested their time and helped build me up while I was in isolation. God used them to make a huge difference in my life.

Once in a while, a bad apple would sneak in with the group claiming to be a Christian. An older gentleman sat in front of my door one Sunday morning and tried to convince me that the Bible was just "fairy tales." He seemed depressed and miserable.

He boasted how he had attended church for fifty years. He boasted of his achievements. The things he said raised red flags in my mind.

"I'd much rather be at home drinking beer and watching the football game, but I decided to come and hang out with you," he said one day. I didn't know if that was a compliment or not. I tried sharing some Scriptures I had been studying, but I could tell he didn't want to hear them. I wanted to show him that the Bible is the infallible Word of God, but he wasn't there to learn anything from me. He was there to give me answers.

I asked him questions about certain Scriptures and let the Word of God contradict everything he said. The best way to fight error is with truth. "Sir, can you help me with some difficult Scriptures?" I asked.

"Sure! Fire away!" he eagerly replied.

"II Peter 1:20, 21. What does it mean?" I asked. He began to read, "Knowing this first, that no prophecy of Scripture is of any private interpretation, for prophecy never came by the will of man, but holy men of God spoke as they were moved by the Holy Spirit."

There was an awkward moment of silence as he stared at what he just read. "Sir?" I asked.

"Hmm. I've never seen this verse before," he answered. He knew this Scripture was speaking about God, the Author of the Bible. Men didn't write what they wanted to write. They wrote what God wanted them to write.

"Can you help me out with II Timothy 3:16?" I asked.

"Oh yes," he confidently replied. "I know the book of Timothy real well."

He flipped through the pages until he found the verse; then began to read, "All Scripture is given by inspiration of God, and is profitable for doctrine, for reproof, for correction, for instruction in righteousness, that the man of God may be complete, thoroughly equipped for every good work."

Again he sat silently, staring at the page. "Hmmm. That's interesting. I've never seen this Scripture before either." He was shocked. This man had gone to church for fifty years and was taught that the Bible was fairy tales. The apostle Peter even wrote in one of his letters, "For we did not follow cleverly devised myths." 2 Peter 1:16

I knew he was being convicted by God's Word, because Hebrews 4:12 says the Word of God is sharper than any double-edged sword. So I continued, "What about 1 Thessalonians 2:13?"

He read, "For this reason we also thank God without ceasing, because when you received the Word of God which you heard from us, you welcomed it not as the word of men, but as it is in truth, the Word of God, which also effectively works in you who believe."

The Bible isn't fairy tales. It is the Word of God. "I see you have been reading your Bible," he said.

"Of course!" I answered. "Faith comes by hearing, and hearing by the Word of God. It is truth that sets us apart from the world; it is truth that sets us free!" His eyes locked with mine, and he wondered why I had joy while sitting in a dungeon, while he was free, yet felt empty and lost. He leaned forward, and I thought he was going to start crying. My heart broke for him,

"Sir?" I asked.

"I'm OK. I was just reading the last verse you gave me. It was Jesus praying to His Father. Jesus said, 'Sanctify them by your truth. Your Word is truth,'" he answered. John 17:17

I didn't say anything, because I wanted those last words to sink in. Either the Bible is fairy tales or it's the truth. It can't be both. It's one or the other! The Bible is unlike any other book. It is unique. It was written by forty different authors over a period of 1,600 years. It was written in different languages, on three continents, yet is perfectly consistent. Coincidence?

In ancient times, people thought the world was flat. Some even believed that the world sat on the back of a large animal. But the Bible said, "He...hangs the earth on nothing." Job 26:7. It wasn't until 1650 A.D. that scientists discovered that the earth actually hangs on nothing.

The Bible also speaks about the hydrologic cycle (Ecclesiastes 1:7); oceanography (Psalm 8:8); the earth is a sphere (Isaiah 40:22); dinosaurs (Job 40:15-24); and many other "discovered" facts, long before scientists agreed. I recommend Ray Comfort's book, <u>Scientific Facts in the Bible</u>.

The Bible is obviously unique. It's supernatural. Open it and see for yourself.

"No other directions are given for our journey through the desert waste of this world than the Word of God."
– Peter J. Pell, Jr.

62 A Lost Soul Wandering the Earth

One night, the guard asked me over the intercom if I wanted to go to the cage on the roof to get some fresh air. It had been over two years since I had been outside. "Yes, sir! I'd love it!" I told the guard.

I was hoping he would follow through this time, since every other time I'd been offered fresh air on the roof nothing had happened. Each day I spent 23 hours in my cell and one hour of day room.

Fifteen minutes later, a guard showed up with belly and ankle chains. "Ready?" he shouted. Finally! It was really happening! I was nervous, but excited.

He shackled me and escorted me to an elevator. As the elevator was going up, I began to wonder about silly things. Will I see birds? Pigeons or seagulls? Crows or sparrows? I laughed to myself, as I realized that people see birds every day; no one gets excited about seeing birds because birds are everywhere. But I felt like a little kid going to the zoo.

The elevator door opened, and I shuffled along taking little steps because of my chains. As the breeze hit my face, all I could say was, "Ahhhhhh." It was unbelievable.

The guard pointed toward a cage in the corner, and I inched my way into it. As he locked the cage, I looked at the lights of Ventura. I saw the mountain that I used to run up and down as I prepared for fights. I could see lights twinkling in the ocean: ships or oil rigs. My eyes turned toward the sky and there they were: my three bright stars.

Now I knew, from Genesis 1:16 and Isaiah 40:26, Who created those stars. My whole life I thought women, a title belt, money, power or fame would satisfy. But, all along it was God, the one who made me. If not for my arrest, I would have been dead. My life had been out of control. For over 25 years I had lived in darkness, but God snatched me away and preserved my life.

Just because I am a Christian now, doesn't mean I am perfect. It doesn't mean I don't face struggles or stumble. I am not sinless, but I will "sin less" because I have the power of God within me.

As I sat on the ground and leaned my back against the wall, my eyes fixed on my stars: Orion's Belt. Suddenly, I began drifting back to my time on The Ultimate Fighter TV show. I remembered sitting in the Jacuzzi in the back of the Ultimate Fighter House. A day or two later, I would be sent home for breaking the rules, but that night I was in the Jacuzzi, watching the planes fly above me in the Las Vegas sky. Travis Lutter came out of the house and sat in the hot tub across from me, making himself comfortable.

We talked about a lot of things, but mostly I just shared my life story with him. He sat quietly, listening and staring into my eyes. After a few minutes, he took some water and rinsed his face with his hands.

"Man, you're like a lost soul wandering the earth," he said. Those words echoed in my mind. Was I lost? Was I just wandering aimlessly through life? No! I knew what I wanted! "Once I get the UFC title I will be content!" I told myself.

Eventually, he got out of the tub and stood to dry off. He was about to walk away, but then stopped and turned around. "Hey, Jay?" he called.

"Yeah?" I answered.

"Thanks for the talk," he said, smiling.

"No, thank YOU!" I answered. He disappeared into the house, leaving me alone to do some thinking. Was I really alone? As I relaxed in the hot water, I watched a waterfall cascading into the Jacuzzi. I laid my head back to rest on the edge. I could see the stars glimmering in the night sky.

"A lost soul wandering the earth?" I asked myself, taking a deep breath. I was mesmerized by the stars. I was about to say my usual prayer, "God, please help me get the UFC title and I'll be happy," when something strange happened. Instead, I found myself praying, "God, I don't know Who You are. I know you created all those stars, though, and somehow You are guiding history." I paused and thought about what I had said. If God is in control of everything, then He obviously knows what's best for me. "If getting the UFC title will truly make me happy, help me get it. But if it won't make me happy, or give me peace, please somehow withhold it from me."

As I sat in a cage on the roof of the Ventura County Jail, tears began to fall. God had answered my prayer from that long-ago night. He removed me from the show.

I'm not saying that the UFC title wouldn't have given me happiness. I'm sure I would have been thrilled. But that wasn't the happiness I wanted or needed. I was seeking a happiness that didn't depend on circumstances. I wanted the kind of peace that transcended understanding. I wanted to know the love that surpassed all knowledge. What I needed was the belt of truth around my waist.

It is the only belt that matters.

63 Doing the Right Thing

My trial finally came at the end of 2010, and it was a very stressful time in my life. So much was going through my mind. My public defender was the best I could ask for. He went in that court room and was winning my case. Guards were telling me they believed I was innocent. Even one of the court reporters believed I was innocent. The jury looked with sympathy at me, and I knew they saw an innocent man.

"I'll have you home in a week or two," my attorney said, and I believed him. Through every second of the trial, he was flawless. If the trial continued one more week, I'd be home before Christmas. The D.A. had already rested the case, and it was our turn to bring in our witnesses.

Something was troubling me, though; something I didn't want to accept, that I had buried. I convinced myself that it was only a dream; that it wasn't real, but deep down, I knew I was guilty and I deserved justice. The stakes were high; if I changed my plea to guilty, I would spend the rest of my life in prison. What should I do?

I knew I could beat the charges, which would make me a free man. "I've learned my lesson. I've spent three years incarcerated," I rationalized. "Surely that's enough. And besides, I've quit cussing, drinking and popping pills. I'm a changed man."

Or, I could change my plea, tarnish my name, and live the rest of my life behind bars.

It would seem like an easy choice, right? Who wants to die in prison? I want to be free! But would I really be free if I continued with the lie, just to win my case? Sure, I'd be a free man outwardly, but I'd spend the rest of my life knowing I was guilty. Inside I'd be a prisoner.

How would I be able to tell my son to always do what's right, no matter what, if I didn't set an example for him? How could I look in his eyes and tell him to live for the truth if I was living a lie? I was tired of being a hypocrite. I didn't want to live chained to a lie. I wanted to live for truth; it's what sets a person really free, as John 8:31, 32 tell us.

I was looking at life in prison, but I'd be free. The truth, which I'd been searching for, would do that for me. No more emptiness or chasing the wind. I have a reason to live. I want to help others who struggle with addictions. I want to help those who are in unhealthy relationships.

There were two roads before me. I know most people would choose the road that offers the least amount of both pain and resistance. I knew, because I walked that easy road for 25 years. I knew what God wanted me to do, but I was terrified. Every time I asked God to show me the way, He would lead me to the book of Romans.

"Everyone must submit himself to the governing authorities, for there is no authority except that which God has established. The authorities that exist have been established by God. Consequently, he who rebels against the authority is rebelling against what God has instituted, and those who do so will bring judgment on themselves….Therefore, it is necessary to submit to the authorities, not only because of possible punishment but also because of conscience." Romans 13:1-2,5; I Peter 2:13,14

I told God, "But what about all the things Liz did to me?" Her verbal and physical abuse scarred me for life. She was the only female I ever feared. She may have weighed only 112 pounds, but she was a fighter. She perfected everything I taught her. She knew how to inflict pain, both emotional and physical.

I tried convincing myself that because of all she put me through, it would be okay to lie during the trial and win my case. I did all I could to justify it, but God kept showing me those same verses in Romans. There had to be another way! I begged and begged God to show me an escape.

My lawyer said if I changed my plea, I'd spend the rest of my life in prison. I didn't think I would survive inside, but then God gave me another Scripture:

"He has showed you, O man, what is good. And what does the LORD require of you? To act justly, and to love mercy and walk humbly with your God." Micah 6:8

Then it became clear: God wanted me to forgive Liz for everything she ever did to me. No matter what, it didn't justify what I did to her. What I did was wrong and the only right thing was to submit to God, which meant submitting to the governing authorities. Trusting God meant prison time, but none of the time would be in vain. I would be doing God's will, following Him.

So, I did what I should have done sooner. Against everyone's advice, I changed my plea[39] from not guilty to guilty and received a 25-years-to-life sentence. When everyone heard the news, they were devastated. It was an emotional day for everyone, including my attorney.

Afterward, some people were allowed into the courtroom, including some of my exes. Maggie was the first one I noticed. She was the one who wrote on the bedroom wall in 2002, "Home is where the heart is. It is what it is…" She was at the trial to support me, and I could see the confusion in her eyes after I pleaded guilty. I wasn't allowed to talk to her, but if she could read my mind she would have heard, "Home is where the heart is, Maggie. It is what it is. My heart is with the truth, and I did what was right."

Joselyn was the second face I saw. I saw the tears in her eyes. They were saying, "Why, Jeremy?" Then my eyes locked with Tarah's. There she was: the mother of my child. All I could do was look at her. A sharp pain shot through my heart, and I wanted to rush to her and hug her. She didn't understand, and I knew that process would take years.

Stephanie couldn't even make it that day because she had to work. I called her on the phone to tell her the news, and it broke her heart. I explained that I still had a lot of changing to do, and I was in God's hands. He wasn't finished with me.

"Stephanie, from this day forward I want to live for the truth, no matter what. I want to be a faithful man. There are other things in my life that God will help me overcome. This is only the beginning. I have overcome alcohol, drugs, and many other things because of God. He even changed my speech. He will heal me in every area. This isn't the end of my life, Steph. This is the beginning of a new life. You can call it "The Real Comeback."

---

39   Earlier in the book I described hitting a pitched ball and hitting my dad in the head. Just because my brother pitched the ball doesn't mean I had to swing. Just because I had an opportunity to manipulate my way out of prison time doesn't mean I should have gone through with it. I needed to do the right thing. Just as my mom made me take back all that I had stolen and suffer whatever the consequences would be, I needed to take responsibility for my crime and accept the consequences.

"Two roads diverged in a wood, and I, I took the one less traveled by, and that has made all the difference."
– Robert Frost

"You must decide if you are going to continue on the easy path, or travel the road the Lord has paved for you."
– Steve Gallagher

"Sometimes we have to do what we know to be right in spite of our feelings."
– Steve Gallagher

64 What Motivated Me?

It wouldn't be until years into my prison sentence that I began to reflect on what really drove me throughout my career. I realized that my motivations had changed over time, so let me break it down in stages.

When I was a teenager, my motive for becoming the best martial artist in the world was fear. "Fear?" you ask. Yes, fear. I was tired of being bullied by other kids and by my older brother. I was tired of feeling helpless and afraid. I wanted to be able to walk down the street, not worrying about someone overpowering me.

When my professional career began in 2000/2001, I had a strong desire to build my name. I wanted to be famous. This doesn't mean I was no longer driven by fear, but my reasoning was that if I were the best fighter in the world, and everyone knew it, who would dare try to bully me? Although I wanted to be famous, I was still motivated by fear. Of course, throughout my career, my dream was to get the UFC title, which would win me the recognition I so badly wanted. It would tell everyone, "I'm the best, so don't disrespect me."

By 2002/2003, I was winning fights against top-level fighters. I was the Scorpion, who was known as a powerful striker. In 2002, I was interviewed by Traci Ratzloff for *Ultimate Athlete* magazine, where I said, "Every time I win, it erases a little bit of the pain."[40] What was that pain? When Zeke Barlow interviewed me in 2007 for the *Ventura County Star,* I said, "I forgot all about who I was as a kid."[41] Winning fights was how I coped with the pain of the past. I didn't want to face that pain; I wanted to bury it. But burying something doesn't make it disappear. It just covers it up. That pain would eventually turn to resentment, and then to anger.

After my older brother died in 2004, my purpose changed again. While we were burying him, the pain of my past was uncovered. I turned to vodka, pain killers and sex to cope. I could barely see my goal through the fog these produced. I continued to pursue my objective to be the best

---

40   *Ultimate Athlete* magazine; interview with Tracy Ratzloff

41   *Ventura County Star,* Zeke Barlow article; 4/15/2007

fighter in the world, but soon forgot what I was fighting for. The vodka, pain killers, and sleeping around with as many women as possible left me confused, and I lacked purpose. Sure, they numbed the pain, but they also numbed me to everything around me. I knew I needed to supply my addictions, so my motivation was to stay drunk, high and in bed. Winning that title belt meant money to pay for alcohol, pain killers and women. It also would mean respect.

So, although my goal to win the UFC title remained the same throughout my career, my motivation changed. People saw me as a strong man, but inwardly I was afraid. I had built my body into a lethal weapon, but never considered building my character.

So how about today? What motivates me now? Put simply, I'd say Jesus Christ. I want to bring glory to God. I do that by living a life that pleases Him, as Romans 12:1, 2 commands. I want to serve Him wherever He puts me. I am able to do this because of God's love flowing into my heart. He never changes. I am able to become the man I am today, a man with character, only because of Christ and what He accomplished on the cross. I am able to love others, because He first loved me.

What is motivating you to get through each day?

65 Repression

I did not want to include this chapter, and I struggled for over a year before I decided to add it. I realized that a big piece of the book would be missing if I didn't include it, because this part of my life had a large influence in shaping the man I was in 2008.

Beginning when I was five, and continuing until I was twelve, my older brother Oscar molested and tortured me. Many of the things he did to me were traumatizing and horrific. Oscar had sadistic tendencies[42], and I was his target. One time when my parents were out of town, he held me down and tortured me for an entire day. I often felt like he was going to kill me.

I remember feeling helpless and afraid. This was the main reason I wanted to learn how to fight. Sure, I wanted to defend myself against bullies, but even more I wanted to defend myself against the one who caused me the most pain: my brother Oscar. Every punch and kick I threw at practice, every time I defended a take down, every submission hold I mastered, was for the purpose of never feeling helpless again.

By the time I was twelve or thirteen, I stood up to Oscar and showed him that I was capable of putting up a fight. I wasn't able to beat him, but he knew that if he tried to assault me, he'd walk away nursing some bruises. Because of this, he turned on his girlfriend, our younger brother Bodi and my pets.

I used to bring injured animals home and care for them. My parents supplied the food and water, and I treated them. I had many animals and Oscar killed them. I stopped bringing them home.

I suffered a lot of guilt for many years because of Oscar's cruelty. I thought it was my fault others were hurt, because I had begun fighting back. I figured if I had let him continue torturing me, they would have been safe.

By the time I began competing as a pro, Oscar didn't stand a chance against me. Occasionally he trained with me, and I could tap him out easily. It was at this time he began to respect me, even becoming supportive and

---

42   I do not know why he became such a sadist.

loving. But it was too late; the abuse had scarred my soul, and I responded with destructive behaviors of my own.

I don't blame my past, but I do put it into its proper perspective. I am not responsible for what my brother did to me; however, I am responsible for my response. I should have sought help, but instead I chose to repress those years of trauma. I thought by pretending these things never happened, I was dealing with them. And, when I committed my crime, I did the same thing – I repressed it. It had become a habit.

I'm not advocating dwelling on the past, which won't help. But don't deny reality. The apostle Paul admitted that he persecuted Christians, calling himself "the chief of sinners." If he had denied his past, those who knew him would have discredited his testimony.

The world doesn't need to know your past, but God already knows it. "Lord, I see it now. This person did this to me, and I hurt someone else. I leave it at Your feet today." You'll feel a weight lifted from your shoulders because you are no longer deceiving yourself by living in denial, something we all have perfected.

Don't ever think it's OK to blame your past for your sins. We are who we are today because of choices we have made. I do not blame my violent behavior on Oscar's abuse, the bullies at school, nor the alcohol, drugs and steroids I consumed. I take full responsibility for my cowardly actions in 2008. Often, inmates will say that they committed crimes because they were beaten or molested as children.[43] I know many who suffered during childhood and grew up to be decent adults who never broke the law. The difference is that they took their pain and chose to deal with it without becoming bitter, or use it as an excuse. Perhaps they sought help.

I feel free today because I've admitted my sin. I shared this story and thought that was enough; then I considered those who may have had similar childhoods and have not dealt with it. The memories are lying dormant right now, and one traumatic event could bring those memories to life. I wanted to let you know that you don't have to suppress those memories with alcohol, drugs, sex, or even becoming a workaholic. You can be honest and say, "It happened, and this is how it makes me feel. It is what it is, but I'm not going to live my life as a victim, imprisoned by my past."

---

43   This trauma may have scarred them, but they chose to commit their crimes.

If a child comes to you and tells you someone is hurting him or her, don't minimize or ignore it. The child looks up to you as a protector and trusts you enough to tell you. Listen, and take appropriate action. If the abuse is against the law, contact the authorities. Take every action to make that child safe. If no one cares, the abuse will continue and that child may develop defense mechanisms that are violent and controlling, and will hurt others, just as I did. This behavior led me to prison.

66 Where Am I Today?

Today, I write this from a prison cell in Chino, California. I have been incarcerated for nearly ten years. It hasn't been easy. I've seen horrible things in here: dead bodies removed in body bags, stabbings, overdoses. It's not pretty, but it's my life. I've spent a total of 3½ years in The Hole – isolation, not because I messed up, but for reasons of safety.

I have found my purpose in life: to serve God wherever He puts me. For now, I serve Him in prison. I've been in five prisons so far, and in each one I've invested my time helping other inmates find purpose in their lives. Walking laps on the yard or sitting in the day room, I share the story of how I overcame my addictions to alcohol and drugs. It is an awesome feeling to see some inmate, who has been "inside" his whole adult life, suddenly turn his life around and choose to live sober. I am grateful to be able to witness this.

It's so easy for an inmate to start thinking he is just a "number." I watch institutionalized men mentally give up. Some are miserable or broken down by the length of their incarcerations. They know that society has given up on them and feel they are just taking up space. It's heartbreaking.

Before I left county jail to come to prison, a Hispanic inmate in his 60s shared something with me. He had done a lot of prison time and wanted to give me some advice. "When a man goes to prison, he has two choices: either he will allow prison to turn him into a beast and come out worse than he went in, or he can use the time to improve himself and come out a better man. No matter which, you will not be the same man when you get out," he said.

"Which did you choose?" I asked.

"I keep coming back to prison, so I obviously came out worse. I choose to kill time in prison by sleeping as much as I can, getting drunk, getting high, fighting, looking at porn, sleeping with trannies. I do whatever I have to do to pass the time until I am released." He paused for a moment; then continued, "But I've seen a few use the time to become better people. They take college courses. They attend church and self-help groups. They avoid drugs, alcohol, violence and prison politics. They use every second for the best. And you know what? When they get out, they stay out! Don't be like me, Homie. I'll always be a screw up."

Obviously, I have chosen to take hold of every second in prison and use it to better my life. If I allow prison to change me into a beast, then all my time here will be in vain. I'm not trying to kill time until I go home. I need every second I can get to transform my life; every second counts! I'm involved in college, self-help programs, church ministry, and I have studied several languages, including Spanish, Greek, Hebrew, Japanese, American Sign Language and Russian.[44]

When I'm getting ready to run some laps on the track, I'm often asked if I have a second to talk. I cancel my plans so I can do that. Sometimes the inmate just wants to do all the talking, so I listen. Sometimes he wants advice. Whatever it is, I give him my time. Dr. John MacArthur once said, "That is how the best learning always occurs. It isn't information passed on; it's one life invested in another."

In 2004, my older brother was addicted to drugs and asked me for help. I was too busy for him and now he is gone. Every time I look at these guys around me, I see Oscar or Bodi. I won't make the same mistake again. I won't be too busy for them. I may not be able to bring my brothers back, but I can make a difference in the lives of the men around me today.

By making a difference, I can help prevent a mother from losing a son, someone from losing a brother, or a child from losing a father. Maybe you know someone who is struggling with addiction. You can make a difference by giving them your time. It is a precious gift.

Looking back at my life, I'm amazed that I'm still alive. I didn't deal as I should have with the death of my older brother in 2004; instead, I turned to alcohol, drugs, steroids, and sex to block the pain. I only thought of

---

44   I also teach a low-impact exercise class to elderly inmates twice a week. Since my incarceration in 2008, I've watched many inmates lying on their bunks all day, staring at the walls. Many have done this for years. I had to try to make a difference, so I spoke with another inmate who was qualified to help me teach a fitness class and asked for help in putting together L.I.F.T. (Low Impact Fitness Team). With the help of others it was approved. The class quickly filled up and now there's a waiting list.

myself and instant gratification, which led to poor choices and deep depression.

Some people envied my sex life. They thought I was one lucky dude! I will tell you that every time I slept with a different woman, I was more empty afterward. The more women I had, the lonelier I felt. I would wake up in a hotel room with a woman in my bed and feel dirty inside. I'd go the bathroom and close the door, looking at myself in the mirror. I hated that person. I wanted to stay in the bathroom until she left. But it never turned out that way; there was always a knock on the door, and I'd open it to see a woman who was a stranger. There was no love or romance; no connection that had any meaning at all.

If I could go back, I would never have had sex before marriage. I wish I would have waited, but I can't change the past. What's done is done. I can live a better life today and make the right choices.

I've overcome my addiction to alcohol and drugs, and with that I've learned to control my anger. But my biggest battle has been sexual temptation. I lost my virginity when I was twelve years old, and had sex almost every day until my arrest. Then I stopped, and I've struggled for years to gain victory in this area.

I've asked pastors in their 70s and 80s, "Will I always struggle with sexual temptation?" Their response is usually something like this, "As long as we are in these bodies, we will struggle with sexual temptation." A book that has helped me in my struggle is *At the Altar of Sexual Idolatry*, by Steve Gallagher.

Although I have joy and peace in my life now, doesn't mean everything is "peachy" in prison. My heart breaks daily, and sometimes it is overwhelming. Anyone who says prison isn't too bad is either lying or is in denial. I understand that there are some who don't mind being in prison, because most of their friends and family members are incarcerated, and they never experienced any decency in the free world. But this is not the environment I'm used to. It's been almost a decade, and I never get used to it. Sometimes at night, I'll think about all I'm missing. The biggest regret is the time I don't get to spend with my son. I've missed all the important events in his life. I also miss walking on the beach or climbing a mountain. I miss simple things like carpet under my feet, a soft chair or a comfortable bed. I live in a concrete and metal world now.

When my heart aches, I remind myself that I'm on the path God has for me. Instead of focusing on the razor wire, gun towers, or the negativity all around me, I focus on God. I know He has a plan and that it is absolutely perfect.

Everything I've experienced in my life has been for a reason. God takes our mistakes and turns them into something good, as Romans 8:28 and Genesis 50:20 tell us. Just because you have messed up your life, doesn't mean it's over; it's not.

All of our suffering is for a purpose. Let me give you a great example. My mom lost two sons, which caused her a lot of pain, but she has taken that pain and used it to help others. She will be standing in a store and start a conversation with a stranger. Some of the women she meets will share how they lost a son or daughter and feel they can't go on. Then my mom comforts them and explains how she has dealt with the same anguish. She has become a blessing to those around her and especially to me.

I know some of you think it was the end of my life when I was arrested in 2008, but it wasn't. It was the beginning of my new life. Being arrested saved my life. If God hadn't interrupted me, my lifestyle would have killed me, and my mom would have no sons left.

When I gave my life to God in 2008, I finally had a purpose for living, and for once in my life I was really alive. I felt the love of God, and it changed me. Words like "faithful," "truth," "love," and "integrity" suddenly had meaning. They were real. I felt like the world had changed in one day, but in reality I was the one who had changed. God Almighty changed my heart, and He can change yours. No matter where you are in life, or what you have done, you are never too far away from God for Him to reach you. Your past doesn't define who you are, nor are you defined by your worst deed. Get back up and make a "Real Comeback."

As for me, I must serve the Lord right here in prison. I can make a difference right here and now; someday soon, the California prison system will say, "It is what it is. Pack your bags, you're going home!"

Res.	Record	Opponent	Method	Event	Date	Round	Time
Win	9-5	Hector Carrilo	TKO (punches)	Total Combat 19	March 31, 2007	1	N/A
Loss	8-5	Pete Spratt	Submission (injury)	The Ultimate Fighter: The Comeback Finale	November 11, 2006	2	1:11
Win	8-4	Christian Vargas	Submission (rear-naked choke)	TC 10 - Total Combat 10	October 15, 2005	1	3:56
Win	7-4	Mark Moreno	Submission (rear-naked choke)	ROH 1 - Ring of Honor 1	November 22, 2003	1	1:30
Loss	6-4	Nick Diaz	Submission (armbar)	UFC 44	September 26, 2003	3	2:04
Loss	6-3	Nick Diaz	TKO (punches)	IFC WC 18 - Big Valley Brawl	July 19, 2003	1	4:17
Win	6-2	Shonie Carter	Decision (unanimous)	WEC 6: Return of a Legend	March 27, 2003	3	5:00
Win	5-2	Nick Diaz	TKO (punches)	UA 4 - King of the Mountain	September 28, 2002	1	0:49
Win	4-2	Mike Penalber	TKO (punches)	UA 4 - King of the Mountain	September 28, 2002	1	N/A
Win	3-2	Zach Light	TKO (punches)	UA 4 - King of the Mountain	September 28, 2002	2	N/A
Win	2-2	Eddy Ellis	TKO (punches)	IFC WC 17 - Warriors Challenge 17	July 12, 2002	1	2:24
Loss	1-2	Joe Stevenson	Submission (punches)	KOTC 15 - Bad Intentions	June 22, 2002	1	1:27
Win	1-1	Peter Delayo	TKO (strikes)	KK - Kage Kombat	April 6, 2002	N/A	N/A
Loss	0-1	Jake Shields	Submission (rear-naked choke)	GC 6 - Caged Beasts	September 9, 2001	1	2:03

"Constantly, life is a matter of decisions. We just pick roads, all the way through life. And so it's fair to say, 'life consists of man at the crossroads.'"
– Dr. John MacArthur, Jr.

This will be a powerful and encouraging book to all who read it.

God certainly changed Jeremy's life. I have been in Prison Ministry for 33 years, and his life story is real. Prison life is no joke. Too many don't turn to God, but Jeremy had a mindset to get healed and delivered from what got him in prison. He got better... not bitter.

He has spent time in five prisons, which is very difficult. These changes did not get him down.

After he invited Christ into his heart, he learned to read and write Hebrew, Greek and Spanish. He also taught Bible studies after spending quality time in the Word.

Jeremy persevered, and all those years his walk with the Lord remained strong. God made Jeremy a new creation, a man of many talents, and a humble man. There is so much value in this book. You will be blessed, as I was blessed.

—Mel Novak

This book hit home for me in many areas, as I have seen and witnessed firsthand so many aspects of which Jeremy writes. My own son was also a very successful, accomplished fighter: smart, kind and caring, extremely talented from a very young age. He seemed to have the world by the tail, yet he also fell victim to some of the very same evils you will read about in this book. For this reason, as well as others, I can relate to every aspect of this amazing story. Jeremy Jackson: the boy, the fighter, the troubled man, who finally became the light of peace.

This is a story of a boy with a dream, who refused to settle and chose sacrifice to fulfill that dream – to become a professional fighter, a champion, and to fight on the biggest stage in the world. Here was a boy, who was constantly bullied while growing up, a boy with impairments and learning disabilities, who eventually defied all the odds. Jeremy Jackson is a young man who ended up fighting for much more than trophies and title belts. His biggest fight was for his own life, for peace and understanding.

This young man sacrificed it all to get it all, only to crumble at the feet of fame and the fast-paced life. Like many others, he could not see beyond the bright lights, big crowds and cheering fans.

While reading this book, I shared in the journey of a young man, who became stronger physically than he ever dreamed, while at the same time experiencing a broken heart, body and soul. As his body became stronger, his mind weakened, and he turned to the evil so available. These vices would become his ultimate trainers and manager; they would become the means by which he fell from the very top to the very bottom.

He cheated people, including his loved ones, and cheated death itself, but he could not cheat his way out of the despair that governed his soul. He describes the emotions of a mother who has had her entire life ripped out from under her through the loss of two of her three boys.

Then, you will join Jeremy in his awakening; the relief and forgiveness he experienced by opening his heart to Jesus Christ, the ultimate Giver of peace.

Jeff DeVore has been studying, training, developing, and teaching martial arts since 1980. He owned and operated a commercial martial arts school and gym from 1989-2010. He is a lifelong student, trainer and combative instructor.

A Note From William D. Moore

Sometimes, after you finish reading a book about a man's life, you sit back in your chair, and you struggle to decide what it would be like to be that man. That is how I felt when I read the final chapter in Jeremy Jackson's book, *The Real Comeback*. But, this I was and am certain of: I haven't yet seen the final chapter of Jeremy's life. That chapter will allow me to better understand the chapters in his book.

I believe you do well to read about Jeremy's past in the light of Jeremy's future. The child of God, no matter his past, no matter his foundation, has a glorious last chapter to his life. Without this understanding, every life's tale is a sad one, not just Jeremy's. Only the mercy, grace, and providence of God cause the sands of self, sin, and shame to sparkle.

Do not be saddened by Jeremy's story; be heartened by it – what a glorious change a new heart makes! Only God can bring such beauty out of chaos.

–William D. Moore
William Moore is a pastor, pilgrim and follower of his LORD